GRASSROOTS
TO GLOBAL

This book is dedicated to
Jill Wrigley

GRASSROOTS TO GLOBAL

Broader Impacts of Civic Ecology

Edited by
Marianne E. Krasny

Foreword by
Keith G. Tidball

Comstock Publishing Associates

An imprint of

CORNELL UNIVERSITY PRESS   **ITHACA AND LONDON**

First published 2018 by Cornell University Press

Printed in the United States of America

Library of Congress Cataloging-in-Publication Data

Names: Krasny, Marianne E., editor.
Title: Grassroots to global : broader impacts of civic ecology /
    edited by Marianne E. Krasny.
Description: Ithaca : Comstock Publishing Associates, an imprint of
    Cornell University Press, 2018. | Includes bibliographical references
    and index.
Identifiers: LCCN 2017056275 (print) | LCCN 2017057141 (ebook) |
    ISBN 9781501714986 (epub/mobi) | ISBN 9781501714993 (pdf) |
    ISBN 9781501714979 | ISBN 9781501714979 (cloth : alk. paper) |
    ISBN 9781501721977 (pbk. : alk. paper)
Subjects: LCSH: Environmental protection—Citizen participation. |
    Human ecology. | Urban ecology (Sociology) | Community development.
Classification: LCC TD171.7 (ebook) | LCC TD171.7 G725 2018 (print) |
    DDC 363.7—dc23
LC record available at https://lccn.loc.gov/2017056275

Cornell University Press strives to use environmentally responsible suppliers and materials to the fullest extent possible in the publishing of its books. Such materials include vegetable-based, low-VOC inks and acid-free papers that are recycled, totally chlorine-free, or partly composed of nonwood fibers. For further information, visit our website at cornellpress.cornell.edu.

Contents

Foreword

As I write this foreword, Washington, DC, our nation's capital and for a time my home (and for a time the home of the editor of this volume, it turns out), is in turmoil. As when the leaves seem to turn over and show their white undersides as the wind picks up announcing the arrival of a thunderstorm, outbreaks of senseless violence are escalating in the United States and throughout the world, such as the shooting of members of Congress and their staffs today while playing baseball, perhaps portending greater disturbance to come in the atmosphere of our politics and our society. But as I think these thoughts, I gravitate to the stories of strangers opening doors to the folks fleeing a deranged shooter bent on destroying, on tearing down. And I am reminded of so many stories where small acts of grace make big differences in contexts such as battle zones, disaster areas, and places Marianne Krasny and I have called "red zones" and "broken places."

This book is about those small acts of grace, and asks whether or not they make a difference beyond the people involved or the patch of landscape they transform. The book is also decidedly about *building*. It's about "culture building" through changing social norms through civic ecology practices. It's about "knowledge building," via its focus on learning while engaged in civic ecology practice. And it's about "movement building," about deploying civic ecology as strategic action. The sum of this focus on building is a decidedly progressive and forward-leaning message of optimism and hope, building upon earlier conceptions of civic ecology as a reflection of the bonds between the traditions of engagement in civil society and of a land ethic based on humans' deep connection to the rest of nature. True to the theoretical origins of these perspectives (Alexis de Tocqueville's *Democracy in America* and Aldo Leopold's *A Sand County Almanac*, among others), this book expands on those earlier notions of civic ecology by opening the conversation to new disciplines, voices, and contexts and illustrates in compelling case studies how civic ecology practices cross traditional notions about social change and institutional boundaries, leading to inspiring new ways to envision the interaction of practices, organizations, networks, and social movements.

This book is also about a kind of clear-eyed honesty and self-reflection uncommon in much of academia today. The editor and coauthor of many chapters grapples with competing instincts to, on one hand, employ an empirical critique, while on the other, offer affirmation and encouragement to practitioners doing laudable work. She charts a course to navigate this challenge by leaning on the tradition of appreciative inquiry, and manages an ecumenical assemblage of chapters that mostly achieve the lofty goals she sets forth to contribute not only to the flourishing of individual civic ecology practice, but also to "understand how such practices contribute to flourishing of the humans engaged, the surrounding community, environmental governance systems," and the environments in which these different levels of activity occur.

When I first offered the term "civic ecology" to Marianne Krasny in 2006, while we were co-teaching and collaborating on an initiative called Science Education for Citizen Participation (which has evolved into the Civic Ecology Lab), I remember saying to her that, someday, civic ecology would be applied and analyzed in national and even international contexts, with global ramifications. This volume brings this prediction into reality, and places Krasny and colleagues at the cutting edge of the science-to-policy-to-practice discussion. I believe that the reader will agree with Krasny that, based on the cases in this book, these practices can and do "make a difference not just to participants' lives, but to Bangalore, India, the anthracite region of Pennsylvania, cities in Iran and the United States, and to our shared planet."

Keith G. Tidball
Cornell University

Acknowledgments

The civic ecology workshop that provided the foundation for this book was supported by the National Socio-Environmental Synthesis Center (SESYNC) under funding received from the National Science Foundation DBI-1052875. Many thanks to Margaret Palmer, Jonathan Kramer, and other SESYNC staff members who supported the workshop, and to Cat Stylinski for encouraging me to apply for SESYNC support. Funding for this research was also contributed by the U.S. Department of Agriculture National Institute for Food and Agriculture administered through Cornell University NYC-14745 and MRP NYC-147859. The views expressed are solely those of the authors.

I also thank Dustin Alger, Caroline Lewis, Jennifer Klein, Anandi Premlall, Carrie Samis, and Carmen Sirianni, who contributed ideas at the SESYNC workshop but were not able to contribute to the book chapters; and the following individuals who provided comments on the chapters: Daniel Daneri Rosenberg, Bethany Jorgensen, Adam Kent, Chankook Kim, Scott Kratz, Jessica Smith, and Bjorn Whitmore. Finally, thanks to David Maddox for facilitating the SESYNC workshop and to Keith Tidball for his long-standing contributions to civic ecology scholarship and practice.

GRASSROOTS
TO GLOBAL

INTRODUCTION

Marianne E. Krasny

My motivation for this book was simple. I am inspired by community gardening, litter cleanups, tree planting, oyster gardening, mangrove restoration, and similar civic ecology practices. Together with my colleague Keith Tidball, I have explored where and why these practices occur and their local outcomes, including provisioning ecosystem services and fostering learning, health and well-being, social capital, and sense of community among participants. We have published papers and two previous books—*Civic Ecology: Adaptation and Transformation from the Ground Up* (Krasny and Tidball 2015) and *Greening in the Red Zone* (Tidball and Krasny 2014). I also practice civic ecology. I started a group called Friends of the Gorge to address stewardship needs in the Cornell campus gorges, and I help out at Friends of the Ithaca City Cemetery cleanups and jog in their Halloween Spook Run fund-raiser.

Yet in exploring civic ecology practices, I was constantly nagged by the fact that these practices are small, perhaps even insignificant, while the problems facing the planet, its people, and other organisms loom large. In an age where humans are a planetary force, seemingly mostly of environmental degradation, do community gardening, tree pruning, litter cleanups, and restoring oysters or mangroves in cities like New York, Shenzhen, and Bangalore make any difference? So you might say shepherding this book was an attempt to justify my enthusiasm—my passion—for these small, community-based environmental stewardship actions in light of my concerns about the future of our planet.

In short, bridging small, self-organized environmental action with larger governance and management impacts is the reason I brought together a group of scholars and practitioners to write this book. The results of our collective efforts are the chapters you are about to read. But before you do, I will introduce you to our authors and to their definitions of civic ecology. And I will share three pathways through which civic ecology can have the kind of broader impacts that emerged through the chapters of this book.

What Is Civic Ecology?

When asked to define civic ecology at the workshop that launched this book, Veronica Kyle had this to say: "When I think of civic ecology I think about engagement of people in their natural environment. That can be everything from engaging in their community park to a local beach to a forest preserve. I think about science and nature; people and nurturing of their environment coming together. Hands-on learning, multigenerational community stewardship. I think about no books, no scientific lectures, no homework. Just lifework in the environment where they live, work, and play" (Veronica Kyle, Outreach Director, Faith in Place, Chicago).

Keith Tidball from Cornell University responded to the same question by stating his long-standing conviction that Aldo Leopold's land ethic serves as the basis for civic ecology. He went on to describe the land ethic as "thinking about the community as more than just the people in the neighborhood or the people on the block. It includes the other life, from the soil to the birds to the bees and the wildlife, the trees, the atmosphere. All of that is the community that we live in."

And Zahra Golshani, a researcher and volunteer with Nature Cleaners in Iran, talked about civic ecology as "activity that connects people to nature and also helps people to build a sense of community and social capital together."

How can we make sense of these disparate perspectives on civic ecology? And how do we take these and other insights to answer the question posed in this book: *In what ways do small-scale civic ecology practices—milkweed planting for monarch butterflies in Chicago, tree planting in Detroit, community gardening in the Bronx, or litter cleanups in Bangalore and Tehran—make a difference beyond the small spaces that they immediately transform?*

To answer this question, I invited a group of twenty-five civic ecology practitioners and scholars to a workshop at the National Socio-Environmental Synthesis Center in Annapolis, Maryland. During our three days together in February 2015, we explored the definition of civic ecology that Keith Tidball and I had proposed in earlier publications within the context of the practices and disciplinary lenses represented at the workshop (text box 1). The goal was to generate understandings of the broader impacts of civic ecology practices by exploring specific stewardship and restoration actions through the lens of academic theories and disciplines. The understandings generated at the workshop and afterward are captured in the chapters in this book, which are coauthored by practitioners and scholars.

Text Box 1   Civic Ecology Definitions

In our earlier writing Keith Tidball and I distinguished between civic ecology practices and civic ecology as a field of study.

Civic ecology practices: *local environmental stewardship actions to enhance green infrastructure and community well-being in cities and other human-dominated systems*

Civic ecology: *study of individual, community, and environmental outcomes and interactions of such practices with communities, governance institutions, and ecosystems*

Sources: Krasny and Tidball 2012, 2015.

I paired one academic with one practitioner at the workshop to begin the process of coauthoring the book chapters. The scholar would apply his or her particular disciplinary or cross-disciplinary lens—environmental governance, environmental psychology, religious studies, among others—to understand and interpret the practice. I tried to create academic practitioner pairs whose members shared common interests. So, for example, human ecologist Karim-Aly Kassam has worked widely in central Asia and is a scholar of the sociocultural history of Muslim societies. He was paired with Zahra Golshani, who shares his Muslim faith and who has volunteered to pick up litter with the NGO Nature Cleaners in public places in Tehran and other Iranian cities. Environmental psychologist Louise Chawla has written widely about childhood engagement in nature and lived for many years in rural Kentucky. She coauthored the chapter with Robert Hughes; together they interpret his work in rural, coal-mining communities in Pennsylvania through the lens of providing youth with significant life experiences that lead them to conservation work later on. And Veronica Kyle engages members of African American, Latino, and other faith congregations in Chicago in reflecting on their migration stories and in planting milkweed to host another type of migrant—monarch butterflies. She was paired with religious scholar Laurel Kearns, who has written about faith traditions that promote caring for God's creation.

For some coauthor pairs, the boundary between scholar and practitioner was blurred. For example, Jill Wrigley was the practitioner in the chapter with ecosystem ecologist Mila Kellen Marshall. Yet in addition to launching the Collins Avenue Streamside Community, Jill was a lawyer and taught food systems at the

University of Maryland, Baltimore County. Philip Silva acted in the role of academic for the chapter with Rosalba Lopez Ramirez on knowledge practices in a community garden in the Bronx. Yet both Philip and Rosalba are community gardeners and garden educators, and both have research experience. They questioned the binary categories of "practitioner" and "academic" and felt that their collaboration clouded the lines between these two ways of making sense of the world. In fact, such merging of different ways of making sense of the world is a means to understand the larger impact of civic ecology practices and thus contributes to the goal of this book.

I also invited two scholars to provide perspectives that would cut across the practices described in the chapters. At the workshop, Emory University professor Lance Gunderson, who has contributed widely to scholarship in ecosystem science, adaptive management, and adaptive governance, referred to civic ecology as "skunkworks," or small groups of people who operate outside the routine procedures of organizations to create innovations (Rogers 2003). In so doing, participants in skunkworks question existing mental models of how things work or how change occurs, and explore possible futures with "novel system configurations" (Gunderson and Light 2006, 332). In using the term "skunkworks," Lance was describing civic ecology practices as small-scale innovations that at least initially emerge outside government bureaucracies. Lance went further to describe civic ecology as evidence that progress can be organic and nonlinear and that "ideas drive policy, and politicians follow ideas." The Ugly Indian, a nonprofit in Bangalore, illustrates Lance's claims in that its core members are a small group of volunteers who developed an innovative way to address the problem of trash dumping in urban public spaces; although they operate outside the confines of municipal government, their work has begun to drive policies about who takes responsibility for public spaces in Indian cities.

Lance's comments about how innovation emerges from nonlinear processes were reinforced by Arjen Wals, a UNESCO sustainability professor at Wageningen University. Arjen was asked to contribute his expertise on social learning and on crossing disciplinary, academic-practitioner, and other boundaries. He emphasized how learning processes that bring together people from different sectors and disciplines—that cross boundaries—often create transformative experiences, practices, and scholarship. Arjen's and Lance's perspectives on how ideas and innovations emerge when individuals work across sectors and disciplines freed from the constraints of mainstream organizational structures are foundational to understanding civic ecology and the chapters in this book. They suggest that civic ecology practices are social innovations generated from the bottom up by crossing traditional boundaries. Their perspectives also reflect the approach used in writing this book. By pairing scholars and practitioners representing multiple disciplines and practices, most of whom had not met before the workshop, I hoped to generate insights about civic ecology practices and their broader impacts.

Civic Ecology Broader Impacts: Pathways Emerging from the Chapters

During the workshop, social scientist Erika Svendsen described civic ecology as "people taking action for themselves and, in that action, thinking beyond themselves and thinking about all the different issues that are important to a community, to a place, and beyond." Erika's research has, in fact, captured the connections among small-scale organizations, communities, places, and broader governance networks. She and her colleagues have mapped the governance network of over seven hundred environmental stewardship organizations in New York City, including small groups engaged in civic ecology (Connolly et al. 2014). Erika's chapter coauthor for this book, Rebecca Salminen Witt, was longtime director of the nonprofit the Greening of Detroit and describes her work with a network of greening organizations that collectively have contributed to civic and environmental revitalization in Detroit. As each coauthor pair like Erika and Rebecca grappled with the grassroots nature of their practice through a disciplinary lens, and attempted to address the question of how the practice could have broader social, environmental, and policy impacts beyond the small space and people involved, three broader-impacts pathways emerged. I refer to these pathways in shorthand as culture building, knowledge building, and movement building.

Farhang-sazi (Culture Building): Changing Social Norms through Civic Ecology Practices

The motto of the Ugly Indian is "See the change you want to be" (riffing off a popular saying attributed to Mahatma Gandhi: "Be the change you want to see"). As depicted in the chapter by Bangalore volunteer and designer Aniruddha Abhyankar and myself, volunteers in Indian cities conduct "spot fixes," or short-term cleanups of small public spaces along streets and sidewalks. Volunteers describe how, by providing visual evidence of what urban public spaces can look like, they "nudge" fellow citizens to take responsibility for their littering behaviors and "provoke" municipal officials into taking action. The officials, who have allowed these spaces to become open trash dumps, are embarrassed when volunteers strategically conduct spot fixes near municipal buildings. As a result, they decide to lend their support to the next spot fix and even strategically leverage the Ugly Indian volunteers to transform additional public spaces.

The Ugly Indian also conducts spot fixes near the homes of prominent Bollywood actors and fields where rugby stars play, with the goal of gaining the support of Indian cultural icons for changing the way Indians treat public spaces. In addition to leveraging these modern aspects of Indian culture, the Ugly Indian invites housemaids to create traditional rice drawings in cleaned-up spaces, not only to demonstrate the beauty of the spaces but, just as important, to influence the maids (and their employers) who often dump their household's trash in these same spaces. Using these strategies of allowing powerful actors and more ordinary citizens to see a change from trash dump to well-tended pocket park, the Ugly Indian hopes to transform the way Indians from all walks of life view their responsibility for the upkeep of urban spaces. The group's approach reflects a large body of research that has shown that "witnessing the actions of other people has a powerful effect on behaviors" (Nolan et al. 2008, 913).

In Iran, volunteers with the NGO Nature Cleaners similarly clean up trashed public spaces. They describe their efforts using the Farsi term "*farhang-sazi*," which literally translates as "culture building," or, more precisely, "a cultural process through which the authorities can reshape and mould values, norms, perceptions, attitudes and, ultimately shape people's behaviour" (Banakar and Fard 2015). In Iran, *farhang-sazi* is associated with government-run campaigns, or top-down interventions to change citizen behaviors (Banakar and Saeidzadeh 2015). In some cases of *farhang-sazi*, for example attempting to build a citizenry disposed to environmental protection in Iran, the government has appealed to Islamic religious writings (Abe 2016), as do coauthors Karim-Aly Kassam and Zahra Golshani in invoking the Shi'ia Islam principle of cleanliness to describe the work of Nature Cleaners.

In referring to their grassroots cleanups as *farhang-sazi*, volunteers for Nature Cleaners express their intent to have broad impacts on Iranian behavioral norms, similar to government-directed social engineering campaigns but outside of government. The Ugly Indian eschews government-directed campaigns in favor of citizen action in describing how it views "the problem of visible filth on our streets as a behaviour and attitude problem that can be solved in our lifetime (or rather, this month). This can be achieved without spending money or changing legislation or systems. It requires coming up with smart ideas to change people's rooted cultural behaviour and attitudes" (Ugly Indian 2010). To build a new culture of people caring for public spaces, Nature Cleaners and the Ugly Indian attempt to change social norms—that is, societal expectations regarding littering and stewardship behaviors—and attitudes. Given the growing number of volunteer trash cleanups in countries throughout the world, and the rampant plastic pollution of our waterways, oceans, and public lands, attempts to change behavioral norms and cultural attitudes toward trash assume an importance beyond the specific practices (cf. Hawkins 2006).

Notions of "history in person" embodied in the efforts of the Eastern Pennsylvania Coalition for Abandoned Mine Reclamation (EPCAMR) also can be viewed through the lens of culture building. Drawing from Holland and Lave (2001), coauthors Louise Chawla and Robert Hughes define history in person as the fact that people's lives reflect the history of the places they are born into, yet people are not entirely captured by this fate but rather retain the possibility of recasting their inherited history and changing conditions through creative action. In the anthracite coal mining region of eastern Pennsylvania, EPCAMR embraces a history and culture of rural mining communities, including a past prosperity, tragic floods and mining accidents, and current-day contaminated streams and pervasive poverty. By transforming mining oxides into ceramic glazes, restoring land to provide food and butterfly habitat, monitoring water quality, and building monuments to the coal miners' past, EPCAMR staff, volunteers, and children participating in their educational programs redirect their shared history while instilling a culture of caring for land and water.

Not far away from rural Pennsylvania's coal region is the city of Baltimore, Maryland. Similar to EPCAMR, which depends on the commitment of its long-term director Robert Hughes, Baltimore's Collins Avenue Streamside Community reflects the vision and commitment of two individuals—Jill Wrigley and Michael Sarbanes. However, this attempt to change social norms uses an approach entirely different from that of EPCAMR, Nature Cleaners, or the Ugly Indian. Here a family headed by two professionals decided to move into a mixed-income neighborhood and form a multicultural intentional community of like-minded professional families. The case of the Collins Avenue Streamside Community is instructive because it entails a family opening access to a private resource—a wooded streamside property adjacent to their home—to the public in their neighborhood. Although not specifically referring to culture building, the families at the center of this effort have dedicated their lives to greening and social justice work, hoping to provide an example for other intentional communities in Baltimore and elsewhere. Like Nature Cleaners and the Ugly Indian, the Baltimore families are contributing to the transformation of social norms by allowing their neighbors, their church, and other actors to "see the change they want to be." The Baltimore efforts, inspired by a Christian faith emphasizing humbleness coupled with justice, appear to be gently nudging others through example, rather than deliberate provocation as employed in the Ugly Indian's strategic cleanups near the homes of powerful government, media, and sports figures.

Similar to how religious values are invoked in the Iranian and Baltimore cases, the work of Veronica Kyle at Faith in Place occurs within the African American and Latino Christian church and other faith-based institutions in Chicago. Veronica also hopes to change social norms, in this case by "nudging" people of color to see not only their deeply rooted connections with nature but also their responsibility to take care of it. She uses the story of monarch butterfly migration as a starting point for discussions about the migrations of black congregants from the southern states to northern cities and of the journeys undertaken by Latino and other immigrants to the United States. Veronica and her coauthor, religious scholar Laurel Kearns, write about how stories incorporate religious references to explain how environmental restoration can have "broader symbolic meanings related to sacred work and to public witness to the collective moral failure of industrial society. This moral failure results in a 'call' to do better."

In sum, drawing on modern secular, traditional, and religious values, civic ecology practices attempt to change social norms and to build a culture of caring for public and degraded spaces. This entails demonstrating through tangible—*visible*—actions what public spaces can become and the value they bring to their stewards, the community, and even a city or region. As noted by the Ugly Indian, civic ecology stewards attempt to change society by letting people "see the change they want to be."

Knowledge Building: Learning in Civic Ecology Practice

Originally, Keith Tidball and I had posited that one means by which a civic ecology practice might have greater influence is through becoming "evidence based"—that is, by incorporating feedback from measuring ecosystem services and other outcomes (Krasny and Tidball 2015, 2012). In particular, we posited that civic ecology stewards would engage in an adaptive management process (Walters 1986; Gunderson and Light 2006) whereby they collect data on the outcomes of their practice and adapt the practice based on what they find. However, the chapter applying an adaptive management framework to the Kelly Street Community Garden in the Bronx echoes what Gunderson and Light (2006) have found for national parks—resource managers experience multiple challenges when faced with the task of collecting data intended to change their practice, including pressure to perform and to not admit mistakes inherent to a management mind-set. In the Bronx garden, coauthors Philip Silva and Rosalba Lopez Ramirez find that even when provided with data-collection protocols designed using input from their peers, community gardeners make limited use of these protocols. That is not to say, however, that they don't incorporate ongoing learning into their practice. The Bronx community gardeners adapted and applied what they found useful at citywide workshops, and in so doing built practical knowledge specific to their garden practice.

Perhaps Keith Tidball's and my earlier focus on established civic ecology practices collecting data to improve their practices started at the wrong place in the adaptive management cycle. We posited that once established, a civic ecology "management" practice would start collecting data on its outcomes, which in turn would lead to adapting the original management practice. The chapter by Rutgers University ecologist Rebecca Jordan suggests an alternative pathway by which data collection can lead to enhancing civic ecology practices. Rebecca describes participants in her Collaborative Science project who collect formal and less formal observations about an environmental problem, and then develop a visual representation of elements impacting that problem. They use hand-drawn diagrams, or "fuzzy cognitive maps," to model outcomes of changing various inputs and processes related to the problem. In Rebecca's chapter, local residents start by collecting data—on water quality in a suburban community or on trash accumulating in an urban neighborhood. They then use their data and Collaborative Science modeling to reflect on and prioritize stewardship actions like trash cleanups, and have gone further to advocate for changes in local and municipal policy. In Baltimore, the volunteers also offered to gather data after the cleanups to assess the results of their actions, and even planned a field experiment to test the effect of art around trash dumpsters in influencing community members' littering behaviors. Rebecca's work suggests that with support from scientists involved in Collaborative Science and similar public participation in scientific research projects (Shirk et al. 2012), volunteer data collectors can use their data to plan stewardship actions, and later may generate additional information about how well their actions work and adapt those actions accordingly. In short, the cycle may start with data collection, which leads to stewardship action, rather than with environmental stewardship per se.

The chapter by Martha Chaves and Arjen Wals describes how multiple civic ecology practices in Bogota and other Colombian cities raise awareness of ecological and cultural memories, including those of indigenous Colombians. At the five-day annual intercultural gathering El Llamado de la Montaña (the Call of the Mountain), groups engaged in civic ecology practices from across Colombia come together to forge alliances, build leadership, share practices, and enact a collaborative project to reinforce skills and knowledge gained through a workshop. In addition to any new knowledge created by informal sharing across practices, participants create a toolbox of approaches for generating sustainability actions and strengthening relations among participants, organizations, and regions. The Colombian initiative also creates learning spaces to promote reflexive learning.

In sum, the community gardening, Collaborative Science, and Colombian cases suggest multiple pathways by which grassroots efforts may build new knowledge. Through creating such knowledge they may strengthen their own practices (Silva and Lopez Ramirez) as well as become empowered to talk with policy makers (Jordan). Further, Jordan's work suggests a pairing of two distinct and increasingly popular participatory activities—citizen data collection and civic ecology stewardship. Sometimes citizen science data collection comes first, with the data providing the impetus to engage in stewardship and to try to influence the policy process. Finally, by bringing together diverse practitioners to share their knowledge and by capturing collective knowledge in a toolbox, the Colombian efforts reflect much of what we attempted at our workshop in Annapolis and in writing this book—through providing platforms for multiple actors with diverse perspectives to exchange ideas, experience, and knowledge, we generated new understandings of civic ecology practices.

Movement Building: Civic Ecology as Strategic Action Field

Civic ecology practices can be considered not only within the context of changing behavioral norms and attitudes and of creating new knowledge, but also from the perspectives of organizations, governance networks, and social movements. Veronica and her colleagues at Faith in Place integrate civic ecology practices, such as church community gardens, with a policy agenda advocating for clean energy in the state of Illinois; in so doing they have formed partnerships with organizations like Interfaith Power and Light. Robert Hughes's EPCAMR also participates in larger governance networks. Although Robert and his coauthor, environmental psychologist Louise Chawla, focus their chapter on educational efforts with young people, Robert is involved in statewide and national networks of nonprofit organizations that attempt to influence government policy regarding abandoned mine reclamation. In spanning hands-on stewardship practices with advocacy and environmental education, these and other organizations integrate aspects of—and blur the lines separating—ecosystem, education, and advocacy-focused environmental organizations (cf. Sirianni and Sofer 2012). They also form governance networks, which play a role in adaptive governance as described in the chapter by Lance Gunderson, Elizabeth Whiting Pierce, and myself.

The chapter by the Greening of Detroit director Rebecca Salminen Witt, environmental sociologist Erika Svendsen, and myself demonstrates how an organization that emerged from an environmental crisis (the decimation of Detroit's urban tree canopy by Dutch elm disease) formed networks with other organizations engaged in community development and stewardship. The Greening of Detroit chapter also offers a cautionary tale about powerful and less-powerful actors in stewardship governance networks, and demonstrates how a reflexive organization can accommodate social justice issues and adapt to changing social, economic, and environmental conditions. Greening efforts after a devastating tornado in Joplin, Missouri, might also be viewed through the lens of local and more powerful actors. As described by practicing architects and university professors Keith Hedges, Traci Sooter, and Nancy Chikaraishi, the more powerful actors, including a national TV network and nearby university, provided much of the impetus for the greening actions, thus situating this chapter in marked contrast to most cases described in this book where the efforts emerge from local citizen efforts. The Joplin case, which entailed creating two gardens—the first to recognize volunteers who helped rebuild after the tornado and the second to provide a space to remember the storm's victims—illustrates how well-resourced organizations can provide visibility for their own work while engaging local volunteers and helping disaster victims. The Joplin Butterfly Garden and Overlook is also part of a national network of "open spaces, sacred places," which seeks to create and conduct research on spaces for healing in communities impacted by crime and disaster.

A visit with Dennis Chestnut in Washington, DC, invariably entails a tour of an emerging network of green spaces connected by an existing network of green organizations along the eight-mile Anacostia River waterfront. The Living Classrooms Foundation, the Washington, DC, Department of Parks and Recreation, the Anacostia Watershed Society, Anacostia Riverkeeper, the Earth Conservation Corps, Groundwork Anacostia River DC, Soilful City, the Kenilworth Park and Aquatic Gardens, the Marvin Gaye Park, the Civil War Defenses—these are but a few of the organizations and green spaces that Dennis, along with his Washington, DC, colleagues Akiima Price and Xavier Brown, have shown me. Partly as a result of their collective grassroots success in cleaning up the Anacostia River and revitalizing surrounding neighborhoods, longtime, low-income African American residents are now threatened by rising housing prices and related aspects of environmental gentrification. In Dennis's and my chapter, we outline how the nonprofit 11th Street Bridge Park is attempting to avert the gentrification that can occur when civic ecology practices become part of expanding stewardship networks, whose success in greening neighborhoods threatens the very social justice principles embedded in the original grassroots civic ecology initiative.

As civic ecology practices grow to become part of regional green space governance networks, they also help shape and are shaped by broader social movements. Congregations planting milkweed to provide habitat for monarch butterflies can be considered as part of a Christian ecological restoration movement (Van Wieren 2013); community gardening in the Bronx contributes to the urban agriculture and social justice movements (Reynolds and Cohen 2016);

and efforts to restore degraded vacant land in Detroit are part of the ecological restoration economy movement (BenDor et al. 2015). More broadly, civic ecology practices can be seen as contributing to a civic environmental movement emphasizing collaboration among nonprofits, government, and business as a means to address environmental and related social problems (Sirianni and Friedland 2005; John 2004).

When civic ecology practices become part of governance networks and social movements, the boundaries between practices, organizations, and movements can become blurred. Such boundary crossing calls out for abandoning questions that focus narrowly on civic ecology practices, networks of stewardship organizations, or a civic environmental movement. The work of the Greening of Detroit is illustrative. Starting with a narrow focus on tree planting and evolving into broader efforts to transform Detroit's myriad abandoned spaces into gardens, orchards, and urban forest, this greening organization has become not only part of a citywide green space governance network but also helps shape and is shaped by a national urban greening and revitalization movement.

Further blurring the lines delineating different levels of organization are new forms of social media. As illustrated by the Ugly Indian's and Nature Cleaners' use of Facebook and Telegram to organize individual cleanups and to connect volunteers over time and place, social media can play a role in expanding the impact of single civic ecology practices and organizations. Social media also can connect actors in different cities and make them feel as if they are part of, and helping to build and shape, a larger social and environmental movement. In this way, civic ecology practices become actors in Internet-mediated or connective social movements, which do not simply use the web to engage more individuals, but become defined by the ways in which they use social and other digital media (Bennett and Segerberg 2013).

In attempting to integrate the literature about organizations and social movements to describe how change occurs across different levels of social organization, Fligstein and McAdam (2011) proposed the term "strategic action field." This term refers to social spaces where individual and collective actors holding common understandings about their purposes, rules, and relationships (including who has power and why) interact and engage in collective action. The notion of fields of strategic action integrates ideas about collective action at the level of individual practices, organizations, governance networks, and social movements. In this way, it helps to shed light on the possibilities for civic ecology practices to become actors whose impacts are felt beyond individual practices.

Summary of Civic Ecology Broader-Impacts Pathways

To summarize, three themes emerge from the chapters in this book that help us address our question about pathways through which civic ecology practices have larger impacts. First, through nudging neighbors into more sustainable behaviors and even lifestyles, and through provoking more powerful government and media actors, civic ecology practices can build cultures of caring for the environment and community and social norms of collective responsibility for what our public spaces look like and what they provide to our communities. Second, civic ecology practices can become more effective in realizing their environmental and civic goals by creating new knowledge; such knowledge is not limited to formal outcomes monitoring but may include adapting what is learned through informal observations and through interactions with other civic ecology stewards at workshops. Finally, civic ecology practices are conducted by organizations, which become part of networks of environmental and civic renewal organizations, and even civic environmental, urban agriculture, Christian restoration, and ecological restoration movements. Here social media can play a role not just in generating engagement of more people in more practices, but in actually defining the shape of the environmental and social movement. Finally, notions of "connective action" and "strategic action fields" reflect how civic ecology practices cross traditional ways of thinking about social change and institutional boundaries, leading to new ways to envision the interaction of practices, organizations, governance networks, and social movements.

Importantly, any one chapter in this book may illustrate multiple pathways to broader impact. Thus, the order of chapters in the remainder of this volume does not always reflect where they are examined in the discussion of the culture, knowledge, and movement-building themes above. For example, above I discuss the Ugly Indian primarily in terms of culture building because its meme, "See the change you want to be," illustrates an attempt to build social norms and cultural attitudes that is useful for multiple chapters. I also mention this chapter in the social-movement-building section above. I decided to place the Ugly Indian chapter at the end of the section on movement building because it illustrates using social media to create a connective social movement and the notion of strategic action fields. It also integrates many of the ideas put forth in the book, as well as tensions faced by civic ecology practices as they scale up—in particular, how to balance framing a consistent message about one's practice while expanding one's activities and becoming part of networks of multiple volunteer and institutional actors.

Appreciative Inquiry

When I apologized for the two and a half years it took to compile this book, Louise Chawla pointed out that bringing together practitioners and scholars as coauthors presents a daunting challenge. Coauthors struggled with how to integrate their "voices" into a coherent chapter, and several authors dropped out along the way. In a few cases, I jumped in to help beyond the usual editorial tasks and was invited to join as chapter coauthor.

Part of the daunting challenge inherent to practitioners working with academics is the difference in our approaches. Practitioners need to talk about their work as successful in order to garner resources, including volunteers and funding. Academics are trained to question and critique, which to practitioners may feel more like inquisition than inquiry.

Appreciative inquiry, defined as "a research method focusing on positive organizational attributes that may fuel change" (Grant and Humphries 2006, 402), has been used in collaborative studies involving health, education, and other practitioners working alongside researchers. Drawing on action research and social constructivism, appreciative inquiry attempts to draw out "what works" in an organization rather than focus on problems, and to share understandings of what works to improve practice. By focusing on the positive, appreciative inquiry offers potential for addressing practitioner concerns about unfair criticism, but becomes subject to academic concerns about distorting the truth and lacking self-reflection and critique.

Encouraging reflection and deliberation during (Reed 2007) and after (Grant and Humphries 2006) the appreciative inquiry process has been used to draw in critical perspectives. According to the authors of one study, "through applications of critical theory we may begin to better understand not just how an appreciative inquiry develops, but to consider also the knowledge and power influences which might be negotiated as the process unfolds and on what basis such negotiation might be used to contribute to the *emancipation and flourishing of humanity*" (emphasis added, Grant and Humphries 2006, 410). This quote reflects what appreciative inquiry and critical theory hold in common—a focus on change, emancipation, and human flourishing. Our chapter coauthors explored what was "working" in organizations and practices, and in so doing sought to understand how civic ecology practices contribute to the flourishing of humans, our communities, and our environment. The authors avoid critiquing the practices per se, with the exception of the chapter about the Greening of Detroit, in which the critique was offered by the practitioner (Rebecca Salminen Witt) rather than by her academic coauthor (Erika Svendsen). Thus, the chapters in this book can be viewed in the tradition of appreciative inquiry.

This does not mean, however, that the chapters lack critical reflection. Our process differs from the approaches described elsewhere, in which an evaluation of power relations in a formal appreciative inquiry process was the source of critical refection. Instead the authors in this book apply disciplinary and theoretical perspectives as a means of critically reflecting on practice. In this way, the chapter authors and I hope our collective work will contribute not only to the flourishing of individual civic ecology practices. We also seek to understand how such practices contribute to flourishing of the humans engaged, the surrounding community, environmental governance systems, and the social-ecological systems in which these different levels of activity occur.

This book has been a journey over several years. Along the way, my coauthors and I not only faced the challenges of working across barriers separating practice and scholarship. We also lost one of our authors prematurely. A lawyer, university professor, and community activist, Jill Wrigley committed her life to living in inner-city Baltimore. Alongside her husband Michael Sarbanes, her three adopted children, and the other members of their Collins Avenue Streamside Community, Jill continues to provide inspiration for those volunteering to clean up a public space, to start a community garden, and more deeply to commit their life to a community, its people, and its nature. Veronica Kyle spoke about civic ecology as "lifework in the environment." Jill's lifework recalls the words scientist Walter Munk shared in reflecting on Pope Francis's call to combat climate change and to "care for our common home" (Revkin 2014). As embodied by Jill Wrigley's lifework, "This requires a miracle of love and unselfishness." We begin with Jill's story.

Acknowledgments

When asked to define civic ecology during the workshop that launched this book, I spoke about inspiration. "Civic ecology to me is the inspiration I derive from people in cities and in stressed communities all over the world who have learned how to care for nature and care for community at the same time." Although compiling this book has been challenging at times, I remain inspired today.

This is the real reason I study, write about, and participate in civic ecology practices. In the spirit of appreciative inquiry, I deeply appreciate civic ecology practices. I also deeply appreciate the authors in this book being willing to share their practices, to help us understand their theoretical context, and to help us envision their larger contributions. I hope that these practices make a difference not just to participants' lives, but to Bangalore, India, the anthracite region of Pennsylvania, cities in Iran and the United States, and to our shared planet.

REFERENCES

Abe, S. 2016. "Management of the Environment (mohit-e zist): An Ethnography of Islam and Environmental Politics in Iran." *Japanese Review of Cultural Anthropology* 17 (1): 63–81. doi:10.14890/jrca.17.1_63.

Banakar, R., and S. N. Fard. 2015. "*Farhang-sazi*: Interviews with Male Taxi Drivers." In *Driving Culture in Iran: Law and Society on the Roads of the Islamic Republic*, edited by R. Banakar. London: I. B. Tauris.

Banakar, R., and Z. Saeidzadeh. 2015. "Culture: Reflections on Individualism and Community." In *Driving Culture in Iran: Law and Society on the Roads of the Islamic Republic*, edited by R. Banakar, 149–77. London: I. B. Tauris.

BenDor, T. K., A. Livengood, T. W. Lester, A. Davis, and L. Yonavjak. 2015. "Defining and Evaluating the Ecological Restoration Economy." *Restoration Ecology* 23 (3): 209–19. doi:10.1111/rec.12206.

Bennett, W. L., and A. Segerberg. 2013. *The Logic of Connective Action: Digital Media and the Personalization of Contentious Politics*. New York: Cambridge University Press.

Connolly, J. J., E. S. Svendsen, D. R. Fisher, and L. Campbell. 2014. "Networked Governance and the Management of Ecosystem Services: The Case of Urban Environmental Stewardship in New York City." *Ecosystem Services* 10:187–94. doi:10.1016/j.ecoser.2014.08.005.

Fligstein, N., and D. McAdam. 2011. "Toward a General Theory of Strategic Action Fields." *Sociological Theory* 29 (1): 1–26.

Grant, S., and M. Humphries. 2006. "Critical Evaluation of Appreciative Inquiry: Bridging an Apparent Paradox." *Action Research* 4 (4): 401–18. doi:10.1177/1476750306070103.

Gunderson, L. H., and S. S. Light. 2006. "Adaptive Management and Adaptive Governance in the Everglades Ecosystem." *Policy Sciences* 39:323–34.

Hawkins, G. 2006. *The Ethics of Waste: How We Relate to Rubbish*. New York: Rowman & Littlefield.

Holland, D., and J. Lave. 2001. Introduction to *History in Person: Enduring Struggles, Contentious Practice, Intimate Identities*, edited by D. Holland and J. Lave, 3–33. Santa Fe, NM: School for Advanced Research Press.

John, D. 2004. "Civic Environmentalism." In *Environmental Governance Reconsidered*, edited by R. F. Durant, D. Fiorini, and R. O'Leary, 219–54. Cambridge, MA: MIT Press.

Krasny, M. E., and K. G. Tidball. 2012. "Civic Ecology: A Pathway for Earth Stewardship in Cities." *Frontiers in Ecology and the Environment* 10 (5): 267–73. doi:10.1890/110230.

———. 2015. *Civic Ecology: Adaptation and Transformation from the Ground Up*. Cambridge, MA: MIT Press.

Nolan, J. M., P. W. Schultz, R. B. Cialdini, N. J. Goldstein, and V. Griskevicius. 2008. "Normative Social Influence Is Underdetected." *Personality and Social Psychology Bulletin* 34 (7): 913–23. doi:10.1177/0146167208316691.

Reed, J. 2007. *Appreciative Inquiry: Research for Change*. Thousand Oaks, CA: Sage.

Revkin, A. 2014. "Tracing the Roots of Pope Francis's Climate Plans for 2015." *Dot Earth* (blog). *New York Times*, December 31, 2014. https://dotearth.blogs.nytimes.com/2014/12/31/tracing-the-roots-of-pope-franciss-climate-plans-for-2015/?_r=0.

Reynolds, K., and N. Cohen. 2016. *Beyond the Kale: Urban Agriculture and Social Justice Activism in New York City*. Edited by N. Cohen. Athens: University of Georgia Press.

Rogers, E. M. 2003. *Diffusion of Innovations*. 5th ed. New York: Free Press.

Shirk, J., H. Ballard, C. Wilderman, T. Phillips, A. Wiggins, R. Jordan, E. McCallie, M. Minarchek, B. Lewenstein, M. E. Krasny, and R. Bonney. 2012. "Public Participation in Scientific Research: A Framework for Deliberate Design." *Ecology and Society* 17 (2): 29.

Sirianni, C., and L. A. Friedland. 2005. *The Civic Renewal Movement: Community Building and Democracy in the United States*. Dayton, OH: Charles F. Kettering Foundation.

Sirianni, C., and S. Sofer. 2012. "Environmental Organizations." In *The State of Nonprofit America*, 2nd ed., edited by L. M. Salamon, 294–328. Washington, DC: Brookings Institution.

Tidball, K. G., and M. E. Krasny, eds. 2014. *Greening in the Red Zone: Disaster, Resilience and Community Greening*. New York: Springer.

Ugly Indian. 2010. "The Ugly Indian." http://www.theuglyindian.com/.

Van Wieren, G. 2013. *Restored to Earth: Christianity, Environmental Ethics, and Ecological Restoration*. Washington, DC: Georgetown University Press.

Walters, C. J. 1986. *Adaptive Management of Renewable Resources*. New York: McGraw Hill.

Part I
CULTURE BUILDING
Changing Social Norms through
Civic Ecology Practices

Chapter 1

COMING HOME TO COMMON GROUND IN STRESSED COMMUNITIES

Intentional Civic Engagement in the
Collins Avenue Streamside Community
of Southwest Baltimore

Jill Wrigley, Mila Kellen Marshall, and Michael Sarbanes

Jill and Michael

On a crisp fall day in the year 2000, in the Irvington community of southwest Baltimore, children were headed on foot to a nature "treasure hunt" in a historic park cemetery, the only publicly accessible green space within walking distance of their neighborhood. They walked through their landscape, past people on porches, kids and youth on bikes, well-kept houses, houses in states of disrepair, vacant houses, tidy and messy front yards, vacant lots full of junk, and a lot of trash on the ground. Six-year-old Ashley tugged on her adult chaperone's sleeve and whispered, "Look, Miss Jill. There are treasures all around." That this little girl was able to see beauty through the disinvested environment around her is a testament to her resilience. The intentionally tended *public* spaces she and other children saw most regularly were the little altars that popped up on telephone poles or chain-link fences adorned with stuffed animals, photos, and candles in the wake of a shooting death. This child deserved more; she deserved access to beautiful and green spaces dedicated to her pleasure and well-being.

Shortly after this experience, the adult chaperone (Jill) and her husband, Michael, who had moved into Irvington in 1994, joined with other neighbors to reclaim an abandoned and trashed vacant double lot at the top of their street. They structured the planning and design process to center on children and youth. Equipped with design elements generated by their young people, the neighborhood residents and community partners undertook many years of grant writing and physical work. Now this once-nuisance lot is the Irvington Peace Park, which serves as a community gathering space and is enriched with elements created by young people, including mosaic art, food gardens, flowering and fruit trees, and a performance/art-making space. In addition, the chaperones on that initial treasure hunt opened up their yard, which is wooded and ringed by a small stream, as accessible green space for their neighbors. All are welcome. The neighborhood's children and young people especially take advantage of this open invitation for playing on a tire swing, exploring the natural setting, and socializing with one another in a relaxing setting.

Irvington Peace Park is located at 506 Collins Avenue, Baltimore. The yard is a wooded area around a stream called Maidens Choice Run, which is part of the Gwynns Falls Watershed and is accessed at the end of the street through the property belonging to 523 Collins Avenue.

Mila

Inner-city environmental programs can accomplish their goals and completely miss the mark at the same time. In my time with Jill, I was both fascinated and saddened in unraveling the reality of the relationship between "environmental allies" and community stewards. I was saddened because we both agreed that there was very little intention and connection between those who wanted to help communities and those who needed the help. We would lament over the savior complex of some so-called partners and gripe about the many ways the relationships were superficial.

Yet I was fascinated with the spirit of compassion Jill and her husband Michael displayed in their shared story, a story that became the impetus of this very shared chapter. I listened often with tears welling in my eyes at the supreme level of care Jill and Michael took to become a part of a system that needed not just allies, but allies who were willing to initiate, negotiate, and facilitate access that was identified by the community. There were moments I thought how special Jill was and how simple the practice was as well: the practice of intention.

It wasn't until I learned of Jill's passing that I understood. I understood Jill had dedicated her life to being of service to those who needed an ally. Much like the ecosystem services that we strive to increase for the benefits of human well-being, Jill taught me that the most important service comes from us: humans being of service to people and nature in an equitable and just way.

The reality of stressed communities is not that people within them are oblivious, or detached from community needs. Rather, the complex, multifaceted, and institutional problems that plague these communities diminish people's ability to mobilize and sustain efforts to address the multiple challenges they face—including challenges related to education, public health, environmental racism, employment, and housing. All these "stressed" communities have people who care deeply and are organized to express that care: there are neighborhood stewards and stalwarts, businesses, social organizations, schools, and churches that have stood firm and remain active in their work to support their own communities. What is apparent is that they are the local champions; however, their capacity to impart effective change that improves the quality of the environment—both natural and built—is limited because of the framework that they too are confined within. The local champions have both remained faithful to their charge and are impeded by structural limitations and constraints. Intentional and careful support from allies may help indigenous processes of empowerment to address some of these barriers by making accessible additional resources including knowledge, financial assets, and networks.

In this chapter, we describe the case of a white couple, motivated by their Christian faith and having grown up with civic-engagement role models, using greening as a means to engage and improve the well-being of a low-income, largely African American neighborhood in Baltimore, Maryland. The case is multifaceted: it draws on Christian and democratic institutions and values; it involves an intentional urban community integrated within the larger neighborhood; and it entails opening up access to public and private property—and to opportunities for civic participation—for children and adults living in the neighborhood. This chapter also incorporates the insights of an African American scholar and environmental justice activist (Mila) into issues of race and civic engagement in communities of color. Although the efforts we describe were temporarily interrupted by the premature passing of the first author of this chapter, Jill Wrigley, her efforts and those of her husband Michael Sarbanes, their friends and church, continue to permeate their neighborhood. This chapter is a tribute to Jill's continuing legacy.

Civic Activism and Race in U.S. Cities

Baltimore shares a social and environmental history with many postindustrial U.S. cities, such as Chicago, Detroit, and Cleveland. For African Americans, historic segregation due to legally enforced separate housing undermined the accumulation of wealth and limited access to city parks, grocery stores, and other amenities (Pietila 2010; Coates 2014; Lichter, Parisi, and Taquino 2015). More recently, disinvestment on the part of industry and municipal government has led to abandoned housing and derelict vacant lots, creating eyesores that foster crime and contribute to negative experiences in one's own neighborhood, negative perceptions of safety and nature, and poor physical, mental, and community health and well-being (Branas et al. 2011; Garvin, Cannuscio, and Branas 2013; Garvin, Branas, et al. 2013; Metro, Dwyer, and Dreschler 1981; Kondo, South, and Branas 2015; Jenerette et al. 2011).

Exclusion from economic, social, and political life helps explain why, after controlling for education and income, African Americans are less likely than whites to participate in civic activities (Foster-Bey 2008). Related to exclusion, volunteering in civic life depends not just on individual characteristics such as income and motivation, but also on simply being asked to volunteer; African Americans are less likely than whites to be asked to volunteer (Musick, Wilson, and Bynum 2000). Further, civic participation often begins during youth, but youth of color experience structural barriers to participation at a young age, including limited opportunities for civic engagement in school and after-school clubs in low-income and minority neighborhoods, lower rates of college attendance, and fewer adult leaders or role models because of high ratios of children to adults and a significant proportion of adult males serving jail time away from families (Flanagan and Levine 2010). These factors may lead to low "outcome expectations"—that is, the expectation that one's actions will make a difference gained through participating in or observing such action (Chung and Probert 2011). Youth have outcome expectations both for themselves and for their community; individual outcome expectations are influenced by prior civic engagement, whereas community outcome expectations are influenced by perceptions of community functioning. Youth living in a neighborhood with multiple incivilities, limited civic participation, and lack of trust among residents can be expected to have low levels of civic participation (Chung and Probert 2011).

Although various forms of exclusion and lower levels of human capital, including income, education, homeownership, and health, may explain differences in civic participation, other forms of capital, both social and cultural, complicate the picture. For example, African Americans attend church more frequently, and church activity builds the social capital that leads to volunteering. African Americans are also more likely than whites to volunteer for church-related activities, which provide training and a "gateway" to other voluntarism (Musick, Wilson, and Bynum 2000; Sundeen, Garcia, and Raskoff 2008). In fact, although whites participate at higher rates in voluntarism related to youth, education, and the environment, African Americans are more active in community action, work-related, and political groups (Sundeen 1992) and have high rates of faith-related voluntarism (Sundeen, Garcia, and Raskoff 2008; Musick, Wilson, and Bynum 2000).

For whites wanting to engage in civic ecology practices, understanding the complex nature of the African American experience in cities, including historical, economic, and cultural barriers to civic participation, as well as cultural traditions and assets related to voluntarism, requires intentionality and a deep commitment. It means more powerful white players finding ways to support efforts that emerge in communities of color without taking credit and dictating practices (Reynolds and Cohen 2016). It may mean living in low-income communities of color, while at the same time taking measures to avert the gentrification that often accompanies better-off citizens moving into such communities (Pearsall 2013).

Collins Avenue Streamside Community

We turn next to the case of the Collins Avenue Streamside Community in the Irvington neighborhood of Baltimore. Because this entails a white couple's life-long commitment to living in and encouraging healing and civic engagement in a predominantly low-income African American community, it brings to the surface issues of race related to civic ecology.

Irvington Neighborhood as Manifestation of "Uncommon" (Hyper-segregated) Ground: The Social and Ecological Context of the Streamside Community

Located in the southwest corner of Baltimore, the Irvington neighborhood has multiple assets: long-term residents who know one another and have friendly relationships, diverse housing stock, many trees, a number of stable local institutions, and access to bus lines. It also faces myriad challenges reflecting a history of residential segregation resulting in 88 percent of residents and 93 percent of public school students being African American. Unemployment, addiction, low incomes, and low education levels are widespread. Much of the housing has been neglected or abandoned, and rental units are often cramped (Baltimore Neighborhood Indicators Alliance 2014). Irvington also has been officially designated as a "food desert" by the Baltimore Food Policy Initiative and its partners (Buczynski, Freishtat, and Buzogany 2015). While the neighborhood contains multiple fast-food and junk-food outlets, it has limited access to fresh fruits and vegetables. A third of households have no car, thus limiting their ability to access healthier foods.

The neighborhood has a wealth of open space that presents opportunities for civic ecology practices. Irvington is bounded to the south by Maidens Choice

Run, a small stream that also runs through a large wooded area owned by Jill and Michael, and by two cemeteries, including the four-hundred-acre Loudon Park Cemetery founded in 1857 as part of the American park cemetery movement (Sachs 2013). At the southern edge of the neighborhood, in the midst of the extraordinary urban green area formed by the stream valley and cemetery woods, is the 500 block of Collins Avenue. This street slopes gently downhill from the subsidized apartment complex at the top of the block, passes the Peace Park, and comes to a dead end at the green space owned by Jill and Michael.

Animating Spirit and Overarching Aims of the Streamside Community

The Collins Avenue Streamside Community is an intentional community whose members are motivated by their desire to enter fully into a life that addresses the challenge put forward by Dr. Howard Thurman in his 1965 treatise *The Luminous Darkness*. Concerned about building the healthy American society in the wake of the end of legal segregation, Thurman wrote,

> The issue then is twofold. The walls that divide must be demolished. They must be cast down, destroyed, uprooted. . . . These barriers must be seen for what they are, a disease of our society, the enemy of human decency and humane respect. . . . Their destruction is such a monumental undertaking and is calling for such huge costs in human lives, resources of money, time, and energy, that an ever-widening weariness is apt to sweep over the land in the wake of the crumbling of the walls. And this is the danger. *When the walls are down, it is then that the real work of building the healthy American society begins.* (Thurman 1965, 91, emphasis added)

According to Michael, the tragedy of the Thurman quote is that ways of building the "healthy American society" are actually quite doable but either are not visible and thus not considered at all, or are framed as the province of exceptional characters. The intent of Streamside Community is to challenge people to consider what can be done.

An intentional community is a self-identified group of individuals who challenge the norms of society (Meijering, Huigen, and Van Hoven 2007). Although such communities are often in rural areas and thus separated geographically as well as psychologically from mainstream society (e.g., eco-villages, religious communities), Streamside Community is in the middle of Baltimore's Irvington neighborhood. The community's two founding members, Jill and Michael, were born during the years when the key civil rights laws were passed, and were raised within family and faith traditions that called them to the challenge of building a healthy multiracial society. In 1994, they moved to Irvington and encouraged like-minded families to follow. Today, the community has grown to encompass more than a half-dozen core households living on the 500 block of Collins Avenue. Members vary in racial, ethnic, and religious backgrounds and are employed in K–12 and university teaching, law, nonprofit management, health care, grassroots activism, and green construction. Because members are employed, the intentional community is economically self-sufficient, requiring neither outside resources nor government action to function (CASC, n.d.).

The core members are joined in their efforts by neighbors within a four-block radius of their homes, and by children and young people who visit friends and family on these blocks or who simply wander into the green spaces created by Streamside Community. Many of these neighbors live in an apartment complex owned and operated by Volunteers of America as long-term affordable rental housing mostly for single-parent households with children. Streamside Community members advocated for this apartment complex to receive and maintain certification as federally funded affordable housing for low-income families. Creation and preservation of decent affordable housing is an important part of Streamside Community's long-term community vision, and Streamside's civic ecology practices depend upon the housing complex's continued presence.

Streamside Community members draw inspiration from secular movements that aim to generate solidarity across race and class lines to support positive social change (e.g., the Freedom Schools in the struggle for civil rights and the Settlement House movement, a leading example of which is Jane Addams's Hull House). They also draw inspiration from faith-based movements in which members seek to embody church-related values (e.g., Dorothy Day and the Catholic Worker tradition) and from various forms of collective living arrangements that focus on ecological restoration (e.g., eco-villages). Streamside Community is aware of how nature and accessible green space can contribute to its goals. According to Jill and Michael,

> Our primary call is to relocate into, or remain in, a stressed (low-income) community in Baltimore City to contribute to the building of that "healthy American society," not just through professional work on policy and programs, but also through relationships, leveraging resources of institutions, and a physical and spiritual commitment to place. Out of this focus, the Streamside Community was born and continues to grow. We are now an intentional, faith-inspired community, seeking to respond to the wounds inflicted by racism and race and class segregation. We live across those lines with the intention to support justice and

reconciliation among people and between people and "nature" (which is the word we use for the surrounding and underlying ecosystem in which we are living).

Civic Ecology Practices Seeking Holistic Neighborhood Improvement while Countering Gentrification

The focus of much urban renewal has been on low-income, African American families moving to higher-opportunity suburban areas, or on creating "improved neighborhood environments" where poverty remains concentrated (Chetty, Hendren, and Katz 2015). Streamside Community represents an alternate route to improving outcomes for low-income communities of color: cultivating healthy, multiracial spaces—what Martin Luther King Jr. called the "beloved community"— in urban areas of concentrated poverty. According to Jill and Michael,

> We understand our practices as contributing to existing efforts by many others in our neighborhood to improve the overall environment, especially for children and youth. Adding to the many ways neighbors in this community provide mutual support to one another, we also offer time and support on simple and complex matters, including out of our own expertise with regard to health care, criminal justice matters, school system and educational advocacy, employment rights, public services, and other matters commonly encountered. We aim to bring our social capital to serve community empowerment. Among the external resources we strategically engage are faith communities, universities, public schools, non-profits, and community and city-wide organizing efforts. Neighbors have reciprocated with gifts of food, time, child care, help on home improvements and friendship. We have benefited immeasurably from these relationships and the experiences we've had living in this community.

Creation of the Peace Park

For many years, the vacant lot at the top of the block, at the corner of Potter Street and Collins Avenue, was a symbol of urban disinvestment. An abandoned and deteriorating house stood on a double lot piled high with garbage and junk. The previous inhabitant had long since left the neighborhood, but retained ownership and used the yard as his informal dump, creating an environmental and visual nuisance. After years of advocacy by the Irvington Community Association (of which Michael was vice president at the time), the house was finally condemned through a public adjudicatory process. Michael and Jill facilitated transfer of ownership of the property to their nearby Episcopal church, which enabled block residents to create and collectively manage the site now known as the Irvington Peace Park. While the vacant lot's repurposing was the subject of some community debate (some sought its transformation into a parking lot), eventually the church decided to dedicate the lot as community green space.

FIGURE 1.1   Author Jill Wrigley and neighbors at the dedication of the Peace Park in 2007. Photo by Michael Sarbanes.

FIGURE 1.2 Neighbors gather for tree planting at Peace Park. Photo by Michael Sarbanes.

The Peace Park's initial design was developed through a yearlong, youth-led "charrette" or collaborative design process facilitated by community residents with support from the Baltimore Neighborhood Design Center (NDC 2016). This process evoked a desire among the community's children and youth for a space to experience beauty, flowers, trees, growing food, open recreational spaces, and opportunities for art, music, and play.

Drawing from the youths' vision and in cooperation with local residents and outside volunteers, Streamside Community members facilitated the transformation of the vacant lot into the Peace Park. They wrote grants and received funding from the TKF Foundation (see chapter 9), conducted cleanups, installed community-created art and garden beds, and planted flowers and trees. Over the years, activities at the Peace Park have included mini–art camps whose participants created a mosaic archway emblazoned with glittering "PEACE PARK"; peace flags representing the professions our children aspire to, and a wishing tree decorated with ribbons that hold neighbors' hopes for the future. Streamside Community members and neighbors also join in recreational activities, including "sprinkler days" on hot summer afternoons, family celebrations, game days, and music and art events that take advantage of the shaded deck built through a youth employment project. In sum, echoing Jane Jacobs's (1961, 271) call to "discern, respect and build upon the forces of regeneration that exist" organically within poor and marginalized communities, youth and adults have created Peace Park, which now serves as a space for play, relaxation, fellowship, and community building.

Streamside Green Space

The other end of the 500 block of Collins from the Peace Park runs into Jill and Michael's wooded streamside property, which they committed to managing as a neighborhood amenity accessible to all. Previously, this parcel bordering the yard surrounding their home was a neglected, municipally owned, informal dump. The prior homeowners purchased the lot from the city for one dollar and hauled out eighteen dump-truck loads of trash in an effort to improve it for their own private use and enjoyment. While Jill and Michael were initially attracted to this green space as a personal resource for urban living, they reconceived and repurposed the streamside ecosystem as a community resource.

The streamside parcel is divided into two areas: (1) an active recreation area comprising a small field, half basketball court, tire swing, and reading circle composed of tree stumps; and (2) a wild area, which is green and lush, though marred for trained eyes by extensive invasive plants. The wild area was a staging ground for a major overhaul of sewage lines, which while critical to restoration of the stream, brought in heavy equipment that disturbed the site, leading to compacted soil and invasive plants. With a multiracial team of three certified permaculturists and a master gardener living on the block, the Streamside Community has begun to restore the land as a perennial food forest serving multiple purposes for humans and other life.

As a result of the sewage system overhaul, fish have returned to the stream, joined by a colony of yellow-crowned night herons, as well as kingfishers, hawks, and owls. Visitors frequently see deer, fox, opossum, raccoon, muskrat, frogs, snakes, and the occasional snapping turtle (whose head was once mistaken for an alligator by a neighborhood child!). Outside visitors are frequently shocked—and neighbors delighted—by the wildlife in this densely populated urban neighborhood just three miles from downtown Baltimore. Waiting for the spring arrival of the herons, watching their nest-building, and spotting the newly born young are now favored activities for neighborhood children.

Collaborative Recovery of and Invitation into Green Space as Civic Ecology Practice

JILL AND MICHAEL

Our civic ecology practice has been to reclaim, improve, and transform these neglected spaces to become multipurpose community resources where relationships are strengthened. We hope that our intentional and ongoing presence, hospitality, and play within these spaces will support people-to-people and people–nature reconciliation, as well as individual, family, and community well-being. *We believe deeply that building the healthy American society requires new forms of community and that the transformation of neglected natural spaces into community-building resources is a potentially powerful civic ecology practice.*

By exercising open-arms hospitality on privately owned land and on the church-owned Peace Park, we seek to foster a sense of communal belonging to the land and to each other. Our model is inspired in part by the Swedish tradition of *Allemansrätt* ("everyone's right"), which holds that all land is accessible for walking, camping, and foraging, to all members of the nation, regardless of private property rights (except land visible from the homestead). We are equally inspired by the South African concept of *ubuntu*—"I am, because we are"—an expression underlining the healthy interdependence and interconnection of human community. By welcoming children and others wholeheartedly into these nature spaces, we seek to communicate their deep belonging to the earth, to one another, and as members of the human community having a relationship with the earth. While we recognize the value that structured programming can provide for engaging communities of color with civic ecology practices, our intention and practices allow for the space to be used in a more intimate and natural way. We believe that interconnectedness and "whole-making" can be nurtured through connection to nature, both for the individual and the collective in the following practices, some formal, some informal.

We have intentionally created and shared a space that allows for unprogrammed practices that are reflected in the dozens of children who flock to any activity in the Peace Park or casually wander its paths, as well as in the constant flow of children who come to play on the tire swing or shoot baskets on our property and then find their way to the stream and woods as a place of wonder, adventure, and peace. Sitting on the benches by the stream, or under the trees at the Peace Park, also provides an opportunity for adults to de-stress and relax in a dense urban environment not designed or maintained for human wellness.

One mother of three expressed gratitude while sitting by the stream: "[Ordinarily] the only place I get a chance to relax is the bathtub, and even then the kids are banging on the door." And a young girl one day sat against a tree in the Peace Park and said, "This is a place where you can just relax and be who God wants you to be." One young man we had known for years, after recently being released from prison and struggling to find work, asked one evening if he could just sit beneath the trees near the stream for a while, saying, "This is the only peaceful place for me in the whole neighborhood." Another young girl, after listening to the sound of the stream with eyes closed for a minute, opened her eyes with wonder and declared, "I heard it tell me to just breathe and be calm."

We engage in a number of intentional practices on our streamside land:

- Actively welcoming children and youth into our green space, speaking with them and spending time getting to know them.
- Answering the daily knocks on our door and taking seriously whoever appears on the other side.
- Providing simple snacks of seasonal, local fruit for any child who asks (and we get multiple requests several days a week).
- Modeling and encouraging participation in informal stewardship efforts, including trail maintenance, tree planting and tree care, vegetable gardening, composting, weed pulling, and stream, park, and street cleanups; and calling the city about sewage leaks into the stream.
- Becoming trained and knowledgeable as "community naturalists" and participating alongside children, youth, and neighbors exploring and learning about our ecosystem. Together we have learned about the native and nonnative plants in our wooded area and wild and cultivated edible plants. ("Can I eat this leaf?" is a surprisingly common question in our herb garden / front yard.) We also have sampled stream insects; trained "Bee Guards" who care for beehives; searched for wildlife such as salamanders, turtles, snakes, spiders, and insects; and listened and watched for birds (hawks and owls are big favorites).
- Encouraging positive forms of conflict resolution and peaceful interactions; communicating norms of mutual respect and endorsement of happy, peaceful play.

- Inviting parents to sit and stay awhile when they come down to our yard to call their children.
- Playing in nature with children and youth: skipping stones, swinging on the tire swing, playing ball games in the yard or hide-and-seek in the woods, and creating works of art with nature objects.
- Creating moments of fellowship with food, music, and conversation.
- Welcoming and engaging in conversation anyone who has wandered into the streamside space.
- Creating short "spa" retreats with food and quiet by the stream for neighborhood women undergoing peak moments of stress.
- Utilizing the space for others in the city to connect to one another, such as a gathering of city public school teachers seeking to collaborate around educating for environmental justice activism.

MILA

The significance of the space lies in the fact that there are no gates or "do not enter" signs; there are no peering fearful eyes from windows but rather smiling faces and sweet hellos. There is no white person lurking behind you investigating what you are doing there, but someone greeting you or letting you know what other spaces are there to explore. People engaging in these spaces do not just experience a structurally transformed space; they have a socially inviting and less interrogative space shared between African Americans and other ethnicities. This I think plays a huge role in the success of the community, but it is also those intentional acts of passive welcoming that are so important for finding common ground.

This practice shows residents they are welcomed by not making them feel like strangers in their own shared backyard. It is a practice that doesn't require a difference in ethnicity; it requires practitioners, even those who look like the community, to have a desire to be present and accessible in a way that challenges the way people of color are engaged in their everyday lives. This model is so new for me and I am so excited because the Streamside Community has set the bar for what it looks like to share and care about the needs of African American urban communities in a meaningful, productive way.

Public Engagement and Public Space in an Intentional Community

We began by talking about the context in which urban civic ecology practices often emerge—segregated neighborhoods whose residents have suffered from years of discrimination and now economic disinvestment leaving behind derelict vacant spaces, poverty, and their attendant social ills (Krasny and Tidball 2015). Although often African Americans and other lower-income residents living in these neighborhoods take the initiative to transform vacant spaces to community gardens (Reynolds and Cohen 2016), in this chapter we describe an effort started by a white couple personally committed to social and economic justice. After moving to the Irvington neighborhood, Jill and Michael adopted two brothers from Ethiopia and an African American girl from Baltimore. They formed an intentional community committed to urban social justice. And along the way they discovered that restoring nature in degraded spaces was a means not only for personal restoration but also for bringing their community together. We next turn to how Jill and Michael's efforts suggest two pathways for how their practice might have impacts beyond Peace Park and their streamside neighborhood: opportunities for public engagement in communities of color and intentional communities in urban renewal.

By providing opportunities for children and families to plan and join in clean-ups, plantings, and neighborhood gatherings at Peace Park and the streamside land, the Streamside Community created not just spaces for healing, but also opportunities for civic engagement among low-income African Americans. Youth engaged in the Peace Park planning charrettes saw the outcomes of their efforts, which could lead to increased individual and community outcome expectancies (Chung and Probert 2011). The planning efforts also allowed Irvington residents to articulate what they perceive and experience as culturally important ecosystem services or disservices (Plieninger et al. 2013). By addressing barriers to civic engagement in communities of color, and thus potentially influencing future engagement of youth and adults in the Irvington neighborhood (cf. Flanagan and Levine 2010), the Streamside Community created the potential for long-term and broader impacts of their local practice.

While the opportunities for people of color to participate in the Streamside Community are important in fostering future civic engagement, it is also important to note that in certain sectors of the environmental movement, people of color are already overrepresented. Much of the research on underrepresentation of people of color in the environmental movement has focused on mainstream environmental organizations (Taylor 2015). Whereas only 12 percent of staff in mainstream environmental organizations were minorities in a 2013–2014 study, in environmental justice organizations, 80 percent of staff, a third of executive directors, all organizational presidents, and two-thirds of board members were minorities (Taylor 2015).

Minority participation in civic ecology practices is also high and may exceed that of white participation in some cities. For example, a study of tree-planting volunteers in New York City found nearly equal percentages of novice (less involved) stewards identified as white (48 percent) and minority (45 percent) (Fisher, Svendsen, and Connolly 2015). Although whites constituted a higher proportion of more committed stewards relative to minorities, after controlling for education and other class-related variables, participation of minorities was higher than expected, based on New York City demographics. Further, Eizenberg (2013) documented the overrepresentation of low-income African Americans and Latinos in the community-gardening movement, and Reynolds and Cohen (2016) describe how African Americans and Latinos have become leaders in the urban agriculture movement in New York City. Interestingly, among African Americans, human capital does not impact volunteer rates in the same way it does for whites—poor and rich, uneducated and educated are just as likely to volunteer in African American communities (Musick, Wilson, and Bynum 2000).

In addition to suggesting how civic ecology practices foster current and future civic engagement, the Streamside Community provides a model for intentional communities interested in building thriving neighborhoods in cities. Whereas many intentional communities involve shared housing, are rural, and represent an escape from urban living, the Streamside Community homeowners purposely located in a low-income city neighborhood, thus demonstrating their commitment to social justice in communities of color. Through advocating for government-supported housing on their block, they countered the potential for gentrification often resulting from professionals moving into and greening low-income urban communities (Wolch, Byrne, and Newell 2014; see also chapter 10 for discussion of environmental gentrification). Whereas some may view Jill and Michael's commitment as exceptional, Michael is aware of two other intentional communities in Baltimore. Both are white, one in a mostly white working-class neighborhood, and the other in a predominantly African American community. Although they have not yet developed the internal racial and religious diversity of Streamside, they have the intention to do so and are in discussion with Michael about pathways for moving forward. Whereas it may always be a relatively small proportion of middle-class whites who choose to live across color and class lines and who conceive of their home and yard as a community space, Jill and Michael have consistently maintained that this approach should be placed in front of people of faith and those concerned about social justice as a realistic option—with its own challenges and rewards.

That Jill and Michael opened up their property to neighbors demonstrates that "public spaces" where people work for the common good (Chung et al. 2005), or "urban green commons" managed for biodiversity and ecosystem services (Colding et al. 2013), depend not on public versus private land ownership but rather on the nature of the activities that take place. Interestingly, by allowing any neighbor to enter their private property or the church-owned Peace Park, Jill and

Michael provide an example of where the ability to exclude outsiders, considered a critical feature of sustainable management of common resources to avoid the tragedy of the commons (Dietz, Ostrom, and Stern 2003), is abandoned in favor of Swedish practices of public access to private property, or "freedom to roam." Perhaps through engaging community members in not only using but also caring for these places, and in some cases in helping to enforce informal rules about responsible use of the space by their peers, the Streamside Community is setting broader, inclusive boundaries that transcend private versus public ownership.

Lessons Learned and Best Practices

Jill and Michael's story suggests how whites can initiate civic ecology practices in ways that are sensitive to the historical and cultural realities of low-income African American communities, including not just the economic and residential exclusion of these communities but also their exclusion from many forms of civic participation. In closing, we would like to share Jill's reflections on how her experiences might inform the continued development of green spaces as community resources. She and Michael felt it is essential that civic ecology practices support experiences in nature that are:

> *Safe.* The space must be safe physically and emotionally, and be distinct in feel and experience from other spaces in the community where violence and fear are all too often present. The core rule for children who are being introduced to the space is to respect each other at all times. When their peers violate this rule, children and youth may be called on to help enforce it.
>
> *Transformational.* The experience of the space must "lead out," by stages, from what may be most familiar to new experiences, awareness, capacities, and confidence. In this context, the Peace Park is a threshold space that leads conceptually into a fuller and wilder natural space by the stream.
>
> *Reconciling.* The space must be welcoming to a diverse group of users, providing a range of ways to connect with the space that embrace people at many different points of awareness, capacity, and need.
>
> *Clean and beautiful.* A significant part of our civic ecology practice involves picking up trash and cleaning up and beautifying neglected areas. Children and youth are regularly invited into this process, where they are volunteers or, for more intense efforts, are paid.
>
> *Nourishing to the spirit and body.* We believe the natural spaces enable neighborhood residents to enter states of mindfulness and meditation without the formality of a program, and that this offers support and resources

to neighbors. One simple expression of this is what we call the "ministry of fruit": households on the block regularly have a supply of fresh fruit for children (who are not at all shy about asking for it). A new member of our community has introduced a practice of encouraging a "giving back" in response to our sharing of fruit. Children are acquiring the habit of letting us know the good things they are doing in response to receiving the fruit (helping a neighbor with a task, picking up trash, or similar benevolent acts).

Accessible in sustained and momentary ways. We seek to create a space that can be transformational for neighborhood residents over a sustained period of engagement and also can spark revelatory moments during a onetime visit.

We close with these words offered in a sermon by the minster at a local church.

> With the renewed earnest conversations about what we can do to address the systemic injustice in this city, the Collins Avenue Streamside Community offers an idea to the rest of us who are looking for a way to work for justice in Baltimore. . . . They say: "One simple way to work for justice is to commit to live for the long term in one of the city communities where poverty is concentrated. Raise your family there. Be a neighbor in all the small and large meanings of that word, to the children and families around you. . . . Honor and nurture the gifts of the youth that are far too often ignored or denied. Learn from your neighbors and be blessed by their strength and compassion. . . . Wrestle with the complexities of relating respectfully, truthfully, and with humility across potential differences of race and class and seek to reconcile across those divides." Nurturing. Reconciling. These words keep coming up this morning. (HRPC 2015)

REFERENCES

Baltimore Neighborhood Indicators Alliance. 2014. "Allendale / Irvington / S. Hilton." University of Baltimore. http://bniajfi.org/community/Allendale_Irvington_S.%20Hilton/.

Branas, C. C., R. A. Cheney, J. M. MacDonald, V. W. Tam, T. D. Jackson, and T. R. Ten Have. 2011. "A Difference-in-Differences Analysis of Health, Safety, and Greening Vacant Urban Space." *American Journal of Epidemiology* 174 (11): 1296–1306. doi:10.1093/aje/kwr273.

Buczynski, A. B., H. Freishtat, and S. Buzogany. 2015. *Mapping Baltimore City's Food Environment: 2015 Report.* Baltimore: Baltimore Development Corp.

Carver, E. 2013. *Birding in the United States: A Demographic and Economic Analysis.* Arlington, VA: U.S. Fish & Wildlife Service.

CASC (Collins Avenue Streamside Community). n.d. In https://collinsavenuestream-side.org/why-community-why-streamside-why-on-collins-avenue.

Chetty, R., N. Hendren, and L. Katz. 2015. "The Effects of Exposure to Better Neighbor-hoods on Children: New Evidence from the Moving to Opportunity Experiment." Cambridge, MA: Harvard University and National Bureau of Economic Research.

Chung, H. L., and S. Probert. 2011. "Civic Engagement in Relation to Outcome Expec-tations among African American Young Adults." *Journal of Applied Developmen-tal Psychology* 32 (4): 227–34. http://dx.doi.org/10.1016/j.appdev.2011.02.009.

Chung, K., R. J. Kirkby, C. Kendell, and J. Beckwith. 2005. "Civic Agriculture: Does Pub-lic Space Require Public Ownership?" *Culture and Agriculture* 27 (2): 99–108.

Coates, T. 2014. "The Case for Reparations." *Atlantic.* June.

Colding, J., S. Barthel, P. Bendt, R. Snep, W. van der Knaap, and H. Ernstson. 2013. "Urban Green Commons: Insights on Urban Common Property Systems." *Global Environmental Change* 23:1039–51. doi:10.1016/j.gloenvcha.2013.05.006.

Dietz, T., E. Ostrom, and P. C. Stern. 2003. "The Struggle to Govern the Commons." *Science* 302 (5652): 1907–12. doi:10.1126/science.1091015.

Eizenberg, E. 2013. *From the Ground Up: Community Gardens in New York City and the Politics of Spatial Transformation.* Farnham, Surrey, UK: Ashgate.

Fisher, D. R., E. S. Svendsen, and J. J. Connolly. 2015. *Urban Environmental Stewardship and Civic Engagement: How Planting Trees Strengthens the Roots of Democracy.* New York: Routledge.

Flanagan, C., and P. Levine. 2010. "Civic Engagement and the Transition to Adult-hood." *Future of Children* 20 (1): 159–79. https://doi.org/10.1353/foc.0.0043.

Foster-Bey, J. 2008. "Do Race, Ethnicity, Citizenship and Socio-economic Status Deter-mine Civic Engagement?" Working Paper no. 62. Boston: CIRCLE.

Garvin, E. C., C. C. Branas, S. Keddem, J. Sellman, and C. Cannuscio. 2013. "More Than Just an Eyesore: Local Insights and Solutions on Vacant Land and Urban Health." *Journal of Urban Health: Bulletin of the New York Academy of Medicine* 90 (3): 412–26. doi:10.1007/s11524-012-9782-7.

Garvin, E. C., C. C. Cannuscio, and C. C. Branas. 2013. "Greening Vacant Lots to Reduce Violent Crime: A Randomised Controlled Trial." *Injury Prevention* 19 (3): 198–203. doi:10.1136/injuryprev-2012-040439.

HRPC (Hunting Ridge Presbyterian Church). 2015. "True Reconciliation Sermon." https://huntingridgechurch.org/2015/05/12/sermon-true-reconciliation/.

Jacobs, J. 1961. *The Death and Life of Great American Cities.* New York: Vintage Books.

Jenerette, G. D., S. L. Harlan, W. L. Stefanov, and C. A. Martin. 2011. "Ecosystem Ser-vices and Urban Heat Riskscape Moderation: Water, Green Spaces, and Social Inequality in Phoenix, USA." *Ecological Applications* 21 (7): 2637–51.

Kondo, M. C., E. C. South, and C. C. Branas. 2015. "Nature-Based Strategies for Improving Urban Health and Safety." *Journal of Urban Health: Bulletin of the New York Academy of Medicine* 92 (5): 800–814. doi:10.1007/s11524-015-9983-y.

Krasny, M. E., and K. G. Tidball. 2015. *Civic Ecology: Adaptation and Transformation from the Ground Up.* Cambridge, MA: MIT Press.

Lichter, D. T., D. Parisi, and M. C. Taquino. 2015. "Toward a New Macro-segregation? Decomposing Segregation within and between Metropolitan Cities and Sub-urbs." *American Sociological Review* 80 (4): 843–73. doi:10.1177/0003122415588558.

Meijering, L., P. Huigen, and B. Van Hoven. 2007. "Intentional Communities in Rural Spaces." *Tijdschrift voor Economische en Sociale Geografie* 98 (1): 42–52. doi:10.1111/j.1467-9663.2007.00375.x.

Metro, L. J., J. D. Dwyer, and E. S. Dreschler. 1981. "Forest Experiences of Fifth-Grade Chicago Public School Students." Saint Paul, MN: North Central Forest Experiment Station, USDA.

Musick, M. A., J. Wilson, and W. B. Bynum Jr. 2000. "Race and Formal Volunteering: The Differential Effects of Class and Religion." *Social Forces* 78 (4): 1539–70. doi:10.1093/sf/78.4.1539.

NDC (Neighborhood Design Center). 2016. www.ndc-md.org.

Pearsall, H. 2013. "Superfund Me: A Study of Resistance to Gentrification in New York City." *Urban Studies* 50 (11): 2293–2310. doi:10.1177/0042098013478236.

Pietila, A. 2010. *Not in My Neighborhood: How Bigotry Shaped a Great American City.* Lanham, MD: Ivan R. Dee.

Plieninger, T., S. Dijks, E. Oteros-Rozas, and C. Bieling. 2013. "Assessing, Mapping, and Quantifying Cultural Ecosystem Services at Community Level." *Land Use Policy* 33:118–29. http://dx.doi.org/10.1016/j.landusepol.2012.12.013.

Reynolds, K., and N. Cohen. 2016. *Beyond the Kale: Urban Agriculture and Social Justice Activism in New York City.* Edited by N. Cohen. Athens: University of Georgia Press.

Sachs, A. 2013. *Arcadian America: The Death and Life of an Environmental Tradition.* New Haven, CT: Yale University Press.

Sundeen, R. A. 1992. "Differences in Personal Goals and Attitudes among Volunteers." *Nonprofit and Voluntary Sector Quarterly* 21 (3): 271–91. doi:10.1177/089976409 202100306.

Sundeen, R. A., C. Garcia, and S. A. Raskoff. 2008. "Ethnicity, Acculturation, and Volunteering to Organizations: A Comparison of African Americans, Asians, Hispanics, and Whites." *Nonprofit and Voluntary Sector Quarterly* 38 (6): 929–55. doi:10.1177/0899764008322779.

Taylor, D. 2015. "Gender and Racial Diversity in Environmental Organizations: Uneven Accomplishments and Cause for Concern." *Environmental Justice* 8 (5): 165–80. doi:10.1089/env.2015.0018.

Thurman, H. 1965. *The Luminous Darkness: A Personal Interpretation of the Anatomy of Segregation and the Ground of Hope.* New York: Harper & Row.

Wolch, J. R., J. Byrne, and J. P. Newell. 2014. "Urban Green Space, Public Health, and Environmental Justice: The Challenge of Making Cities 'Just Green Enough.'" *Landscape and Urban Planning* 125:234–44. doi:10.1016/j.landurbplan.2014.01.017.

Chapter 2

THE BITTER AND THE SWEET OF NATURE

Weaving a Tapestry of Migration Stories

Veronica Kyle and Laurel Kearns

The Bitter . . .

Running from the trees . . . lynching trees . . . strange fruit

Trees were saviors, I hid in the top to hide from Mr. Whoever owned the land, or when they were chasing me to tell where my brother had gone, or to get some shade and a bit of rest from picking cotton and peaches.

I saw my family member drown in them waters . . . I'm never going get in nothing but my bath tub.

My daddy worked in those tobacco fields and smelled like a walking cigar.

Remember Emmitt Till?

I was a share cropper—I am not going to touch the dirt.

The Sweet . . .

Every summer we go back home to pick fruits, can and quilt.

I loved sitting under that weeping willow tree in my grandparents' yard.

Nothing like picking and shelling pecans and digging up peanuts.

My grandfather made the best peanut brittle I ever tasted.

We used to go fishing all day and sometimes didn't catch much, but it was just nice to be out there on the river.

I was so sad to go back home and see that all those magnolia trees were gone.

These bitter and sweet memories and similar African American migration stories inspired Veronica Kyle to create Migration, Monarchs, Birds & Me, a program that connects the migration stories of butterflies, birds, and people to inspire environmental action among faith communities. In this chapter, we use the stories of African Americans and Latino Americans to illustrate the role of faith and narratives in creating engagement in urban restoration—in healing the land and the soul—and in a broader spiritual restoration movement. Our program— now called simply Migration & Me—is one of many programs of Faith in Place, a nonprofit organization that since 1999 has empowered "Illinois people of all faiths to be leaders in caring for the Earth, providing resources to educate, connect, and advocate for healthier communities" (Faith in Place 2017). Veronica is the Chicago outreach director at Faith in Place, while Laurel is an academic and activist concerned with religion and ecology who teaches at Drew Theological School in New Jersey. Because we bring mutual interests but very different backgrounds and experiences to this chapter, we have chosen to write some text in the first person. We think it is important to attach our names to what has shaped our own involvement and perspectives related to environmental efforts among faith groups.

Veronica

My name is Veronica Denise Brown Kyle. My own story is filled with experiences and thoughts similar to those in the bittersweet reflections above that are common to many African Americans. I knew that as the outreach director for Faith in Place, I needed to create a program and space where folks could risk being able to tell the bad about nature—the bitter—to perhaps get to the sweet spots. I joined Faith in Place in 2008 after spending nearly twelve years working overseas for another faith-based organization engaging diverse and marginalized communities in all forms of development. I had a particular passion for empowering youth to pursue higher education and for supporting women in economic development.

When I reflect back to my time abroad and to the years leading up to such an amazing opportunity at Faith in Place, I now realize how my work has continually woven a thread in the tapestry of sustainability in all the communities I served. It seemed whether I was working on the Southside of Chicago in my early years, on the East Coast, or overseas, I found myself gravitating around communities where environmental injustices were paramount issues. Whether it was cleaning up vacant and abandoned city lots and planting an urban food garden in Chicago or in a South African township, beach cleanups in Chicago or the Caribbean, or advocating for clean air in Illinois, working to make the world a more sustainable place for all just seemed to be my calling.

As a person of faith who happens to be married to a minister, I've heard that word "calling" often, yet never did I attach it to what I do. But as the years have rolled by and I am now in the third trimester of my life, I realized that perhaps all the work around empowering and engaging my people and other marginalized groups just might be what life coach Stephenie Zamora describes as not a whim, but a calling. A whim is impulsive, fleeting, temporary. In contrast, in her words, "A calling is magnetic and all-consuming. Callings draw you toward them. The core focus of a calling is always present; it will always drive you, regardless of how you choose to act on it. Callings are about contribution. This is why they matter" (Zamora 2016).

That calling to make the environment a better one for all is why Reverend Clare Butterfield, a Unitarian Universalist minister, founded Faith in Place. The need to level the playing field around environmental justice and access to nature, clean air, healthy food, outdoor recreation, green spaces, and a sustainable life for everyone is what drives us to do this work. I also believe that most of us have arrived in the space that some refer to as "civic ecology" because of our passion to do all we can to make things better.

But before I dive into the story of Migration & Me, I feel compelled to share my own personal migration story and how that journey has led me to this very moment where I am sitting at my desk after hours trying my best to share through these words my passion, my commitment, and my struggles with civic ecology. It is my hope that by the end of this chapter you will be able to find encouragement and inspiration to continue to do the work needed to make this earth a more just and sustainable place for all who inhabit it.

So here is where the formation of my calling began. . . .

As an African American southern-born female, I can clearly recall my family's migration story from Anniston, Alabama, to Atlanta, Georgia, and finally to Chicago. I was seven years old, just a few months shy of my eighth birthday.

I, along with four younger siblings and our mom, who was only twenty-five at the time, boarded a train to come and join my father and other maternal relatives who had settled in the big city.

I also look back and realize that we left behind the red clay–like dirt that I made into "edible" mud pies to share with my best friend Audrey and my siblings. Dirt roads and dusty sidewalks. I left behind the pecans that we shelled to make pies and eat during the holidays. The peach tree in my grandparents' yard with the juiciest peaches I have ever tasted, which I saw the women can into jars and make into pies and preserves. Today, I'm still chasing that juicy peach! The peanuts that we harvested, ate raw, roasted, or made into peanut brittle. Juicy watermelon that we didn't even wait to get a knife to cut. The men would simply throw it on the hard ground to burst it open, and we would dig in, sweet juice running down our chins. And I left behind wooded areas that were forbidden by our parents, but called us into them anyway when no one was looking. At seven I wasn't fully aware of Jim Crow, but I do remember learning to distinguish the "white only" signs on water fountains and other public places in my hometown in Alabama.

I can still remember my dad saying that he was taking us to Chicago for a better life and to get an education so we could "use our heads not our hands." The problem was that digging in the dirt was connected with being poor and work, so especially for new northern immigrants like my family and thousands of others, they didn't want to be seen with their hands dirty.

Back in Alabama, I had seen lots of "dirty hands." My paternal grandfather and most of the other men in my family were farmers, either full time or on the side. I saw the women work their gardens, harvest peas and greens, and shuck corn. This background, combined with the older generation's desire for the next generation to use their heads, not their hands, to get ahead in the world, reinforced that gardening and getting one's hands dirty were to be avoided.

Fast forward to Chicago, 1962, and what a difference in my visual landscape! Tall buildings, so tall I couldn't see the top of them. Concrete sidewalks decorated with pastel chalk and little chocolate- and caramel-colored girls playing hopscotch and jumping rope. The sun felt hotter with fewer trees to cover me, and I quickly learned to enjoy swinging, climbing monkey bars, and gliding down steel sliding boards so hot from the sun that the back of my legs would tingle for minutes afterwards. My past and present connection to nature changed drastically, as with most African Americans who left the South to seek better opportunities for their families in the North.

As a child of the fifties and turbulent sixties, I heard the stories of my people's encounters and misfortunes in nature. When, in 2008, I joined Faith in Place with a real passion to connect my people to their work and mission, these stories of nature, the environment, and our history came flooding back again.

I was troubled, yet in some ways not surprised at the responses, when I went to talk to churches about the Faith in Place stewardship program. "I ain't going in the woods where bad things have happened, I ain't going to get my hands dirty." "Why should we care about some woods, when folk don't care about our neighborhoods?" "I promised the good Lord that if I made it north, I would never get my hands dirty again. I ended up still cleaning white folks' toilets and taking care of their children, but when it came to digging in the dirt I drew the line."

I knew from my own story that many of my people not only remembered and shared their negative experiences in nature in the South; they also encountered negative nature experiences in their newfound homes. While growing up in a housing project on the outskirts of Chicago, my teenage brother was shot in the back playing in the nearby forest preserve with our younger brother and their friends. As they were hiking in the woods, the boys came upon a group of white men hunting rabbits and perhaps other animals. For some reason one of them turned toward the group of young boys, smirked, and fired his rifle. Fortunately, my brother lived to tell about it. The bullet is still lodged in his back now at the age of fifty-nine, too close to his spine to remove.

Despite such horrific incidents in nature, I was also very much aware of just how many African Americans and other people of color were fully engaged in all aspects of nature, from gardening and farming, to hiking in national parks and forests. I knew that we fished, hunted, boated, canoed, and kayaked, skied and ice skated, and more. So when I started at Faith in Place, instead of coming into churches to encourage folks to come out and steward nature, I would ask about their experiences related to nature. Often, part of what they had been trying to get away from by moving to Chicago was related to nature. I noticed when people started talking about what they were getting away from, then they were able to release that pain. It was like watching someone extract puss from an infected sore. The stories started oozing out, and they all ended up relating to the bitter and sweet realities of their encounters with nature.

Laurel

My name is Laurel Diane Kearns. As a researcher, teacher, and movement participant in religious environmentalism, I was excited when the civic ecology book project brought me together with Veronica Kyle. I have long researched the interface of religion and the environmental movement, with a particular interest in organizational aspects and how to get people to act. This focus stemmed from my own youthful alienation from evangelicalism when I was chastised by the church for my environmental activism and plans to study environmental science. I had known of Faith in Place since its beginnings in 1999, and considered it to be a very effective organization with wide impacts on Chicago and Illinois. Early on, it had established the capacity to work with multiple racial, ethnic, and faith groups—black, white, Latino, Christian, Muslim, Jewish. Faith in Place uses the vocabulary and worldview of multiple faith perspectives to translate a range of environmental issues, from gardening to energy use to the treatment of animals, into religious thinking and acting.

The bitter and sweet stories, the menacing threat of the strange hanging fruit, are not the stories told by white middle-class environmentalists like me. I grew up on Sanibel Island, Florida, watching Flipper, Gentle Ben, and Jacques Cousteau television shows, and learned about gentle animals that needed saving. The only bad things in the swamp I tromped through were copperheads, rattlers, and gators. I was surrounded by people who had the power, privilege, and desire to conserve natural spaces, and viewed going into the swamp as an opportunity to see rare orchids and beautiful wading birds—with little worry that the woods and swamps were places to be feared, where people did bad things to others.

When dominant groups don't listen or seek to hear the stories that challenge their view of the world, important perspectives are excluded. That is why Veronica and I felt it important to tell the story of the work of Faith in Place in encouraging those who are either excluded or who do not see environmentalism as having anything to offer their worlds, and in enabling them to become part of ecological and community restoration. In *Sisters of the Yam*, one of many books that influenced both of us, bell hooks (2014, 172) comments, "Without the space to grow food, to commune with nature, or to mediate the starkness of poverty with the splendor of nature, black people experienced profound depression. Working in conditions where the body was regarded solely as a tool (as in slavery), a profound estrangement occurred between mind and body." Our task in the remaining sections is to put the work of Faith in Place and Veronica's program Migration & Me in conversation with the sociology literature. We focus on diversity within the environmental movement, stories of ecological restoration, and how Migration & Me illustrates civic ecology principles, faith-based environmentalism, and faith-based institutions as movement assets.

Diversity within the Environmental Movement

Laurel

When we first met, Veronica told me about the awakening environmental awareness and activism in several large, predominantly African American United Churches of Christ and other denominational churches in the Chicago area.

Although I knew some of what was happening in black and Latino churches because of my own research and teaching on environmental justice issues for over thirty years, I was excited by the breadth and depth of what was happening in Chicago. Whereas just ten years ago, the majority of my students of color were not interested in environmental issues, today I constantly meet students and scholars of color with environmental awareness and commitments. My students reflect the reawakening and growing environmental concern among people of color in the United States, as evidenced by a flurry of recent publications (Glave 2010; Enderle 2007; Melosi 2006; Baugh 2016; Taylor 2016); the special issue of the journal *Worldviews: Global Religions, Culture and Ecology* on ecowomanism (Harris 2016); and church statements including the ten-thousand-plus signatures on the "Black Church Climate Statement" in support of President Obama's Clean Power Plan (MSR Online 2015; Tolbert et al. 2015), the "African American Clergy Open Letter on Climate Change" (GreenFaith 2015), and the Climate Resolution of the 2.5 million-member African Methodist Episcopal denomination calling for swift action on climate change (Blessed Tomorrow 2016).

Additionally, recent data show that among religious groups in the United States, black Protestants have the second-highest level of concern about climate change, topped only by Hispanic Catholics (Jones, Cox, and Navarro-Rivera 2014). These faith groups are also the most likely to have heard something about climate change from the pulpit. Further debunking the myth that people of color lack concern about environmental issues is a nearly forty-year research record. In 1994, Jones and Carter (1994, 561) claimed that a number of widely held beliefs about race and concern for environmental quality are largely collective myths "that blacks are disinterested in environmental issues; that a 'concern gap' for environmental issues exists between blacks and whites; and that minority group members would be more likely to be influenced than others to withdraw support for environmental protection during economic downturns." The detailed historical work of environmental justice scholar Dorceta Taylor (2016) also counters notions that people of color don't care about the environment.

Stimulated by the United Church of Christ report *Toxic Waste and Race in the United States* (UCC 1987), the environmental justice movement (Mohai 1990; Enderle 2007; Bryant and Mohai 1992) coalesced in 1991, when over one thousand environmental-justice activists gathered for the First National People of Color Environmental Leadership Summit and confronted the major environmental organizations with the lack of diversity in their staffs, boards, and the issues they addressed (Enderle 2007; Bullard 2005; see Taylor 2015, for lack of progress). Although the emergence and growth of the environmental justice movement demonstrate a concern about environmental degradation and those impacted by it, the perception persisted that people of color were not interested in the conservation, restoration, or preservation aspects of environmentalism (Melosi 2006). In short, the dominant narrative of the environmental movement and the demographic expectations of who is an environmentalist have erased counternarratives and often silenced or obscured voices of people of color. Veronica's own story, and the stories she has readily listened to, illustrate this and contrast with my own story of being raised a white environmentalist.

Veronica's work at Faith in Place, which began with efforts to incorporate discussions of food and health in Bible study groups in African American houses of worship, is motivated in part by her desire to move beyond a singular focus on environmental racism, which has come to dominate discussions about the environment and people of color (Baugh 2016). Her work is consistent with civic ecology practices, which demonstrate African American and other people of color's active stewardship of the environment (Reynolds and Cohen 2016; Eizenberg 2013; Saldivar and Krasny 2004). In focusing on social-ecological memories (Barthel, Folke, and Colding 2010) and nature connectedness (Mayer et al. 2008), such stewardship or restoration practices build on the "sweet" narratives Veronica has uncovered. Yet Veronica's work at Faith in Place is directed at African Americans and others who are still entrapped by "bitter" narratives and, as Carolyn Finney (2014, 90) points out, might be influenced by the lack of representation of African American participation in mainstream environmentalism and outdoor activities, and by "how African American concerns and interests in relation to the environment have not been articulated, invited, or understood in the accepted context of the environmental movement."

Migration & Me

Veronica

When the program first started, it seemed impossible to get much traction; very few people would show up for the stewardship and nature outings. I had to redirect my outreach efforts to the congregations where we had helped start community gardens, a sure sign that some folks in the faith community were accustomed to getting their hands dirty and being outdoors. So I began doing special outreach to garden groups, because their members had already grown to have a nature connection. People working in gardens understand conservation, backyard habitat, and the need to care about what is happening to the food they grow. They care about sunshine, shade, having access to water, and how the weather will impact their harvest.

It was at that time that Mike Rizo, an urban and community program special-
ist with the U.S. Forest Service, approached Faith in Place about the plight of the
monarch butterfly. He saw the need for folks to grow milkweed to provide natural
habitat. I learned about the monarch flyway and that parts of Illinois, including
the urban areas, were along the butterflies' path. I discovered that the milkweed
was the only plant that the female would lay her eggs on and how essential it was
to the caterpillars' diet. Monarchs migrate each year from Mexico, and it is usually the fourth generation that actually makes the trek back home.

A lightbulb moment for me was when I realized that like the mighty monarch, African Americans had also migrated for survival reasons. Not so unlike the
monarch, we too enjoy cultural foods that make us feel at home and connected.
But what really blew my mind was to learn that it is the fourth generation of the
monarch clan that makes the trek back home to Mexico. This was precisely how
it often happens in my community; my grandparents migrated, my parents came
later after my grandparents were settled, they brought me at age seven, and it was
my siblings and I who felt the need to take our children to see where we had all
come from. Four generations later, my family made the thirteen-hour drive to
Anniston, Alabama, where it all began!

That was the turning point for me to create a program where we let folks
share their stories and I then share the story of this beautiful delicate creature, the
monarch. I share where the monarchs come from, why they migrate, what they
need along their journey to survive, and how we as humans could provide such
"hospitality." This was no different from what our kinfolks and friends did for us
as we traveled north seeking a better opportunity and a more sustainable future.

The storytelling is the key. Story circles can take place in forest preserves, in
a church basement, on the beach, over a meal, just about anywhere the group
wants it to be. The program now has a toolkit with a set of questions that are used
during story circle sessions. The facilitator of the circle might ask: "What were
the things that were welcoming? What made you feel comfortable when you got
here?" Participants learn that hospitality for the monarchs and other creatures
means clearing the invasive plants, planting milkweed, perhaps planting a butterfly native garden, and providing hospitality in terms of familiar desired foods,
both for caterpillars and people. Participants in my program make the connections. And when they join us in clearing invasive species or planting milkweed,
they walk away feeling like they have made a difference. Ranging from preschool
to senior citizens, representing a diversity of race, class, religious affiliation, and
cultures, they understand the need to do good for " the least of those" in our
ecological community. The program now averages at least a dozen major stewardship and recreational outings a year to our local forest preserves, beaches, and
city parks, which have hosted hundreds of individuals.

FIGURE 2.1   Chris Burrel, Faith in Place eco-ambassador leader, at a Migration & Me event. Photo by Faith in Place staff.

Stories of Ecological Restoration

Laurel

Veronica's work and that of Faith in Place offer insights into how stories can engage parishioners and their congregations. Through the use of story circles, seemingly disconnected issues—butterfly and bird habitat and migration

(Veronica also brings bird migration into her programs)—become personal, leading individuals to become involved. As Veronica points out, her use of storytelling is the key, reflecting a growing realm of research demonstrating the role of stories in social movement participation (Polletta 2006; Stoknes 2015). Joseph Davis (2002, 24) points out in *Stories of Change* that "stories can embed moral messages, engage our moral imagination (answerable to the sufferings of others), and call forth powerful moral reactions. Similarly, with their personal immediacy and symbolically evocative renderings of experience, stories can stimulate strong emotional responses in hearers—sympathy, which can heighten common identity, and anger, which can spur or increase the motivation to work for change."

Similarly, James Jasper (2011) has focused the attention of social movement researchers on the complex role of emotions, moods, and reactions. His work suggests that by linking personal and familial emotions of hardship and hospitality with religiously shaped moral sensibilities of care and justice, Veronica's story circles spur collective actions that open up new experiences and overcome barriers to participation in environmental restoration. Faith in Place, through recognizing the powerful emotions and insights bound up in migration stories, creates the space for a sympathetic hearing of the plight of migratory monarchs and birds, as well as for the emotion and energy to strengthen communities and repair degraded places.

Our focus on the role of stories in place-based, spiritual ecological restoration of degraded lands in cities and elsewhere also illustrates Gretel Van Wieren's (2013, 139) claim that "developing restorative communities of place will need to be accompanied by the creation and narrating of new stories with accompanying individual and cultural-symbolic meaning related to a healing nature and humanity." These stories often incorporate religious references to explain how restoration work becomes a personal experience of transformation and renewal, and thus gains broader symbolic meanings related to sacred work and to public witness to the collective moral failure of industrial society. This moral failure results in a "call" to do better, perhaps not unlike the "call" to her work that Veronica describes above. Such public witness to injustice is unique in being situated within embodied practice rather than expressed as protests or civil disobedience, although its practice and accompanying stories also contribute to social movements.

Showing how stories give meaning to the connection between healing the land, healing one's community, and healing ourselves, Van Wieren (2013, 177) continues: "Christian communities working restoratively, for instance, may narrate the ways in which experiences of divine presence are opened in and through the collective process of working to bring naturally evolving life back to land.

Restorationists may describe experiences of forgiveness, grace, and healing by 'living with' and observing land's self-healing capacity and emerging, dynamic beauty. Through regenerating degraded natural landscapes, one might experience regeneration, a biological and theological term, within one's own self and within the community."

The participants in Migration & Me tell stories of regeneration of self and land experienced through civic ecology practice. These stories lay the basis for an ecological identity to grow, or help to revive an earlier one, perhaps left behind in childhood or another place. It is important to note that such an identity need not necessarily be "environmentalist," but rather the formation of a bond or connection with the natural world that leads one to further care (Clayton 2003; Van Wieren 2013). Reverend Debbie Williams, the Migration & Me program coordinator, describes in an e-mail how the program transformed her:

> Since being involved with the Migration & Me program, I have experienced nature, people, and purpose in exciting and unexpected ways. I would not consider myself an "outdoorsy" person. I do consider myself a "people" person. The Migration & Me program has allowed me to embrace the present but in some ways undeveloped "outdoorsy" part of me. Since connecting with this program, the marriage of the hidden and the obvious that has occurred within my heart and spirit has been a breath of fresh air. The Migration & Me program's intangible but very evident pull allows the connection of people to people, people to nature, and people to themselves. It is a regular occurrence to see individuals be drawn into the essence of others as they tell the good, the bad, and sometimes the ugly of their migration stories. However, by virtue of them being present to tell the story, they offer testimony that in spite of it all "I'm still here!" Also, not only that, but that others are benefitting in unknown ways by my journey.
>
> So it is in nature. Connecting to nature through education and experience allows for the quiet personal revelations of creation, and for me the Creator. It has been absolutely amazing to engage with the power of possibilities and transformation when talking about the life cycle of the Monarch butterfly. To watch smiles that emerge on the faces of people of all ages while they listen to the story of the Monarch is a powerfully peaceful and encouraging experience. Then to watch people who just met and sometime don't even speak the same language partner up to accomplish a given task during a nature outing speaks loudly to the power of what still is good and possible in human engagement. This season of opportunity in my life to experience the mystery of the Migration & Me program has been a blessing!

Veronica and I are both firm believers that when people are allowed to tell their story and share their plight, they are much more inclined to listen to others; and in telling their stories, they open up new ways of thinking and acting for others to follow. Yet Veronica realizes that her transformational work is bigger and more complex than the story circles. "It takes time, patience is crucial, and being

FIGURE 2.2   Veronica Kyle of Faith and Place preparing to lead a story circle at the Cook County Forest Preserve. Photo by Faith in Place staff.

open and welcoming of different viewpoints, people's history, and the cultural relevance of civic ecology is key." She continues, "The Migration & Me program is continuing to evolve far beyond what I envisioned. I'm still learning right along with the wonderful and amazing people that Faith in Place has attracted to this program."

Civic Ecology

The Migration & Me program provides a link between the work of civic ecology and a spiritual practice of restoration, starting with the civic ecology principle: "Because of their love for life and love for the places lost, civic ecology stewards defy, reclaim, and recreate these broken places" (Krasny and Tidball 2015). To understand, however, all the brokenness that the Faith in Place program "mends" is to go beyond the immediate places of Chicago's Southside. Migration & Me creates a space for African Americans and other people of color to reclaim a lost heritage, to reclaim a place in the natural world that is healing and not harmful, and to reclaim the connection to land interrupted by slavery and forced migrations from place after place, then uprooted once again in the migrations to the cities. And it helps to break open the "white spaces" of the environmental movement and nature preserves—preserves often created, as Dorceta Taylor (2016) points out, by moving indigenous people, communities of color, and poor people out of them first. Quoting bell hooks (2014, 173), we need to see the "correlation between the struggle for collective black self-recovery and ecological movements that seek to restore balance to the planet."

Migration & Me also addresses how civic ecology stewards "draw on social-ecological memories to recreate places and communities" (Krasny and Tidball 2015), as well as work to change the bitter memories. By acknowledging migrants' social-ecological memories of bad things happening in the woods, of the land being punishing and a place of hard labor, and of something to be left behind, the program can balance these bitter memories with the sweet—the memories of fresh-picked garden produce, of canning, of fresh air and open spaces. It also can help to create new social-ecological memories among those who have been displaced.

Reflecting another civic ecology principle (Krasny and Tidball 2015) and Van Wieren's (2013) spiritual restoration practice, Migration & Me helps to re-create a sense of community or connectedness. This includes a sense of community within families as generations are brought closer together within churches, which are given new ways to create wellness through gardening and connections to God's creation; within neighborhoods or cities that now look beyond cultural and linguistic differences to see their places blooming with new life; and within nature, now beginning to reflect the diversity and creativity needed to restore ecosystems. Further, Christian traditions offer notions of stewardship and caretaking, of partnership with other creatures and the land, and of intercon-nectedness through the presence of the divine to support a restoration spiritual-ity ethic and practice (Van Wieren 2013).

A Migration & Me participant's e-mail vividly illustrates how the program builds such partnerships or connections:

> As a Mexican American first generation woman, learning about my own parents' migration story from south to north I knew firsthand the impact migration had on my family. It was hard and illegal for my par-ents to come to this country, but because my parents were poor they were looking for a better quality of life, they had to migrate. Along with my three siblings they made their journey here to Chicago. This was a story I knew since I can remember, and from a young age I knew this was a hard migration journey. Learning and working in the Migration & Me program has been an eye-opener and it has been empowering to me and my family. Connecting with firsthand accounts of migration stories of Latino and African Americans in our story circles and their hard journeys to the north has given me even a deeper appreciation. These connections between the African American and Mexican migra-tion have parallel experiences, starting in the early part of the twentieth century. Nothing was given, and we worked hard to make it in the north. As a first generation, I truly appreciate the sacrifice of my parents and those who had to make a journey for a better life here in Chicago. I am the result of that, and for that I am truly grateful. Making connections in faith, taking ownership by being good stewards to the Earth, for a better environment is where we meet, share our common experiences. [This] leads me to believe that no matter if you are brown or black we can share this home with each other and our migrating birds and butterflies.

Another initially reluctant participant's e-mail aptly expresses how multiple connections—with her nephew, nature, and other participants—motivates her restoration work:

> I wanted to go on a Nature Outing when I first heard about them, but getting up that early in the morning after a week of work was just too exhausting to think about. I wanted my Saturdays to myself, if I wasn't performing a tabling somewhere [presiding over tables of literature about Faith in Place and environmental problems]. I began mentioning the Nature Outings to my family, and my nephew wanted to go imme-diately. He wanted something different and exciting to do. So I said "Yes" to the Nature Outing scheduled for Sat., Dec. 13, 2015! That morning turned out to be a wet, misty, foggy, dim day. But we went anyway. We

FIGURE 2.3 Latino/Hispanic congregation on a nature outing led by Faith in Place Waukegan outreach director Susana Figueroa. Photo by Faith in Place staff.

went with church members from a Latino United Methodist Church in Chicago. Everyone greeted each other as they boarded the bus. I was thinking they are a friendly bunch of people even though we quickly found out there was a language barrier. We arrived at the Forest Preserve and were told we would have to cut down some invasive plants and my nephew and I were not feeling that, because it was cold, wet and muddy out there. But we decided to push forward because we are NOT Quitters. We got our work gear on and picked the tool that we wanted to use to cut down the Buck Thorn & Honeysuckle. I was freaking out about this soft and, in some places, muddy soil. Ack! So I pressed on anyway and began to cut down the invasive plants. Well, I got very warm and began to see that others were helping me out as I tried to cut down a thicker plant/tree. No language was needed . . . we just cut, kept each other's safety in mind and carried the wood to a pile to be burned. Now that's Teamwork! We just nodded, said Thank you or Gracias and smiled and it got the job done. My nephew was off deep in the woods helping others and meeting new people, so much so, that he forgot all about his Auntie. My nephew said he had so much fun and that he felt good about helping to save the Forest from invasive plants. He said he definitely wants to go again.

I have since been on two other Nature Outings and they were just as enjoyable! Nothing like being in nature at the start of a Saturday morning or meeting & getting to know another culture.

In sum, through Migration & Me, participants redefine community and connections. This occurs through actions including gardening and growing your own food. It also occurs through stories—whether they are the nearly lost stories of one's elders, the story of one's community and church, the story of the importance of pollinators and native plants, or the incredible migration story of multiple generations of monarchs. These actions and stories lead to the realization that nature can be safe, indeed spiritually uplifting and inspiring, and that one's faith can expand to include all of God's creatures.

Faith-Based Environmentalism

Laurel

It is exciting to see how Migration & Me and the broader work of Faith in Place expands the notion of human community to a community of creation, of interconnectedness between human creatures and other creatures. This work helps people expand their faith and theology, their sense of prayer, and what counts as religious practices. At the same time, the work of spiritual ecological restoration offers new possibilities for a larger civic and religious environmental movement. Faith in Place sees its work as inspiring "religious people of diverse faith to care for the Earth through education, connection and advocacy" (Faith in Place 2017). The focus on advocacy suggests that the work goes beyond embedded practice to encompass a "religious environmentalism."

The story of religious involvement in environmentalism is a somewhat parallel story to the unrecognized environmental concern of African Americans and Latinos—many don't expect it. Many within the environmental movement see people's religious faith as part of the problem—reacting to some conservative theologies that place more value on the next world over this world and to a religious conservative hostility toward environmentalism that is expressed in support for antienvironmental politicians (Kearns 2013). Admittedly, social scientists wrestle with how much religious attitudes that dismiss this world, see it as fallen, or see the chief religious task to be attaining salvation lead to a dismissal of environmental concern (Taylor 2016), or alternatively, with how much an ethic of caring, including for all of God's creation, leads to pro-environmental behavior (Kearns 2011).

In fact, extensive survey research yields mixed results on churchgoers' environmental involvement and behaviors, and concludes that in the United States, political ideology is more important than religious engagement per se (Taylor, Van Wieren, and Zaleha 2016). Most white, politically conservative church members tend not to support environmental policies or engage in environmental activism. In contrast, black Protestants and Hispanic Catholics, who hold similar beliefs on dominion, biblical literalism, saliency of religion, and religion versus science, do support environmental policies and the scientific consensus on climate change and related action, as do theologically liberal Protestants, although to a lesser degree (Jones, Cox, and Navarro-Rivera 2014).

Whereas conservative ideology often appears to trump church support of environmental policies and activism, non-policy-related environmental behaviors such as recycling and reducing energy use appear to be more common among churchgoers relative to the general public (Kearns 2011). It is possible that civic ecology and spiritual ecological restoration (Van Wieren 2013) also may cut across the conservative/liberal divide, in that both conservative and liberal congregants are engaged in such volunteer practices. Many houses of worship in Faith in Place's network and across the country grow food for their communities and for food pantries and soup kitchens. Nor is such activity limited to Christian churches. Encouraged by Faith in Place, Chicago's Taqwa Islamic Center connected with organic farmers to provide healthy food for its members and to feed the hungry during Ramadan; such ethical food actions are common in "green Islam" efforts in the United States (Green Muslims 2015). Similarly, the Jewish organization Hazon has a commitment to connecting Jews with gardening and sustainable agriculture (Ayres 2013).

Such faith-based environmental practices grow to incorporate more than gardening or hands-on restoration, as Veronica describes for congregations in Chicago:

Covenant United Church of Christ, my church, is a three-thousand-member congregation with forty-three different ministries and a viable Green Team of fourteen members. It has embraced not only the Migration & Me program, but also hosted a cross-section of Faith in Place programs, including the Community Climate Change Initiative and workshops on the effects of climate change on the African American community and the role we play to slow down its effects.

I could go on. Vernon Park Church of God, an African American congregation located in a suburb on the Southside of Chicago, has a CSA (community supported agriculture), and about an acre is devoted to native plants, including milkweed. They also have a bee colony and harvest honey. In fact, Faith in Place has contact with over sixty green teams in congregations in Chicago and Illinois.

Faith-Based Institutions as Movement Assets

Faith-based institutions bring multiple assets to the work of restoration and to social movements more broadly (Smith 1996). These assets relate to shared values and identities, leadership, and mundane things like spaces to meet. Together these assets come together in networks that cross multiple boundaries and foster collective action.

Religions are the carriers and shapers of values that motivate and provide moral imperatives for action, making religion a potent force in bringing about change. Religious people share moral frames about concern for their neighbor, ethical relations, and justice for those who are marginalized, and which expect self-discipline and provide transcendental motivations that go beyond the self. As Helene Slessarev-Jamir (2011, 7) states, "Religious commitments create possibilities for people to act in ways that defy the dominant models of rational, self-interested actors found in most current theories of political behavior." Members of faith-based groups share collective practices, language, music, symbols, and rituals that can be tapped to create collective identity (Smith 1996). They have experience working together, building community, and organizing programs that get people involved. Built into many religious groups is not just a sense of "who we are," but "who can we be" and what it means to act on that identity.

Religion also provides trained leaders who carry moral authority and a privileged legitimacy in the public eye. The "Pope Francis effect" of the *Laudato Si* encyclical on climate change is real, as is the impact of the leadership of Faith in Place. Getting one minister or one house of worship in a community involved can provide a significant boost to a cause or campaign because religious leadership is often respected, and religious leaders and members are part of social networks that persuade and recruit others and even transmit ideas and practices to other locales. Churches can also lead by example, as Veronica describes for the black megachurch Trinity United Church of Christ:

> They were one of the first to install a butterfly garden, named after a minister who had passed away who loved butterflies. Faith in Place introduced them to the concept of a "green team"; their team is about thirty strong. They have a big garden and host a summer farmer's market as well as a summer youth farming program engaging six eco-ambassadors. Trinity United Church of Christ hosted the Obama Climate Change kickoff. They are now installing a green roof, and with our assistance and some collaborative funding, they will be installing two engineer-designed rain gardens and will host a rain barrel giveaway where one hundred households that surround the church will receive a free rain barrel.

Trinity is known by some for being President Obama's home church, but it is just as noted as a leader in the Green the Church campaign founded by Rev. Ambrose Carroll. Carroll worked with Van Jones's Green for All organization, Faith in Place, and Trinity's Rev. Otis Moss III and their green team to organize the 2015 national "Green the Church" summit in Chicago (Dream Corps, n.d.). The involvement of a megachurch like Trinity can first touch thousands of people in its own congregation, then bring others into its circle as it demonstrates the success and creativity of a new path. Its pastors meet others in religious leadership councils, and congregation members tell friends (who are likely to be members of religious organizations) and others in their organizational networks.

Religious groups may also serve as "movement midwives" in that they help new organizations and relationships form. For community, advocacy, or protest groups, houses of worship can provide critical meeting space, financial and organizational resources, and fund-raising opportunities, as well as communication channels such as bulletins, Facebook pages, and member directories to aid in sharing information or announcing events. At the mundane level, they have "enterprise tools"—copiers, computers, storage space, secretarial or legal help, and organizing know-how. Perhaps more important, church members carry an expectation of involvement (Smith 1996).

Finally, houses of worship have denominational, trans-denominational, interfaith, translocal, and transnational networks that make people feel part of a larger whole that offers an alternative to societal norms. Often these networks cut across boundaries of race and ethnicity, class, nationality, and even religion.

Indeed, religious groups and congregations have been referred to as "free social spaces" where the hierarchies and expectations of the larger world can be overthrown and different identities and leadership honed—for example, the black church during the civil rights movement (Törnberg and Törnberg 2016; Polletta 1999). In turn, transcendental or collective identities can make strangers seem familiar quickly and overcome social divides, further enabling collective work. Congregations can mobilize quickly, host and feed large groups, and are filled with people used to volunteering and motivated to make a difference through collective action. For all these reasons, religious organizations can play key roles not only in restoration practice but also in spreading the stories and providing the infrastructure needed to expand such practices (Smith 1996).

At the end of her treatise on the spiritual practice of ecological restoration, Van Wieren (2013) claims that we are entering a new "restoration era" in which restoration (and civic ecology) practices help society move beyond narratives of environmental destruction, guilt, and hopelessness. She proposes three ways in which stories of connection to and healing the land can contribute to this new era, including their contribution to forming human and in particular ecological identities (cf. Clayton 2003), their ability to engage the imagination in ways that connect people to local place and foster avenues for personal and social change, and by framing a restoration or civic ecology movement. Stories, such as those of diverse churchgoers engaged in restoration in Chicago, play an important role in this new era.

Multiple religious narratives can be used to explain why humans ought to restore the environment, including because the earth and its creatures are intrinsically valuable and sacred and because human spirituality is nurtured by a thriving and regenerating natural world. Further, restoration is a form of service to other than human nature, a devotional practice to heal wounds of past ecological and social sins. It is also a form of justice making and community revitalization, as well as public witness to ways in which good can be enacted in today's individualized and globalized society (Van Wieren 2013).

Van Wieren (181–84) offers six elements for stories of a spiritual restoration, "from wounded land and spirit to healing land and spirit":

Local but woven together. Stories weave specific examples of ecological degradation and recovery together into a broader narrative.
Grieving and celebration. Narratives recognize grief for what has been degraded and celebrate what can be regenerated.
Evolving. Stories recognize that the relationship between humans and the natural world is dynamic and evolving.

Multidimensional. Stories portray the complexity and multidimensionality of human and earth relations.

Human-nature partnerships. Narratives show how people and natural processes are interwoven to promote human and ecological wellness.

Sacredness. Stories remind us of the earth's sacredness and our human experience of that sacredness.

Faith in Place occupies a unique place in civic ecology and a broader restoration era. It is not a religious organization per se, but is well-versed in the perspectives of religious communities and environmental concerns. Its committed staff bring to a congregation their skills, vision, cultural and religious knowledge, time and energy, and stories that can make something new and unfamiliar, like restoration practices, inviting.

We have shown how organizations such as Faith in Place can provide the theological visions, textual/biblical foundations, and related practices for a socially just restoration theology, which takes a seemingly secular concern related to the environment and embeds it in congregants' shared religious worldviews and experiences. In these ways, the work of Faith in Place embodies Van Wieren's (2013, 186) broader vision that restoration practices and the accompanying narratives may "provide fuel for the re-storying of society and building of a restoration age." Returning to where we began this chapter, it is the new stories being generated by Faith in Place and others that intertwine with the old bittersweet stories to create a tapestry of spiritual ecological renewal and inspiration.

REFERENCES

Ayres, J. 2013. *Good Food: Grounded Practical Theology.* Waco, TX: Baylor University Press.

Barthel, S., C. Folke, and J. Colding. 2010. "Social-Ecological Memory in Urban Gardens—Retaining the Capacity for Management of Ecosystem Services." *Global Environmental Change* 20:255–65.

Baugh, A. J. 2016. *God and the Green Divide: Religious Environmentalism in Black and White.* Berkeley: University of California Press.

Blessed Tomorrow. 2016. "AME Climate Resolution Press Release: July 13, 2016." http://blessedtomorrow.org/ame-resolution-press-release.

Bryant, B., and P. Mohai, eds. 1992. *Race and the Incidence of Environmental Hazards: A Time for Discourse.* Boulder, CO: Westview.

Bullard, R. D. 2005. *The Quest for Environmental Justice: Human Rights and the Politics of Pollution.* San Francisco: Sierra Club Books.

Clayton, S. 2003. "Environmental Identity: A Conceptual and Operational Definition." In *Identity and the Natural Environment,* edited by S. Clayton and S. Opotow, 45–65. Cambridge, MA: MIT Press.

Davis, J. E. 2002. *Stories of Change: Narrative and Social Movements.* Albany: SUNY Press.

Dream Corps. n.d. "Green for All, Green the Church." https://www.greenforall.org/green_the_church.

Eizenberg, E. 2013. *From the Ground Up: Community Gardens in New York City and the Politics of Spatial Transformation*. Farnham, Surrey, UK: Ashgate.

Enderle, E., ed. 2007. *Diversity and the Future of the U.S. Environmental Movement*. New Haven, CT: Yale School of Forestry and Environmental Studies.

Faith in Place. 2017. www.faithinplace.org.

Finney, C. 2014. *Black Faces, White Spaces: Reimagining the Relationship of African Americans to the Great Outdoors*. Durham, NC: University of North Carolina Press.

Glave, D. D. 2010. *Rooted in the Earth: Reclaiming the African American Environmental Heritage*. Chicago: Lawrence Hill Books.

Green Muslims. 2015. http://www.greenmuslims.org/about/.

GreenFaith. 2015. "African American Clergy Open Letter on Climate Change." http://www.greenfaith.org/programs/environmental-justice/african-american-clergy-open-letter-on-climate-change.

Harris, M. L. 2016. "Ecowomanism: An Introduction." *Worldviews: Global Religions, Culture and Ecology* 20 (3): 1–3.

hooks, b. 2014. *Sisters of the Yam: Black Women and Self-Recovery*. Florence, KY: Routledge.

Jasper, J. M. 2011. "Emotions and Social Movements: Twenty Years of Theory and Research." *Annual Review of Sociology* 37:285–303. doi:10.1146/annurev-soc-081309-150015.

Jones, R. E., and L. F. Carter. 1994. "Concern for the Environment among Black Americans: An Assessment of Common Assumptions." *Social Science Quarterly* 75 (3): 560–79.

Jones, R. P., D. Cox, and J. Navarro-Rivera. 2014. *Believers, Sympathizers, and Skeptics: Why Americans Are Conflicted about Climate Change, Environmental Policy, and Science; Findings from the PRRI/AAR Religion, Values, and Climate Change Survey*. Washington, DC: Public Religion Research Institute.

Kearns, L. 2011. "The Role of Religions in Activism." In *The Oxford Handbook on Climate Change and Society*, edited by J. Dryzek, R. B. Norgaard, and D. Schlosberg, 20 (online). London: Oxford University Press.

——. 2013. "Green Evangelicals." In *The New Evangelical Social Engagement*, edited by B. Steensland and P. Goff, 157–73. New York: Oxford University Press.

Krasny, M. E., and K. G. Tidball. 2015. *Civic Ecology: Adaptation and Transformation from the Ground Up*. Cambridge, MA: MIT Press.

Mayer, F. S., C. M. Frantz, E. Bruehlman-Senecal, and K. Dolliver. 2008. "Why Is Nature Beneficial? The Role of Connectedness to Nature." *Environment and Behavior* 41 (5): 607–43. doi:10.1177/0013916508319745.

Melosi, M. V. 2006. "Environmental Justice, Ecoracism, and Environmental History." In *To Love the Wind and the Rain: African Americans and Environmental History*, edited by D. D. Glave and M. Stoll, 120–32. Pittsburgh: University of Pittsburgh Press.

Mohai, P. 1990. "Black Environmentalism." *Social Science Quarterly* 71 (4): 744–65.

MSR Online. 2015. "Black Churches Show Support for Obama's Clean Power Plan." *Minnesota Spokesman-Recorder* (Minneapolis). http://spokesman-recorder.com/2015/11/03/black-churches-show-support-obamas-clean-power-plan/.

Polletta, F. 1999. "'Free Spaces' in Collective Action." *Theory and Society* 28:1–38.

——. 2006. *It Was Like a Fever: Storytelling in Protest and Politics*. Chicago: University of Chicago Press.

Reynolds, K., and N. Cohen. 2016. *Beyond the Kale: Urban Agriculture and Social Justice Activism in New York City*. Edited by N. Cohen. Athens: University of Georgia Press.

Saldivar, L., and M. E. Krasny. 2004. "The Role of NYC Latino Community Gardens in Community Development, Open Space, and Civic Agriculture." *Agriculture and Human Values* 21:399–412.

Slessarev-Jamir, H. 2011. *Prophetic Activism: Progressive Religious Justice Movements in Contemporary America*. New York: NYU Press.

Smith, C. 1996. *Disruptive Religion: The Force of Faith in Social Movement Activism*. New York: Routledge.

Stoknes, P. E. 2015. "Use the Power of Stories to Re-story Climate." In *What We Think about When We Try Not to Think about Global Warming: Towards a New Psychology of Climate Action*, edited by P. E. Stoknes, 132–50. White River Junction, VT: Chelsea Green.

Taylor, B. 2016. "The Greening of Religion Hypothesis (Part One): From Lynn White, Jr and Claims That Religions Can Promote Environmentally Destructive Attitudes and Behaviors to Assertions They Are Becoming Environmentally Friendly." *Journal for the Study of Religion, Nature and Culture* 10 (3): 268–305. doi:10.1558/jsrnc.v10i3.29010.

Taylor, B., G. Van Wieren, and B. Zaleha. 2016. "The Greening of Religion Hypothesis (Part Two): Assessing the Data from Lynn White, Jr, to Pope Francis." *Journal for the Study of Religion, Nature and Culture* 10 (3): 306–78. doi:10.1558/jsrnc.v10i3.29011.

Taylor, D. 2015. "Gender and Racial Diversity in Environmental Organizations: Uneven Accomplishments and Cause for Concern." *Environmental Justice* 8 (5): 165–80. doi:10.1089/env.2015.0018.

———. 2016. *The Rise of the American Conservation Movement: Power, Privilege and Environmental Protection*. Durham, NC: Duke University Press.

Tolbert, S., J. Bottoms, S. Lartey, R. Cunningham, C. Baltimore, and L. Lovett. 2015. "The Black Church and Climate Change." http://www.blackchurchclimate.org/black-church-climate-statement.html.

Törnberg, A., and P. Törnberg. 2016. "Modelling Free Social Spaces and the Diffusion of Social Mobilization." *Social Movement Studies* 16 (2): 1–21. doi:10.1080/1474 2837.2016.1266243.

UCC (United Church of Christ). 1987. *Toxic Wastes and Race in the United States: A National Report on the Racial and Socio-economic Characteristics of Communities with Hazardous Waste Sites*. New York: United Church of Christ Commission for Racial Justice.

Van Wieren, G. 2013. *Restored to Earth: Christianity, Environmental Ethics, and Ecological Restoration*. Washington, DC: Georgetown University Press.

Zamora, S. 2016. "How to Uncover Who You're Here to Be and the Work You're Here to Do." http://stepheniezamora.com/2013/01/tell-difference-between-life-calling-and-whims/.

Chapter 3

GRASSROOTS STEWARDSHIP IN IRAN
The Rise and Significance of Nature Cleaners

Karim-Aly Kassam, Zahra Golshani, and
Marianne E. Krasny

This chapter outlines the civic ecology practices of Nature Cleaners, an urban grassroots civil society organization that emerged from a community-based initiative in Iran. Kazem Nadjariun founded Nature Cleaners in June 2012, having returned from Lake Chooret in northern Iran. He had witnessed a startling decline of a beautiful habitat that had become enveloped in trash and suffered from neglect and indifference on the part of visitors and other users alike. Disturbed by what he saw, Mr. Nadjariun and his family decided to clean up the area around the lake. Upon his return to Tehran, he posted pictures of the cleanup on Facebook. The post went viral and became the impetus for the creation of the civil society organization called Nature Cleaners. In a span of just one week, two thousand members joined the Nature Cleaners Facebook group. Within two weeks, the first cleaning event took place in Tehran, Iran's capital city. In a matter of three months, Mr. Nadjariun helped establish thirty-one Nature Cleaners chapters covering all Iran's provinces. By January 2017, Iran's Nature Cleaners Facebook group had more than 18,500 members (Nature Cleaners 2017a), while the Tehran Facebook group had 12,200 members (Nature Cleaners 2017b), including members from outside Iran. Over a span of three and a half years, Nature Cleaners held 183 events in Tehran involving five hundred volunteers, and a total of 1,645 events throughout the country.

In telling the story of Nature Cleaners, we integrate Zahra's fieldwork in Iran with Karim-Aly's insights gained through studies conducted with indigenous communities in the Canadian, Russian, and U.S. Arctic and boreal forest

(Kassam 2009) and among ethnically diverse societies in the Pamir Mountains of Afghanistan, China, Kyrgyzstan, and Tajikistan (Kassam 2010, 2013, 2015). Shi'ism, Suni'ism, and the poetical and mystical threads of Sufism represent the pluralistic Islamic heritage, and Zoroastrianism and Buddhism have influenced the cultural fabric of these Central Asian communities. Persian culture has extended beyond Iran and also been prominently integrated into the religious as well as the social fabric of these regions. How cultural values can be expressed through a social structure within the context of environmental stewardship is the focus of Karim-Aly's work. In the case presented in this chapter, cultural values reflect the history, politics, and religious traditions of Iran, and the social structure that enables their expression is the grassroots organization called Nature Cleaners. Before delving into our own work, we first describe the Iranian context of how cultural norms and government policies shape civil society and voluntarism.

Iranian Context

Increasingly in Europe and North America, the Middle East conjures up ill-informed images of "the other"—of Islam, oil, and violence. However, this region shares much with the rest of the world, including processes of urbanization leading to the fracturing of social bonds and of a self-centeredness within the fabric of society (Dien 2003, 113). Historically Iran, like much of the historic Silk Road lands in Asia, has boasted a vibrant and vital urban culture; in fact, prominent Persian cities predate many northern European and North American cities (Hodgson 1974; Lapidus 1984, 2002). Therefore, it would be anachronistic to view Persian urban culture only through the lens of colonial industrial development. Nonetheless, with the rise of European colonization, Iran's urbanization has occurred in the context of a unique turbulent political history and, since 1979, under the influence of revolutionary Twelver Shi'ism. In this chapter, we briefly explore how Iran's recent political history and historic cultural values might explain the rampant littering that Nadjariun and his family encountered at Lake Chooret. Then we turn to a study of Nature Cleaners and address the question: How do Iran's dynamic cultural values engender a civil society response to this environmental desecration?

Personalism and *Farhang-sazi* (Culture Building)

We begin by examining issues of culture and norms of social responsibility using Banakar and Saeidzadeh's (2015) sociological explanation for Iran's high automobile accident rate (twenty times the global average). Noting the absence of teamwork and defiance of government-imposed rules in Iran, these authors propose that having endured centuries of foreign invaders and political instability, Iranians have developed a unique form of individualism. Iranian "personalism" is manifested in collectivist tendencies, loyalty, and trust related to family and close peers but individualistic actions geared toward strangers, authorities, and the larger society. In addition to being influenced by political instability, the authors argue, personalism reflects Twelver Shi'ite philosophy shaped by the perception of having suffered perennial injustices, not unlike Judaism. This outlook, in turn, "shapes the formations of a politics of opposition at the level of the State and a defiant attitude to social order at the level of the individual" (Banakar and Saeidzadeh 2015, 5). In everyday exchanges, Iranian personalism continuously searches "for ways of transgressing the norms of society at large and beating the system, whose legitimacy and secular authority it cannot recognize" (8). Arguably, personalism may help explain Iranians' defiant vehicle driving culture and possibly their rampant littering of public spaces.

Whereas personalism serves to promote continuity in the face of ongoing turmoil and uncertainty, authorities are challenged to address the resulting disorder. Iranian drivers in Banakar and Saeidzadeh's study frequently used the term *farhang-sazi* (literally "culture building") to describe authorities' attempts at social engineering campaigns to bring about reform and progress. When citizens see the benefit of such government information campaigns for their families, such as the campaign to reduce birthrates, which brings socioeconomic advantages, *farhang-sazi* has been successful (Iran's fertility rate declined dramatically from 7.0 in 1980 to 2.17 in 2000; see Shavazi, n.d.). However, when citizens see no advantage to their families, for example the government campaigns to impose strict Shi'i Islamic moral codes, the authorities have had to rely on force and violence. In short, because of a general lack of trust in authorities, "*farhang-sazi*, which started with a revolutionary cultural ethos and a belief in controlling social change, must be brought down to earth and turned into factually based ideas to be implemented at the discretion of the family" (Banakar and Saeidzadeh 2015, 13).

Whereas Banakar's and Saeidzadeh's explanation does not fully take into account rich and dynamic Persian history, including its urban culture, it does illustrate how individual action manifests cultural values in continually changing social circumstances, including foreign intervention in Iran. With the notion of personalism, Banakar and Saeidzadeh show how anxiety and instability have strong effects on social structures that govern society. In defying norms dictated by the authorities, Iranians follow values based on interpersonal trust and mutual dependency in the extended family and, increasingly in cities, in a small group of neighbors or peers. As Iranians move from the countryside to cities, they attempt to re-create traditional rituals and a sense of community through close, daily interactions and collective activities. These activities might include eating and the supervision of children in the public spaces of their new neighborhoods (Banakar and Saeidzadeh 2015)—or perhaps joining in activities of groups like Nature Cleaners, as we will suggest below.

Civil Society and the Environmental Movement in Iran

In addition to social and cultural changes, urbanization and industrialization in Iran have led to profound environmental destruction. Tehran is among the ten most polluted cities in the world, and water issues continue to plague Iran. However, relative to other Middle Eastern countries, Iran has more aggressively addressed its environmental problems at the policy level; regrettably, implementation of policies has been spotty at best (Foltz 2003). In an attempt to link environmental policy to civil society action, Iran's Department of Environment called for "promotion of NGOs and community participation" (Foltz 2003, 261) and established a Public Participation Bureau (Fadaee 2012) under the reformist president Mohammad Khatami during the late 1990s. Civil society organizations grew rapidly; by 2005, Iran was home to over fifteen thousand NGOs, over six hundred of which focused on the environment. Reflecting Iran's tumultuous political history, the rise to power of a conservative government in 2005 led to a precipitous decline in the number of civil society organizations (Fadaee 2012). The work of the remaining NGOs is more constrained in Iran than in Europe or the United States. Not unlike in China and the former Soviet bloc countries, NGOs are required "to remain nonpolitical, impartial, and have various interactions with government ministries for registration and monitoring, including approval for work involving international cooperation" (Namazi 2005). Describing how NGOs face both financial and political obstacles, Shadi Mokhtari states, "There are few NGOs in Iran that can really be considered NGOs because they are mostly dependent on the government both substantively and financially. . . . Therefore, NGOs that served to hold state agencies accountable or protest the status quo were virtually non-existent" (Shadi Mokhtari, personal communication, November 15, 1998; quoted in Foltz 2006 / 2010 online, 872).

Despite these constraints, within a limited sphere of action that coincides with the authorities' attempts at *farhang-sazi*, civil society has been encouraged and achieved successes in Iran, sometimes beyond what the authorities intended. Shortly after the 1979 revolution, Iran's government promised universal health care, education, and other social welfare rights; however, these pledges were thwarted when eight years of war and subsequent U.S.-led sanctions took their toll on Iran's society, infrastructure, and economy. To meet its promises, the revolutionary government called on women to volunteer in literacy, reproductive health, and rural development (Asya 2017). Through the Volunteer Women's Community Health Workers Organization, women not only helped to successfully reduce Iran's birthrate, but also redefined their roles and demonstrated civic responsibility and duty. This led to increased mobility, status, and independence for women, which triggered social transformations through networking and negotiating with the authorities. According to Asya (125), "since the efforts of volunteer-run organizations and projects cannot be fully subsumed or controlled by state authorities, volunteers generated alternative ideals about women's decision making and mobilized women in a way that the state could not wholly subvert."

Despite the cycles of crackdowns and reform-minded governments, a discourse of civil society and public-sphere action has persisted in Iran, aided by a new urban, highly educated middle class and by the use of the Internet as a mobilizing tool (Fadaee 2012). Further, the environmental movement was among the few social movements that were partially tolerated after the conservative turn in 2005, perhaps because it was seen as supporting government policy. This environmental movement "calls not only for reform and alteration of the relationship between nature and humans, but also between government and citizens" (Fadaee 2012, 90). The movement's goals are twofold: education and awareness of the general populace, and pressuring government to become more effective in implementing environmental policies. Motivations for establishing environmental groups often focus on social responsibility and include "participation in public life" and "doing something for the nation" (Fadaee 2012, 94). In a 2004 study of twelve hundred Tehran residents, over 50 percent engaged in readily performed individual environmental behaviors such as turning off water while brushing teeth, buying beverages in returnable bottles, and talking with friends about environmental problems, whereas about 20 percent reported engaging in conservation behaviors. Conservation behaviors tended to be public and noncontroversial, and included planting trees on roadsides and courtyards (11 percent of survey respondents), taking part in a campaign to restore a polluted place (4 percent), and cleaning streets and alleys (2 percent). Only 0.4 percent cited membership in environmental groups (Calabrese et al. 2008).

In sum, Nature Cleaners was launched within a context of cultural values that support building community through a small family network and drawing in new friends through socioculturally and ecologically informed action. Despite the fact that involvement in environmental organizations was not high among residents of Tehran (Calabrese et al. 2008), the group found itself in a social context of government openness to limited civil society activity in areas like women's reproductive rights and environmental quality that the government saw as priorities. Instead of defying *farhang-sazi* as imposed by the government, an Iranian civil society organization, we contend and will show, reframed and took ownership of the notion of "culture building" to reflect the continuing evolution of traditional Persian religio-cultural values in modern-day Iran. In essence, Nature Cleaners is a bottom-up redefinition of *farhang-sazi* manifested through environmental consciousness and concomitant action. We turn next to a study of the perceptions of Nature Cleaners' leaders and participants about the role of their actions in present-day Iranian society.

Nature Cleaners: A Case of Civil Society Action in Iran

I (Zahra) am an Iranian American living in the United States. I first encountered Nature Cleaners via Facebook in 2013 and immediately established an online relationship with the group's founder, Kazem Nadjariun. During a trip to Iran in the summer of 2013, I spoke with Mr. Nadjariun for several hours, as well as with the leader of Nature Cleaners in Hamadan, a city in northwest Iran. I also participated in three cleaning events in Hamadan, Karaj, and Tehran (Golshani and Krasny 2013; Krasny et al. 2015; Krasny and Tidball 2015). I continued to be in touch with Nature Cleaners through their Facebook group from the summer of 2013 to the summer of 2015, and used the posts and comments to learn more about their work as well as about the members' opinions and values.

At Karim-Aly's suggestion to gather empirical evidence, in the summer of 2015 I returned to Iran and attended three cleanup events, including of a riparian area (Latiyan Dam), an urban park (Boostan-e Parvaz), and a village outside Tehran (Ahar). During the cleanups, I conducted informal discussions and semi-structured interviews with ten participants (five males and five females) who had been active in Nature Cleaners for a sustained period of time and four leaders (two males and two females). In addition, I interviewed Mr. Nadjariun, the founder, at a café.

I began my interviews with general questions at a Nature Cleaners event to put the interviewee at ease and then continued our conversation via telephone or Telegram (a popular text-based social media tool in Iran). We had two separate sets of questions for participants and leaders, which were jointly developed by Karim-Aly and me based on my preliminary (2013) findings. These questions were designed to be brief, not burdensome, and conscious of the changing political situation in Iran. At the same time, we sought to understand participant

FIGURE 3.1   Cleaning event at Ahar village, Tehran Province. Photo by Zahra Golshani.

motivations for volunteering in cleanups and how Nature Cleaners reflected participants' values and beliefs. Specifically, I asked participants

- Why did you join Nature Cleaners?
- In how many events have you participated?
- What is it that you like most about participating in cleaning events?
- What makes you continue your participation?
- How does your participation reflect your values and beliefs?

To ascertain the leaders' values and perspectives, I asked them:

- How do you select a place to be cleaned, where do you usually clean, and why do you select that place?
- What is the level of participation in your group?
- What are the main motivations for participants to join?
- Does organizing events reflect certain beliefs or values that are important to you?

As we attempted to tease out the cultural factors that are manifested in Nature Cleaners as a social institution, three themes emerged: (1) cleanliness, culture, and civil society; (2) changing others' behavior through "culture building" (*far-hang-sazi*); and (3) sense of community as a social force. We report these findings within the Iranian context described above, and then briefly summarize them from the perspective of creating positive environmental stewardship narratives. Finally, we describe how Nature Cleaners illustrates the connections between cultural systems and social structures in Iran, and use this framework to understand the potential broader impacts of Nature Cleaners on Iranian society.

Cleanliness, Culture, and Civil Society

Other studies have revealed multiple motivations for engaging in volunteer environmental stewardship, including creating social connections, caring and learning about the environment, acting on one's sense of place, and leaving a legacy (Asah and Blahna 2012; Liarakou, Kostelou, and Gavrilakis 2011; Warburton and Gooch 2007; Krasny et al. 2014). Whereas several of these motivations were also reported by Nature Cleaners volunteers, a previously unreported motivation, cleanliness, links to Iranian religio-cultural values.

Volunteers repeated over and over the importance of wanting to protect the environment as an important motivation for joining Nature Cleaners.

> I joined to clean the nature because I have a great interest in nature. I like nature a lot, because I want to protect the environment. (volunteer, female)

Similar to other civic ecology stewards in cities (Fisher, Svendsen, and Connolly 2015; Krasny et al. 2014; Asah and Blahna 2012), Nature Cleaners participants saw nature as encompassing their urban surroundings.

> The first motivation is conserving the environment, not only physical environment but urban environment and our surroundings in which we live. (volunteer, male)

Cleanliness emerged as an important motivation for environmental action in urban spaces.

> Being clean is important to me, at either my home or my car or the environment, which is the most important part, so I wanted to do something for cleanliness of the town that I am living in. (volunteer, female)

> I liked to help with cleaning. It always bothered me when I saw trash on the ground. (volunteer, female)

A focus on cleanliness was also found in a survey of Egyptian environmental attitudes. Respondents, the majority of whom were likely Muslim, spoke of cleanliness as a key part of a healthy environment. Unlike the idea of "nature" existing outside of culture found in environmental discourse in Europe and North America, these respondents linked personal cleanliness with a clean urban habitat (Rice 2006).

According to Nadjariun, many Nature Cleaners volunteers had individually undertaken cleaning of ecological spaces during outings with their families; thus, cleaning one's habitat was already part of their behavior.

> I used to do individual cleanings with my family when we traveled. So when I learned about the group I thought it's great that there is a group doing this, and I joined. (volunteer, male)

Joining Nature Cleaners provided a social context to continue and expand this work while increasing participants' impact on their habitat through collective action and mutual support. Cleaning the environment also was associated with a responsibility toward future generations.

> We should believe that the dirtiness in the environment is a cost to us, and by not caring for the cleanliness of the environment we are responsible to future generations. (volunteer, male)

Although working in a significantly different context (with Australian stewardship volunteers), Warburton and Gooch (2007) found a similar motivation associated with leaving a legacy for the environment and for children and grandchildren, which they labeled a "generative response." Further, indigenous peoples have rejected oil and gas development on their lands, from the 1970s in the Mackenzie River delta in the Arctic (Berger 1977) to recent opposition to the Dakota Access Pipeline near the Standing Rock Sioux tribal lands. These and other actions across multiple settings may reflect fundamental human impulses and a universal disposition toward environmental stewardship to safeguard the habitat for future generations. While outside the realm of this chapter, further study examining cultural values and social structures that engender this behavior in diverse societies would inform broader discussion of civic ecology.

Returning to Nature Cleaners, the focus on cleanliness reflects Iranian Zoroastrianism and Shi'i Muslim beliefs incorporating ritual cleanliness of the body and surrounding environment, which are linked to ethical human behavior and to engagement with the divine (Burge 2010; Naguib 2007; Powers 2004). Whereas pollution of the body or the habitat is degradation, the act of cleaning is an expression of spiritual intent and ethical behavior. Thus, the act of cleaning is a form of praxis linking values with social action having a direct impact on an individual's environment. Nature Cleaners provides the communal and social framework to implement long-established religio-cultural traditions of cleanliness, and in so doing, provides evidence of how traditional values of cleanliness persist in modern-day Iran.

FIGURE 3.2 Cleaning event at Javan Park, Tehran. Photo by Zahra Golshani.

A focus on nature and cleaning also may explain why Nature Cleaners has been tolerated and even received national government recognition. For example, the Department of the Environment invited Nadjariun to the inauguration of its new head in 2013, and recognized his work with a national prize in 2014. In a television interview (Ba Tabiat, June 7, 2013), Nadjariun explains: "Protecting the environment is not just the responsibility of the Department of the Environment but the responsibility of all members of the society. We have been taught that cleanness is part of our religious teachings. We should keep nature clean both for future generations and for ourselves."

Working in the environment—one of the few spheres in which civil society was allowed to remain active during the Ahmadinejad regime (Fadaee 2012)—Nature Cleaners may have posed a negligible threat to, and even provided support for, implementing the state's strong environmental policies (Foltz 2003). This is not unlike how the women's health volunteers supported government family planning policy during the post-1979 repressive era (Asya 2017). In contrast to the federal government, the Tehran municipal government has been more reticent and even resisted Nature Cleaners' early attempts to hold cleanups in city parks. Similar to the situation faced early on by the civil society group the Ugly Indian in Bangalore (see chapter 12), Tehran's government feared that a volunteer organization cleaning a park, generally considered a municipal government responsibility, would reflect negatively on the city's image. This issue was resolved, and Nature Cleaners is now able to hold cleanups in Tehran's public spaces. However, the municipal government has provided little material assistance, only occasionally offering garbage bags or access to a garbage truck.

Changing Others' Behavior through "Culture Building"

Reflecting the ethical framework for human behavior in the Quran (Dien 2003; Izutsu 1987; Özdemir 2003), female Nature Cleaners volunteer and university professor Dr. Jafri, in a television interview on October 18, 2014, called on Iranians to honor their own humanity through fulfilling their role as God's stewards and tending to their own care as well as that of other creatures:

> The reason that people don't care for nature and leave their trash is that they do not like themselves. If one does not like oneself, he or she can't like the world, nature and his or her surroundings. We should like ourselves, we should respect ourselves and value ourselves. We need to know that we are a valuable creature in the natural cycle, and God has given us the responsibility to not only take care of ourselves, as his *khalifa* [deputy or steward], . . . but also take care of nature and animals.

While grounding their actions within religious ethical conceptions of cleanliness and stewardship, Nature Cleaners volunteers sought to foster broader behavioral and social change by demonstrating stewardship action.

> I like it a lot when people come to us and ask what we are doing, where are you coming from, why are you doing this? This way we'll have a great positive influence on them. I can't have such impact when I do the cleaning on my own. (volunteer, male)

Interestingly, in describing the change they are seeking, leaders use the term *farhang-sazi*, or "culture building."

> Their main motivation is first *farhang-sazi* and next cleaning the areas that are full of trash. These people have a high level of environmental literacy and are aware of the negative impacts of trash on nature. They are determined to clean up the natural places and tourist sites first for the visual beauty and next for health, to bring back the health to the environment. (leader, female)

Given that *farhang-sazi* is a term used to describe government-directed campaigns that incorporate indoctrination and education to change Iranians' moral behaviors (Banakar and Saeidzadeh 2015), it is noteworthy that Nature Cleaners leaders see "culture building" and societal-level change as potential outcomes of volunteer cleanups. This suggests that leaders and possibly participants envision a role for civil society in effecting major shifts in culture and behavior; the efforts of Nature Cleaners are seen as a nationwide information and education campaign originated by a grassroots organization. This is an illustration of how Iranians have redefined and taken ownership of the traditional notion of "culture building" and how culture becomes an active process of societal engagement. Whereas a culture ceases to exist if it loses its vitality and becomes calcified, Iranian societies, urban and rural, reflect historical dynamism by negotiating and renegotiating cultural values, making them relevant to their temporal and spatial context (cf. Geertz 2000; Kassam 2009).

Leaders also attribute unselfish motives to Nature Cleaners volunteers. For example, volunteers "are involved in cleaning activities with love and no expectation." This comment is interesting in light of Iranian norms of personalism, which suggest that actions are taken to benefit one's family but not larger society (Banakar and Saeidzadeh 2015). Another leader's comment reinforces the idea that volunteers act in ways that challenge perceived cultural norms of modern Iranian society.

> Their main motivations include love for nature and *farhang-sazi*. They like to do something useful. They are humble selfless kids with no ego, because if someone has ego they would not bend and pick up trash. (leader, female)

Finally, Nadjariun refers to Nature Cleaners as having a larger impact through collective action and teamwork, again challenging notions of Iranians having little experience with working together and not going beyond actions that benefit their extended family (Banakar and Saeidzadeh 2015).

The motivation is keeping the environment clean and protecting it. There were people who would do this alone, and when they found this group they joined so they can do this in a group together. The group makes it official through teamwork. (leader and founder, male)

Sense of Community as a Social Force

Through providing an opportunity for teamwork—for volunteers to work collectively to "build culture" and create larger social change—Nature Cleaners provides a means for urban Iranians, whose traditional village and family bonds may have been disrupted (cf. Banakar and Saeidzadeh 2015) and who are likely to be from small families, to re-create a sense of community with peers (cf. McMillan and Chavis 1986). When the concept of community is invoked, the individual also becomes significant, because individual interests and actions form the complex of relations that make a community. That community arises from individuals is widely recognized, but what is not easily grasped is that the notion of individual cannot exist outside a simultaneous understanding of community (Williams [1976] 1983). Even the notion of "personalism" in Banakar and Saeidzadeh (2015) cannot be discussed devoid of the idea of a wider community, whether it is extended family or neighbors. Community provides the social structures for individual actions and encompasses holding something in common through the social relations of a particular group or civil society organization (Williams [1976] 1983; Kassam 2009). Nature Cleaners, as a community, provides the social structures for its individual volunteers' actions.

Nature Cleaners members often referred to their local chapter as a "family." Social activities such as sharing food after cleaning events help build this sense of community. Participants saw the value of cooperation as extending beyond their environmental work.

> First, becoming friends with those who have the same concerns for nature and the environment. Second, working in a group has a better energy and it's more beautiful. Third, extending this cooperation and education throughout Iran sometimes happens with other benevolent work such as collecting bottle caps. (volunteer, male)

Further, teamwork was viewed as a potential "attractor" to the work and its value for others.

> We have one aspiration, and that is a clean Iran, Iran without trash! Teamwork is very weak in Iran; since we work together as a team and we are coherent, people like to join us. (volunteer, male)

Reflecting the possibility of having a larger societal impact, one participant remarked:

> I feel that I am having a positive impact, I am being useful, and I am participating in society instead of being a stay-at-home mom. (volunteer, female)

Nature Cleaners has expanded its activities linking care for the environment with care for others. This indicates that environmental consciousness generated through community is amenable to actions related to social justice. Ironically, some local chapters promote safe driving, whose importance in Iran is undoubtedly why it was used by Banakar and Saeidzadeh (2015) in their study of cultural norms. Local Nature Cleaners chapters also engage in outdoor activities with children and youth, visit orphanages and homes for the elderly, and collect bottle caps to sell to recycling companies to earn money to buy wheelchairs for people with disabilities. Nature Cleaners is thus defining itself as a civil society organization where care for one's environment includes care for one's community. In this sense, as described by Dr. Jafri above, the act of caring for oneself, for another individual, the community, and the habitat, is part of a continuum of environmental stewardship.

FIGURE 3.3 Volunteers eating and socializing after a cleaning event. Photo by Zahra Golshani.

Creating Positive Narratives and Accepting Responsibility

Through their reflections, Nature Cleaners volunteers create positive narratives about what is generally considered a distasteful task, namely picking up some-one else's trash. These narratives revolve around cleanliness, family, sense of community, and having a positive impact on broader society through creating new cultural norms (*farhang-sazi*). They replace narratives of guilt and envi-ronmental degradation, as well as recent Iranian cultural narratives around lack of teamwork and disregard of societal rules. Given the long-established cultural values of cleanliness and stewardship in Iranian society supported by evidence from Zahra's interviews with Nature Cleaners volunteers, and drawing on previ-ous work in other settings, we now turn to a broader perspective from which to understand the actions of this civil society organization.

Linking Culture and Social Structure in Iran

Through my applied research work in the circumpolar Arctic and boreal for-est (Kassam 2009) and central Asia (Kassam 2015, 2013, 2010), I (Karim-Aly) developed a model linking cultural systems and social structure (figure 3.4). In so doing, I draw upon Pitrim Sorokin's and Clifford Geertz's writings on cultural systems and social structures and how their relationship can provide a theoretical framework for interpreting sociocultural change. Culture is an ordered system of symbols, values, and beliefs from which individuals draw meaning and interpret their experience of the world and which guide individuals' actions. The social

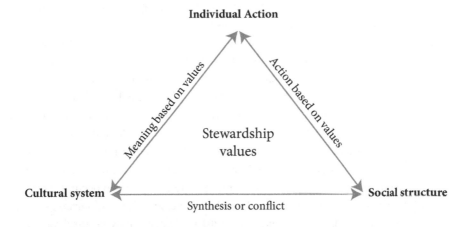

FIGURE 3.4 Connectivity of cultural system, social structure, and individual action. Graphic by Karim-Aly Kassam.

structure is where individual action turns into group activity in the context of a network of human relations (Geertz 2000; Sorokin [1937] 1962). Although interdependent, cultural values and social behaviors are not the same. To quote Geertz (1973, 144–45),

> On the one level there is the framework of beliefs, expressive symbols, and values in terms of which individuals define their world, express their feelings, and make their judgments; on the other level there is the ongoing process of interactive behavior, whose persistent form we call social structure. Culture is the fabric of meaning in terms of which human beings interpret their experience and guide their action; social structure is the form that action takes, the actually existing network of social relations. Culture and social structure are then but different abstractions from the same phenomena. The one considers social action in respect to its meaning for those who carry it out, the other considers it in terms of its contribution to the functioning of some social system.

In short, culture "is an ordered system of meaning and of symbols, in terms of which social interaction takes place," and the social structure is the "pattern of social interaction itself" (Geertz 1973, 144). Flyvbjerg (2001, 43) summarizes this well when he writes: "The rules of a ritual are not the ritual, a grammar is not a language, the rules for chess are not chess, and traditions are not actual social behavior." Hence, a cultural value is not social behavior, but it informs that behavior (figure 3.4). In this sense, poor driving behavior as described by Banakar and Saeidzadeh (2015) is not a complete explanation of a society's value system, and the actions of Nature Cleaners' volunteers cannot be extrapolated for all Iranians. Together, however, they may give us valuable insight into environmental behavior in contemporary urban Iranian society.

To Sorokin's and Geertz's thinking about cultural systems and social structures we add the foundational role of ecological systems (figure 3.5). In short, sociocultural phenomena take place in ecological space. Cultures, like social structures, are embedded within nature; they do not exist outside the habitat. Therefore, a habitat forms the basis from which a social group, like Nature Cleaners, can adapt to and influence change. When there is synthesis between the cultural system and social structure of a community or group—that is, when meaning is effectively integrated into social structure in a specific ecological context—collective action and adaptation are possible. In instances where this fails to occur, there is potential for conflict (Kassam 2009). The ideas of personalism and *farhang-sazi* as described by Banakar and Saeidzadeh (2015) illustrate how cultural values came into conflict with social structures imposed by government in a "politics of opposition." A tension arose because the social structures created by the

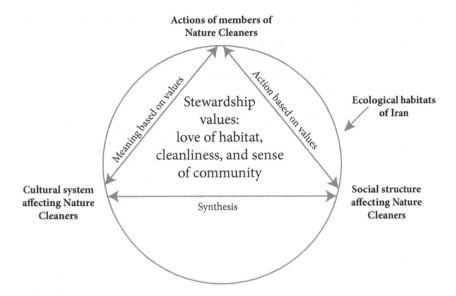

FIGURE 3.5 Dynamics of cultural values and social cohesion in their ecological context. Graphic by Karim-Aly Kassam.

government through top-down *farhang-sazi* did not suit the values of individual citizens, and citizens sought to "beat the system." The case of Nature Cleaners is the opposite—it is an example of synthesis, as the stewardship values involved in bottom-up *farhang-sazi* are rearticulated through the actions of this civil society organization (figure 3.5).

In the case of Nature Cleaners, the value of cleanliness linked to love of habitat is a cultural force that inspires volunteers, whereas a sense of community and the potential for broader impact drive Nature Cleaners as a social organization. Thus, the work of Nature Cleaners operationalizes cultural meaning through collective actions to impact the local environment and society, and volunteers see the potential for their work to influence society more broadly. Interestingly, Nature Cleaners participants use the term *farhang-sazi*—culture building—to describe the potential of their actions for effecting this larger change. They have appropriated and repurposed top-down government policy in one sector (strict moral codes) by rearticulating it in a new context (environmental stewardship).

Nature Cleaners operates within the context of a larger set of Iranian cultural values and social structures. According to Banakar and Saeidzadeh (2015), Iranian society is marked by lack of trust for those beyond one's immediate family, the absence of a tradition of teamwork, and defiance of government-imposed norms and government-directed campaigns that do not directly benefit one's family. In this explanation, the activities of Nature Cleaners may be viewed as an attempt to re-create "family" or the social cohesion Iranians lost when they moved from traditional villages to cities. Cleaning up litter is seen to benefit one's extended "family" and close-knit group of peers.

More broadly, we propose that Nature Cleaners is an expression of bottom-up empowerment driven by dynamic and continuous rearticulation of cultural values that manifest principles of stewardship and responsibility. Nature Cleaners is operating within the policies and rules set by the state. Although civil society has at times been encouraged by the central government when seen as promoting government policies, it has also been constrained by lack of laws and confusion regarding government policies toward NGOs. Fortunately, the environment is one of those sectors where civil society organizations have been allowed to operate, and a fledgling national environmental movement has emerged (Fadaee 2012). Nature Cleaners is one of many environmental organizations that are part of this movement. It has, however, demonstrated independence from government institutions in its day-to-day activities. Municipal cooperation was not necessary for Nature Cleaners to undertake stewardship activities in Tehran and quickly gain membership. Moreover, its rapid spread across the nation illustrates that the central government was not effective in providing social infrastructure for effective implementation of environmental policy. This created space for civil society organizations, such as Nature Cleaners, to demonstrate immediate impacts. Through participating in cleanups and related social media, Nature Cleaners volunteers have demonstrated social connections not based on family but rather on a community of interests driven by values that extend beyond kinship. Membership is more akin to kindredness than to kinship (Kassam 2009).

The case of Nature Cleaners suggests a more pluralistic outlook to Iranian society. We add the dimension of dynamic cultural systems acting in tandem with evolving social structures operating within ecological space. Nature Cleaners has extended the notion of "caring" and "stewardship" to include the self, other individuals, the community as a whole, as well as the habitat. While its activities may seem small in scale, Nature Cleaners is certainly not irrelevant to an emergent, twenty-first-century Iranian society.

REFERENCES

Asah, S. T., and D. J. Blahna. 2012. "Motivational Functionalism and Urban Conservation Stewardship: Implications for Volunteer Involvement." *Conservation Letters* 5:470–77.
Asya, A. 2017. "Embodying Change in Iran: Volunteering in Family Planning as a Practice of Justice." In *Bodies in Resistance: Gender and Sexual Politics in the Age of Neoliberalism*, edited by W. Harcourt, online only. London: Palgrave Macmillan.

Banakar, R., and Z. Saeidzadeh. 2015. "Culture: Reflections on Individualism and Community." In *Driving Culture in Iran: Law and Society on the Roads of the Islamic Republic*, edited by R. Banakar, 149–77. London: I. B. Tauris.

Berger, T. R. 1977. *Northern Frontier, Northern Homeland: The Report of the Mackenzie Valley Pipeline Inquiry*. Vol. 1. Ottawa: Department of Indian and Northern Affairs Canada.

Burge, S. R. 2010. "Impurity/Danger!" *Islamic Law and Society* 17 (3–4): 320–49.

Calabrese, D., K. Kalantari, F. M. Santucci, and E. Stranghellini. 2008. *Environmental Politics and Strategic Communication in Iran: The Value of Public Opinion Research in Decisionmaking*. Washington, DC: World Bank.

Dien, M. I. 2003. "Islam and the Environment: Theory and Practice." In *Islam and Ecology: A Bestowed Trust*, edited by R. C. Foltz, F. M. Denny, and A. Baharuddin, 107–20. Cambridge, MA: Harvard University Press.

Fadaee, S. 2012. *Social Movements in Iran: Environmentalism and Civil Society*. London: Routledge.

Fisher, D. R., E. S. Svendsen, and J. J. Connolly. 2015. *Urban Environmental Stewardship and Civic Engagement: How Planting Trees Strengthens the Roots of Democracy*. New York: Routledge.

Flyvbjerg, B. 2001. *Making Social Science Matter: Why Social Inquiry Fails and How It Can Succeed Again*. Cambridge: Cambridge University Press.

Foltz, R. C. 2003. "Islamic Environmentalism: A Matter of Interpretation." In *Islam and Ecology: A Bestowed Trust*, edited by R. C. Foltz, F. M. Denny, and A. Baharuddin, 249–80. Cambridge, MA: Harvard University Press.

——. 2006 / 2010 online. "Islam and Environmentalism in Iran." In *The Encyclopedia of Religion and Nature*, edited by B. Taylor, 869–72. London: Continuum.

Geertz, C. 1973. "Ritual and Social Change: A Javanese Example." In *The Interpretation of Cultures: Selected Essays by Clifford Geertz*, edited by C. Geertz, 142–69. New York: Basic Books.

——. 2000. *The Interpretation of Cultures: Selected Essays*. New York: Basic Books.

Golshani, Z., and M. E. Krasny. 2013. *Civic Ecology Practice in Iran: The Case of the Nature Cleaners*. Baltimore: North American Association for Environmental Education.

Hodgson, M. G. 1974. *The Venture of Islam: Conscience and History in a World Civilization*. Chicago: University of Chicago Press.

Izutsu, T. 1987. *God and Man in the Koran*. Salem, NH: Ayer.

Kassam, K.-A. 2009. *Biocultural Diversity and Indigenous Ways of Knowing: Human Ecology in the Arctic*. Calgary, AB: University of Calgary Press / Arctic Institute of North America.

——. 2010. "Pluralism, Resilience, and the Ecology of Survival: Case Studies from the Pamir Mountains of Afghanistan." *Ecology and Society* 15 (2): 8.

——. 2013. "Keeping All the Parts: Adaptation amidst Dramatic Change in the Pamir Mountains." In *Continuity and Change in Cultural Adaptation to Mountain Environments: From Prehistory to Contemporary Threats*, edited by L. R. Lozny, 303–17. New York: Springer.

——. 2015. "Engendering a New Generation of Public Intellectuals: Speaking Truth to Power with Grace and Humility." In *Speaking Power to Truth: Digital Discourse and the Public Intellectual*, edited by M. Keren and R. Hawkins, 129–54. Edmonton, AB: Athabasca University Press.

Krasny, M. E., S. R. Crestol, K. G. Tidball, and R. C. Stedman. 2014. "New York City's Oyster Gardeners: Memories, Meanings, and Motivations of Volunteer Environmental Stewards." *Landscape and Urban Planning* 132:16–25. doi:10.1016/j.landurbplan.2014.08.003.

Krasny, M. E., P. Silva, C. W. Barr, Z. Golshani, E. Lee, R. Ligas, E. Mosher, and A. Reynosa. 2015. "Civic Ecology Practices: Insights from Practice Theory." *Ecology and Society* 20 (2): 12.

Krasny, M. E., and K. G. Tidball. 2015. *Civic Ecology: Adaptation and Transformation from the Ground Up.* Cambridge, MA: MIT Press.

Lapidus, I. M. 1984. *Muslim Cities in the Middle Ages.* Cambridge: Cambridge University Press.

———. 2002. *A History of Islamic Societies.* Cambridge: Cambridge University Press.

Liarakou, G., E. Kostelou, and C. Gavrilakis. 2011. "Environmental Volunteers: Factors Influencing Their Involvement in Environmental Action." *Environmental Education Research* 17 (5): 651–73. doi:10.1080/13504622.2011.572159.

McMillan, D. W., and D. M. Chavis. 1986. "Sense of Community: A Definition and Theory." *Journal of Community Psychology* 14:6–23.

Naguib, S. 2007. "And Your Garments Purify: Tahāra in the Light of Tafsīr." *Journal of Qur'anic Studies* 9 (1): 59–77.

Namazi, B. 2005. "The State of Civil Society and NGOs under Iran's New Government." Wilson Center, Middle East Program. https://www.wilsoncenter.org/event/the-state-civil-society-ngos-under-irans-new-government.

Nature Cleaners. 2017a. "Nature Cleaners Iran Facebook Public Group." https://www.facebook.com/roftegranetabiateiran/.

———. 2017b. "Nature Cleaners Tehran Facebook Public Group." https://www.facebook.com/groups/R.T.Tehran.

Özdemir, I. 2003. "Towards an Understanding of Environmental Ethics from a Qur'anic Perspective." In *Islam and Ecology*, edited by R. C. Foltz, F. M. Denny, and A. Baharuddin, 3–38. Cambridge, MA: Harvard University Press.

Powers, P. R. 2004. "Interiors, Intentions, and the 'Spirituality' of Islamic Ritual Practice." *Journal of the American Academy of Religion* 72 (2): 425–59.

Rice, G. 2006. "Pro-environmental Behavior in Egypt: Is There a Role for Islamic Environmental Ethics?" *Journal of Business Ethics* 65:373–90.

Shavazi, M. J. A. n.d. "Recent Changes and the Future of Fertility in Iran." http://www.un.org/esa/population/publications/completingfertility/2RevisedABBASIpaper.PDF.

Sorokin, P. A. (1937) 1962. *Social and Cultural Dynamics.* 4 vols. New York: Bedminister.

Warburton, J., and M. Gooch. 2007. "Stewardship Volunteering by Older Australians: The Generative Response." *Local Environment* 12 (1): 43–55. doi:10.1080=13549830601098230.

Williams, R. (1976) 1983. *Keywords: A Vocabulary of Culture and Society.* New York: Oxford University Press.

Chapter 4

RETURNING ORANGE WATERS TO BLUE

Creating a Culture of Civic Engagement
through Learning Experiences

Louise Chawla and Robert E. Hughes

This chapter presents the concepts of *history in person, ecological identity*, and *social environmental identity* as a framework for understanding civic ecology practices. These concepts help us investigate the following questions: How do people's lives reflect the history of their place? What significant life experiences contribute to people's development of personal bonds with their locality and the motivation to protect it or restore it when it has been degraded? What experiences lead people to join with others in action for the environment, and once engaged, how does a person's identity as someone who actively cares for the environment deepen over time? And finally, how can collective action influence widening circles of social consciousness and even redirect history?

We explore these questions through the story of the Eastern Pennsylvania Coalition for Abandoned Mine Reclamation (EPCAMR) and its founding executive director Robert Hughes. Robert's life illustrates significant experiences that contribute to an individual sense of ecological and social environmental identity, while EPCAMR as an organization creates opportunities for many others to have similar formative experiences. Through the collective efforts of its participants, EPCAMR increases public awareness of local history while steering current history in new directions.

Central to EPCAMR's mission is gathering and disseminating information about abandoned mine land reclamation and opportunities for watershed restoration. Its staff, interns, and volunteers assess water quality, monitor the flow of discharges from abandoned mines, share reclamation technologies with other watershed coalitions, and create three-dimensional models of underground mining to guide the reclamation, planning, and development decisions of local munici-palities, industry, and community groups. EPCAMR also scans, digitizes, and geo-references mine maps and makes them publicly available through the Pennsylvania Mine Map Atlas and other databases. The organization works at multiple levels simultaneously, sharing information with congressmen, state legislators, local gov-ernment officials, civic leaders, members of the coal and cogeneration industries, local residents, educators, and students from elementary through graduate school.

But EPCAMR does more than share its technical expertise. It cultivates a culture of civic engagement around reclamation and abandoned mine drainage remediation by bringing people in coalfield communities together and igniting a "constructive hope" that, by working collectively, they can restore the region's social, economic, and environmental health. Constructive hope is different from unrealistic optimism. It involves gathering information to understand a problem, believing that one's personal actions can make a difference, and trusting that people in responsible positions are also working on solutions (Ojala 2012).

EPCAMR's origin and practices illustrate a large body of research about how people learn to understand and care for the environment and work effectively with others to address environmental problems. On the level of the individual, the study of *significant life experiences* has explored life events that motivate envi-ronmental awareness, concern, and action. Examining the backgrounds of diverse groups of people, it shows that experiences similar to those that propelled Robert to help establish EPCAMR characterize other people who show committed care for the natural world (Chawla and Derr 2012). These formative experiences help us trace how both an *ecological identity* and *social environmental identity* develop, as people form emotional bonds of connection with local places and learn how to play an active role in working for their protection and restoration (Thomashow 1995; Clayton 2003; Kempton and Holland 2003; Williams and Chawla 2016). Not least, the lives of Robert and others involved with EPCAMR illustrate the con-cept of *history in person*—that people's lives reflect the history of the places they are born into, but people are not entirely captured by this fate. People retain the possibility of recasting their inherited history and changing conditions through creative action (Holland and Lave 2001). We begin by sharing Robert's story and then interpret it through the framework of these constructs.

Learning the Land and Its People: Robert's Story

Robert was born in Wilkes-Barre, a city along the Susquehanna River in the Wyoming Valley of northeastern Pennsylvania. For the Lenni-Lenape, Mahi-can, Nanticoke, and Shawnee tribes of the region, it was a land of fertile soils, clear-flowing creeks and streams, abundant fish, and thick forests of oak, pine, and laurel (Chapman 1830). Conditions began to change after European settlers moved into the valley in 1762 and discovered "hard coal," or anthracite. It is estimated that sixteen billion tons of coal lay under an area of almost seven hundred square miles—the richest deposit of anthracite in the world. By 1917, anthracite production peaked at more than one hundred million tons a year. The coal from these seams brought an economic boom to Pennsylvania and fueled U.S. victories in two world wars.

But booms lead to bust, and today the legacy of this coal-fired prosperity is mine fires, mining pits full of toxic waters, more than 5,500 miles of degraded streams, 252 miles of dangerous mine highwalls, over 1,200 open mine portals and vertical shafts that leak toxic waters, deserts of black silt and pink ash, thousands of acres of waste piles, subsidence-prone land, and the elimination of entire ecosystems (EPCAMR 2016). More than 180,000 acres across Pennsylvania have been left in this condition, with aquatic systems most severely impacted. The water that drains from underground mine pools almost always contains iron hydroxides that cover streambeds with sediment in hues from red to orange, killing aquatic life. Sometimes it also contains toxic doses of aluminum hydroxides that stain streambeds white.

This is the world Robert was born into, but as the following account of his life in his own words shows, he and others are working together to build a more promising future. They are repairing the damage of past mining practices, communicating an appreciation for local history and local landscapes, and improving the quality of life of those who have suffered the most from the legacies of coal.

Childhood Beginnings

I (Robert) was born on June 23, 1972, the day of the historic Agnes Flood when the Susquehanna River topped its banks by forty-three feet, damaging and destroying twenty-five thousand homes and businesses in the Wyoming Valley of Luzerne County (O'Boyle 2009). My family lost all our possessions, and moved from one temporary shelter to another during my infancy, sometimes living in tents in relatives' backyards on higher ground and sometimes in Federal Emergency Management Agency (FEMA) trailers. By the time I reached school age, we had moved into the Heights section of Wilkes-Barre, eventually settling into the O'Karma Terrace, a low-income housing project in the Heights. My father was a truck driver and mover who spent long days on the road. My mother initially worked as a seamstress in a textile factory, later becoming a housewife. She took care of me and many of my siblings' children, so that I grew up with nieces and nephews. When I was sixteen, my father died of a massive heart attack, leaving me to take care of my mother as we sought strength and love from one another amid our struggles. I supplemented my mother's welfare payment, Social Security disability payment, and small widow's pension by working as a paperboy and finding other part-time and summer jobs. I did not want to burden her with any additional stress. During this time in my life, nature in the outskirts of the city became my escape and a place where I could find solace. Ironically, I was attracted to long hikes along abandoned mine lands, mine fires, and orange-colored streams. Little did I know, these unsafe havens would become integral parts of my adult life.

An important person in my early years was Ms. Elizabeth Stevens, an elderly neighbor who taught me how to garden, identify plants and fossil rocks, and bake banana bread and oatmeal raisin drop cookies. Her home was another safe haven in the housing complex for me and many of my friends. She showed me how to use a 1970 Imperial typewriter and encouraged me to write stories about my experiences in the outdoors and adventures with my friends. She was soft-spoken, gentle, caring, and created a sense of calm around her. She initially sparked my interest in anthracite coal by teaching me the names and types of different fossils that her son collected from the coal banks and brought home for her gardens.

From the time I was ten, my friends and I backpacked, hiked, and pedaled miles on our bikes across the Wyoming Valley, drawn by our love of adventure and curiosity about the abandoned landscapes that we could see on the distant mountainsides. We were also eager to escape the alcohol and drug scene in our neighborhood and avoid getting mixed up with the wrong crowds. Our parents encouraged us to take off on our bikes to find creeks to swim in and to pick grapes, blackberries, blueberries, and other fruit to bring home for jams and pies. I went fishing along the banks of the Susquehanna River almost every other day in the summers. Older brothers and sisters took us camping and hiking in the surrounding woods and along abandoned railroad beds. In addition to the region's beauty, we discovered mine fires, open mine shafts, mine tunnels, and orange-colored, sulfur-laden creeks. Less often, farther up the mountainsides, we found pristine trout waters. As I roamed the region from ages ten to fourteen, I stored up what I witnessed, tasted, smelled, and touched. I developed a connection with these abandoned, mine-scarred landscapes and wanted to know more. Being naturally inquisitive, I wanted to digest all knowledge that I could find about coal mining history, rivers, streams, forests, and aquatic ecosystems.

Academic Directions

My friends named me their token naturalist, as I had a fascination with all things living. I began spending hours in the city library, reading about plants, animals, and other subjects of interest, and then walking next door to the Wyoming Valley historical, geological, and genealogical societies to learn more. I strove for high honors in high school, and played basketball, baseball, and football and ran cross-country. In 1991, I graduated in the top five of my class at E. L. Meyers High School and won a scholar-athlete award, and most importantly, the F. William Remington Scholarship, named after a former president of the Wilkes-Barre Commission on Economic Opportunity. It provided me with money to go to Pennsylvania State University for four years on a full academic scholarship. I was the first person in my family to go to college. When I earned a bachelor of science degree in environmental resource management, with a technical area of water pollution control, it made my mother and siblings very proud, knowing all the struggles we endured in our lives. They knew that I wanted to make a difference in the environment that surrounded my community, as I had often shared this passion with them.

At Penn State University, I learned to understand what my friends and I had seen when we explored the forests, river, streams, and glacial rocks of our region. I found dedicated professors in environmental geology, hydrogeology, soil chemistry, pollution control, and agricultural systems management, who encouraged me to get my hands dirty on field trips and watershed tours. Through internships during school and summers, I found my future path and calling. My first internship was at the Pennsylvania Department of Environmental Protection's Bureau of Abandoned Mine Reclamation in Wilkes-Barre, followed by work with the district mining office in Hawk Run in Western Pennsylvania's bituminous coal region. As an intern, I researched abandoned mine discharges and drainage treatment systems, monitored mine fire gases in the historic town of Centralia, investigated mine subsidence, and got to know people in dozens of coalfield patches and towns across Pennsylvania who wanted to see their communities reclaimed and restored.

After I graduated, I worked for two years for the Pennsylvania Environmental Council, a statewide nonprofit whose director suggested that I organize a conference on abandoned mine reclamation near our regional office in Wilkes-Barre. On the second day of the conference, regional conservation district representatives and community leaders, initially led by the Pocono Northeast Resource Conservation and Development Council, decided to form a coalition to take action on this issue. Coalition members met every month for a year, with me assisting them by writing bylaws, a strategic plan, scope of work, and funding applications. With a grant from the Pennsylvania Department of Environmental Protection, EPCAMR was established in 1996. I was its first executive director, hired in May 1997 at the age of twenty-two. Today, with its regional office in Ashley, Pennsylvania, in the center of a catchment region with a population of about

FIGURE 4.1   Robert Hughes, EPCAMR executive director, demonstrating the value of cattails in abandoned mine drainage remediation on an educational field tour, Luzerne County, Pennsylvania. ILCP.com / photo by Miguel Angel de la Cuerva.

one million people, EPCAMR is a nonprofit environmental organization that services an area of sixteen County Conservation Districts and dozens of regional nonprofit and watershed organizations, municipalities, active anthracite mining companies, utility companies, cogeneration facilities, and mining-impacted communities.

Significant Life Experiences in the Formation of an Ecological Identity and Social Environmental Identity

Robert's story is consistent with the results of more than thirty-five studies from around the world that have examined the backgrounds of people who show active care for the environment (Chawla and Derr 2012). Whether these people choose to turn off lights when they leave a room, vote for pro-environmental policies, enhance wildlife habitat on their farms, choose careers in environmental education or conservation, or invest countless hours as a volunteer activist, a recurring experience that they share is many hours spent playing and exploring in nature as a child. This is the most common experience that distinguishes more environmentally active people from the less active.

Other frequently reported significant experiences are also evident in Robert's story. People who show active care for the natural world usually report childhood role models demonstrating appreciative attention to nature. It is often a family member, but it can also be a mentor such as Ms. Stevens, who taught Robert how to garden and identify plants and rocks. By paying attention to elements of nature in a closely observant and respectful way, these people communicate that nature has value (Chawla 2007). For children like Robert who are fascinated by everything they discover in woods and fields, these role models affirm the importance of their interests.

These experiences lay a foundation for an *ecological identity*, or a bond of emotion and life history that connects people to the natural world (Clayton 2003; Thomashow 1995). Although influenced by social interactions, an ecological identity is anchored in direct experiences of nature and emotional connection with the earth. In Clayton's (2003, 45–46) words, this sense of connection "affects the way we perceive and act toward the world; a belief that the environment is important to us and an important part of who we are."

The anthropologist Dorothy Holland (2003, 34) cautions, however, that sentiments like a sense of connection to nature are not by themselves enough to propel people into a lifetime of "sustained and generative environmental action." For that, people also need to develop a *social environmental identity* that involves affiliating themselves with an environmental group and learning how to act skillfully (Kempton and Holland 2003). James, Bixler, and Vadala (2010) concur, noting that people need a sequence of opportunities for "environmental socialization" that begins with childhood play and exploration in nature, and then continues with learning about the environment through formal education, apprenticeships, environmental clubs, or hobbies. Through mentors at school, work, or in a volunteer organization, people need to learn how to take action on the environment's behalf. A study by Chawla (1999) of environmental leaders in the United States and Norway came to a similar conclusion, while Stapleton (2015) described the importance of social interactions, taking environmental action, and being recognized for that action in the formation of social environmental identity.

Like Kempton and Holland (2003), James, Bixler, and Vadala (2010) believe that a critical step is developing "role awareness" of oneself as someone who knows about and actively cares about the environment. This self-identity may begin in childhood, but it deepens as people take on formal roles such as volunteer in an environmental organization, teaching assistant for a conservation biology professor, or staff member of an environmental agency. Holland and Lave (2001) describe these successive experiences as a "thickening of identity."

This sequence of experiences can follow many paths. Like Robert, some people have significant experiences as youth and later as university students, when they find opportunities to deepen their understanding of the natural world, choose a career path in an environmental field, and meet mentors who show how knowledge can inform action. Some people find mentors among family members. Some enroll in an environmental organization or initiative at the encouragement of a friend, only to find that participation transforms their sense of themselves and their relationship to the environment. There are as many paths into a social environmental identity as there are forms of collective care for the environment, and the identities that form may be general (such as a responsible hunter or gardener) or specific (such as a member of EPCAMR). The development of a bond with one's place (an ecological identity) and coming to self-identify as someone who joins with others to protect or restore local places (a social environmental identity) could also occur through engagement in civic ecology practices, although this possibility has yet to be explored (cf. Krasny and Tidball 2015).

Embodying and Influencing History

Holland and Lave (2001) note that a social identity embodies the concept of *history in person*. Drawing on ethnographic work that initially focused on the civil rights and women's movements (Holland et al. 2001), these authors observe that people's identities are fashioned in the context of long and complex social, political, and economic struggles. The environmental movement is another example of a long-term struggle to transform societies. Although this struggle spans national and even global scales, people experience it at their local level, from different points of view, with different interests, and using different cultural languages. According to the concept of history in person, history acts through individuals as they engage in local practices, but individuals also have opportunities to shape history creatively. Everyone both inherits history and shapes it, for better or for worse—not only people who become recognized as leaders of change. Residents of eastern Pennsylvania, for example, might see the environment as something external to the self, something that is "not me" and that merely exists for human use, and treat degraded mine lands and streams as convenient dumping grounds for old tires and other waste, accepting and perpetuating the history of the region's abuse. Or they could feel connection with the environment, realizing that their well-being is related to the condition of the land, and shift their own behavior and the behavior of their communities in more fertile directions. An organization like EPCAMR can help people see themselves as agents of the second kind of history shaping.

The concept of history in person applies to people's actions at all levels—local to national and even international. As the director of EPCAMR, for example, Robert works to strengthen state and federal policies that govern mining for coal, oil, and gas; land reclamation; and water quality. Current laws that require mine operators to restore disturbed lands descend from the passage of the U.S. Surface Mining Control and Reclamation Act (SMCRA) in 1977. EPCAMR networks with other coalitions, such as the Western Pennsylvania Coalition for Abandoned Mine Reclamation, the National Coalition for Abandoned Mine Reclamation, the National Association of Abandoned Mine Land Programs, and the Interstate Mining Compact Commission, to maintain support for strong regulations and adequate funds for reclamation and mine drainage water-quality improvement. This network lobbied successfully for reauthorization of SMCRA in 2006. By themselves, Robert and his staff could never have this kind of impact. Participation in a national network gives them leverage—but this network of organizations exists because Robert and others like him created it.

As an example of statewide impacts, during the 2014 legislative session, Robert provided public comments and scientific documentation to legislators across Pennsylvania regarding EPCAMR's opposition to the injection of abandoned mine water into gas wells for hydraulic fracturing (hydrofracking). A bill that would have authorized this practice failed to pass. In addition to influencing national and state history, these actions create supportive policies for EPCAMR's local initiatives.

For the public in eastern Pennsylvania's anthracite region, EPCAMR seeks to increase awareness of and appreciation for local history as well as possibilities for more sacred, protective, and restorative relationships with the land. Past and future are physically represented by Robert and his staff's current work with the Huber Breaker Preservation Society in Ashley, Pennsylvania, to construct an Anthracite Region Miners Memorial Park at former colliery grounds that were

FIGURE 4.2   Robert Hughes, EPCAMR executive director, provides testimony before the Pennsylvania Senate Environmental Resources and Energy Committee to preserve an adopted tax credit measure and to explore other opportunities for economic support and regulatory relief to help keep cogeneration plants operating and assist in reclaiming abandoned mine lands in Pennsylvania.

dismantled in 2014 (Hughes 2016). The three-acre park will contain a replica powder house, an engine house foundation, old colliery signs, a shiftman's shanty, sections of iron rail, restored coal cars, a building for educational and community events, an amphitheater, a green infrastructure parking lot, community gardens,

FIGURE 4.3   Robert Hughes, EPCAMR executive director, speaking at the former Harry E. Colliery about a proposed reclamation project in Luzerne County, Pennsylvania.

low-impact trails, and interpretive signage. A natural playground will be built to look like the outline of the former coal breaker—large machinery that broke coal into pieces, sorted it by size, and removed impurities. At sites like this, the region's coal history remains visible, while promising practices for the future are displayed.

Providing Significant Environmental Experiences for Contemporary Children

Sites like the Anthracite Region Miners Memorial Park provide opportunities for informal learning as local residents and visitors walk the grounds and read the interpretive signs, but they also form destinations for school programs (cf. Forsström 2016). Environmental education is an important part of EPCAMR's mission. Most children in the region come from families that are struggling to make ends meet, and few go on to college. In typical school classes, they never hear about the history of anthracite and the reign of "King Coal," never learn to see how past history continues to pervade the present, and lack opportunities to participate in envisioning how their future could be better. They don't understand why local streams run orange, or how the water could ever run clear again. EPCAMR brings these opportunities to local schools as its staff visit classrooms and lead students on explorations of the world beyond classroom walls to engage in hands-on learning about local history and culture and respond to the social and environmental issues that they encounter.

By bringing students into the field, EPCAMR staff are addressing a dilemma that significant life experience research presents. This body of research shows that people like Robert are motivated by childhood experiences that happened outside of school when they autonomously engaged with their environment through play and exploration. Later teachers or mentors deepened their understanding of what they had encountered. Many children today, however, lack similar experiences. They lack the freedom that Robert and his friends enjoyed to roam their surroundings widely, discovering both the beauty of the natural world and evidence of damage (Louv 2008). Many children lack family members or friendly neighbors like Ms. Stevens who direct their attention to the natural world and its value. Later in life, many lack opportunities to go to universities where they can learn to understand the environment in depth and have internships that guide them into meaningful environmental careers. Facing these limitations, how can organizations like EPCAMR make the experiences they offer to children and youth as formative as possible—both in terms of forming ecological and social environmental identities and reinforcing notions of history in person?

Research about environmental education has repeatedly uncovered three characteristics of programs that are most likely to move students to act on the environment's behalf on their own time, after program activities have ended (Chawla and Derr 2012). These programs engage students for an extended duration of time beyond one-day field trips or onetime classroom activities. They connect learning experiences to students' homes, communities, or regions, involving students in issues that matter to them, that they can see with their own eyes. Not least, they engage students actively. Students learn action by taking action, investigating local issues, discussing options, gaining skills like water monitoring, analyzing data, and presenting their ideas to decision makers. They have opportunities to try ideas and learn by trial and error—just as adults do. When they see their efforts bear fruit, they enjoy "mastery experiences" that strengthen their sense of self-efficacy, or their belief that they can achieve important goals that they set for themselves, working as individuals and as a group (Bandura 1997).

These characteristics of effective programs reproduce some of the significant experiences associated with the formation of ecological and social environmental identities. Field trips enable students to learn local cultural and natural history through hands-on experiences and see how their life fits into this larger context, which can promote a personal bond of connection to their place, an aspect of an ecological identity (Thomashow 1995; Clayton 2003). According to Kempton and Holland (2003), a social environmental identity develops along three interdependent dimensions: (1) environmental issues and the cultural world of people who are working to protect and restore the environment become salient; (2) people begin to identify themselves as an actor in this world of environmental threats and problem solving; and (3) in the course of engaging in action, they gain practical knowledge about how to take action effectively. Stapleton (2015) has shown how adolescents in an immersive climate-change education program that involved both general knowledge and field-based learning progressed on all three dimensions. She also observed that a fourth step in the formation of a social environmental identity occurred when families, friends, and communities began to give the teens social recognition as environmental actors with valuable expertise to share.

For hands-on experiences of local issues, EPCAMR staff take elementary school students on watershed tours, showing them how to test water chemistry and sending them into creeks in wader boots to sample aquatic insects and catch and identify fish. They teach students how to make systematic visual assessments of watershed quality, and they tell stories about the history of mining and mining communities. When staff describe how the transport of coal shifted from river to rails, they take students to see where old railways are now being turned into trails for biking and hiking. EPCAMR also provides curricula that meet state standards, so that teachers can involve their classes in similar activities.

A challenge for organizations like EPCAMR is how to provide more than one-day classroom visits or field trips. How can students become engaged in environmental activities for an extended duration of time? EPCAMR is grappling with this problem, and its evolving response is evident in the partnership that it formed with the Greater Nanticoke School District to bring environmental studies and art together. In this district characterized by high poverty rates, EPCAMR worked with all 365 fourth and fifth graders during the 2014–2015 school year over a period of nine months.

In the fall, the fourth- and fifth-grade students toured abandoned mine sites, viewing sources of mine drainage and impacted streams as well as a large water treatment system. For a close-to-home experience of water treatment, they collected buckets of orange water and took them to the EPCAMR office to be processed in a solar kiln, where the water evaporates and leaves iron oxide powder behind. For the first time, the students understood why streams in their school district run orange. Later in the winter, EPCAMR staff visited each classroom, working in partnership with a local art studio to teach the children how to make pinch pots and glaze them with the extracted iron oxide powder. The pots emerged from the kiln with a beautiful cherry-blossom color. Students organized an exhibit of their work and invited parents to come and share their pride in the products they had created.

A similar plan to involve students in extended activities began in the 2016–2017 school year, this time combining ecological restoration with the study of biology and earth sciences. Called "Release the Monarchs! Monarchs on Minelands," it involved more than two hundred middle and high school students in raising monarch butterflies in their classrooms, monitoring their growth and metamorphosis, learning how to tag the butterflies so that their migration patterns could be traced, and learning how citizens were working in other places to protect this species. The students released the butterflies on a mine site, and then planted milkweed on the abandoned mine land to feed future generations of monarchs.

These projects share common features. They involve students in extended processes of learning and action. They give them firsthand experience of the environmental devastation in their region, but do not stop there. In the first case, students learn how to turn polluting sediments in local water into a valued product. In the second case, they learn how to turn abandoned mine lands into habitat for a treasured species. They begin to try on a social environmental identity as they are encouraged to see themselves as environmental actors who can respond resourcefully to the problems they discover. The larger lesson is that the region's degraded environment does not need to be passively accepted; it contains opportunities for reclamation, ecological restoration, practical applications, and artistic expression—for history in person.

Again targeting middle school and high school students, EPCAMR works in partnership with Pennsylvania State Parks in a program called Community Connections to Our Watershed. Students sign up as volunteers for the yearlong program, which includes a daylong field trip led by EPCAMR. At the end of the year, students can elect a culminating service project with EPCAMR, such as a weekend of stream cleanups or riparian tree planting. Some students decide to become regular EPCAMR volunteers, returning to do service projects year after year. In the sequence of environmental socialization experiences that James, Bixler, and Vadala (2010) describe, these students are deepening their "role awareness" as environmental actors. In the words of Holland and Lave (2001), they are "thickening" their social environmental identity.

Passing Opportunities for Agency Forward

Robert works most closely with EPCAMR interns and staff. Remembering how formative his own internships were, and how the Pennsylvania Environmental Council gave him freedom to show leadership at a young age, he seeks to create similar opportunities for others. He and his seasoned colleagues, Michael Hewitt, Kelsey Biondo, Gabby Zawacki, Denise Hernandez, and Gavin Pellitteri, train college interns and new hires, usually recent graduates who take part-time positions for the chance to learn new skills, work in teams, and build their résumés. Most plunge into the technical work of water quality monitoring, water treatment, land reclamation, and generating mining maps. Some focus on environmental education, and others coordinate partnerships for community development, rallying conservation districts, local government agencies, and local environmental organizations to involve people from nearby communities in initiatives like cleaning up creeks and illegal dumps, restoring habitat, planting trees, and establishing community gardens (Comp 2001). These young adults have moved further along the stage of role awareness where they are trying on formal positions in an environmental organization, acquiring advanced skills, and exploring professional environmental identities.

The major lessons that Robert hopes to pass on to his interns and young staff reflect the values that he learned as a native son of the region who knows the challenges that many of its families face, as well as their resilience. He seeks to instill in them that EPCAMR is an organization that works *with* communities, not one that initiates and supervises community efforts from the outside. This means that staff work shoulder to shoulder with local residents to haul tires out of creeks, dig gardens, and host barbecues when the work is over. They listen to people share their lives, sense of place, and ideas about how to continue to shape their landscapes in positive ways. These activities build EPCAMR's most important asset, which is trust.

Another core value is resourcefulness. EPCAMR typically operates on a shoestring, so Robert is always encouraging his staff and interns to come up with new ideas for affordable ways to accomplish their aims. If Plan A isn't possible, then what is Plan B? Recent examples of low-cost plans for habitat restoration involve planting milkweed in community gardens, introducing beehives on reclamation sites, and teaching children in low-income housing how to make bird boxes and stain them with iron oxides. For fertilizer, a young staff member suggested installing a compost bin on a mine site to turn food scraps that EPCAMR generates into rich soil for restoration efforts, closing the loop of the cycle of plant growth, decay, and regeneration. Seeking ideas from staff and interns creates teaching opportunities and demonstrates that practical knowledge does not just travel from senior mentors down, but radiates from every level.

As EPCAMR moves forward, Robert and his staff hope to persuade local community leaders and politicians to make greater investments in coalfield communities through job creation, job training, and green infrastructure projects to reclaim mine-scarred lands. For this purpose, EPCAMR will need to continue to serve as a liaison to state and federal government agencies that can contribute much-needed funding to local communities, and to provide a base for meaningful internships and educational experiences in cooperation with local schools and community development and environmental groups. EPCAMR is committed to improving not only the quality of water and land in the coalfields, but also the quality of life of its hardscrabble people who want to remain in the places they call home, to raise their families there, and to live, work, play, socialize, and come together to improve their conditions. This sense of pride in one's community resonates with Robert on a deep personal level. He hopes that he will be able to see his three children swim, hike, and restore their spirits in some of the same areas he explored as a boy, so that they will share this common bond when someday he looks back and entertains his children and grandchildren with tall tales about his life's journey through the coal mining regions of Pennsylvania.

How does Robert and EPCAMR's work answer the questions we posed at the beginning of this chapter? We have seen how Robert's life reflects the interconnected environmental, social, and economic history of the anthracite region of eastern Pennsylvania and how he attempts to create significant life experiences for others so that they can work with him to redirect that history. In so doing, he designs environmental education programs that include elements known to lead people to take action—that is, programs that occur over an extended duration; that connect learning experiences to participants' lives, homes, and communities; and that actively engage participants. The programs also encompass the steps needed to create a social environmental identity—helping individuals to recognize the salience of environmental issues, to become actors in environmental problem solving, to gain practical knowledge about how to take action effectively, and to receive recognition as environmental actors with expertise to share. Importantly, Robert is creating these experiences not in the context of a past, minimally supervised childhood such as he experienced, but in the context of the contemporary constraints of children's lives.

Perhaps the most important question in the context of this book on broadening impacts of civic ecology practice is how can collective action influence widening circles of social consciousness and even redirect history? By embracing the region's coal mining tradition, yet trying to redirect that history through collective actions reflecting notions of history in person, EPCAMR can have broader impacts on its own and set an example for other coal mining regions. Further, Robert and EPCAMR are notable in that they work at multiple levels. Whereas in this chapter we have emphasized creating significant life experiences and building a social environmental identity among children and youth in eastern Pennsylvania, Robert and his staff are active in regional, state, and national networks of government agencies and nonprofits that have successfully advocated for environmental policies concerning abandoned mines and current resource extraction. In this way, while redirecting history in place, EPCAMR is also a player in adaptive governance and the civic environmental movement, themes we explore in other chapters in this book.

REFERENCES

Bandura, A. 1997. "Self-Efficacy: The Exercise of Control." New York: W. H. Freeman.
Chapman, I. A. 1830. *A Sketch of the History of Wyoming*. Wilkes-Barre, PA: Sharp D. Lewis.
Chawla, L. 1999. "Life Paths into Effective Environmental Action." *Journal of Environmental Education* 31 (1): 15–26.
———. 2007. "Childhood Experiences Associated with Care for the Natural World." *Children, Youth and Environments* 17 (4): 144–70.
Chawla, L., and V. Derr. 2012. "Developing Conservation Behaviors in Childhood and Youth." In *The Oxford Handbook of Environmental and Conservation Psychology*, edited by S. Clayton, 527–55. New York: Oxford University Press.
Clayton, S. 2003. "Environmental Identity: A Conceptual and Operational Definition." In *Identity and the Natural Environment*, edited by S. Clayton and S. Opotow, 45–65. Cambridge, MA: MIT Press.
Comp, T. A. 2001. "Eastern Pennsylvania Coalition of Abandoned Mine Reclamation." In *Hope and Hard Work: Making a Difference in the Eastern Coal Region*, 16–17. https://brownfieldstsc.org/pdfs/Hope%20and%20Hard%20Work.pdf.
EPCAMR (Eastern Pennsylvania Coalition for Abandoned Mine Reclamation). 2016. www.epcamr.org.
Forsström, S. 2016. "Planting at Atlas Coal Mine." In *Civic Ecology: Stories about Love of Life, Love of Place*, edited by M. E. Krasny and K. Snyder, 98–109. Ithaca, NY: Cornell University Civic Ecology Lab.
Holland, D. 2003. "Multiple Identities in Practice: On the Dilemmas of Being a Hunter and an Environmentalist in the U.S.A." *Focaal—European Journal of Anthropology* 42:31–49.
Holland, D., W. Lachicotte, D. Skinner, and C. Cain. 2001. *Identity and Agency in Cultural Worlds*. Cambridge, MA: Harvard University Press.
Holland, D., and J. Lave. 2001. Introduction to *History in Person*, edited by D. Holland and J. Lave, 3–33. Santa Fe, NM: School for Advanced Research Press.

Hughes, R. 2016. "Development of the Anthracite Region's Huber Miner's Memorial Park: Paying Homage to Our Mining Heritage." In *Civic Ecology: Stories about Love of Life, Love of Place*, edited by M. E. Krasny and K. Snyder, 128–36. Ithaca, NY: Cornell University Civic Ecology Lab.

James, J., R. Bixler, and C. Vadala. 2010. "From Play in Nature to Recreation, Then Vocation." *Children, Youth and Environments* 20 (1): 231–56.

Kempton, W., and D. Holland. 2003. "Identity and Sustained Environmental Practice." In *Identity and the Natural Environment: The Psychological Significance of Nature*, edited by S. Clayton and S. Opotow, 317–41. Cambridge, MA: MIT Press.

Krasny, M. E., and K. G. Tidball. 2015. *Civic Ecology: Adaptation and Transformation from the Ground Up*. Cambridge, MA: MIT Press.

Louv, R. 2008. *Last Child in the Woods: Saving Our Children from Nature-Deficit Disorder*. New York: Algonquin Books.

O'Boyle, B. 2009. "Agnes Now a Flood of Memories." *Wilkes-Barre Times Leader*, June 22. http://timesleader.com/archive/265255.

Ojala, M. 2012. "Hope and Climate Change: The Importance of Hope for Environmental Engagement among Young People." *Environmental Education Research* 18 (5): 625–42. doi:10.1080/13504622.2011.637157.

Stapleton, S. 2015. "Environmental Identity Development through Social Interactions, Action, and Recognition." *Journal of Environmental Education* 46 (2): 94–113. doi:10.1080/00958964.2014.1000813.

Thomashow, M. 1995. *Ecological Identity: Becoming a Reflective Environmentalist*. Cambridge, MA: MIT Press.

Williams, C. C., and L. Chawla. 2016. "Environmental Identity Formation in Nonformal Environmental Education Programs." *Environmental Education Research* 22 (7): 978–1001. doi:10.1080/13504622.2015.1055553.

Part II
KNOWLEDGE BUILDING
Learning in Civic Ecology Practice

Chapter 5

THE NATURE OF TRANSFORMATIVE LEARNING FOR SOCIAL-ECOLOGICAL SUSTAINABILITY

Martha Chaves and Arjen E. J. Wals

Learning seems to be the talk of the town nowadays. Once the exclusive domain of the educational sciences and learning psychology, and restricted to formal education, learning has become a key mechanism for realizing change, adaptation, innovation, and transitions in the context of the grand sustainability challenges of our time. Such challenges include slowing down the extinction crisis, ensuring food and nutrition security, and countering rising inequality and runaway climate change. Sustainability can be understood as an emergent property of complex interactions that bring about the well-being of planet Earth, including all forms of life, now and in the future. Such well-being necessitates the processes of living within the constraints of a dynamic equilibrium between continuity and discontinuity, growth and decay, uncertainty and clarity, and disruption and adaptation.

Dealing with such seemingly intractable challenges or "wicked" problems (Brown, Harris, and Russell 2010; Rittel and Webber 1973) calls for a wide range of learning configurations: *learning individuals, learning organizations, learning networks, learning communities,* and even *learning societies.* This, however, does not imply just any kind of learning; the learning required for breaking with dominant and resistant unsustainable routines and systems is learning that makes explicit—and asks us to continuously reflect on—our assumptions, values, and ways of seeing the world (Wals 2015). This is learning that also reveals the powers and inequities that tend to keep things the way they are or force us in directions we may not want to go—in other words, learning that questions what is taken for granted, the normalized, the hegemonic, and the routine. Further, it is learning that enables us to make changes and to transform others and ourselves, while learning from this process.

To complicate things, all this needs to happen in a world that is in constant flux—a world where what we thought was true yesterday turns out to be quite different today. This is a world where what we think works well in the Bronx in New York may not work very well in de Bijlmer in Amsterdam, and not at all in Temeke in Dar es Salaam, or in an eco-village in Colombia. We might call this *reflective learning*, or more introspective and interactive *reflexive learning* (Ryan 2005; Dyke 2009). Reflexive learning can assume a critical and even disruptive quality, transforming and transgressing stubbornly resistant patterns and systems based on undesirable foundations and values (Lotz-Sisitka et al. 2015).

Being or becoming reflective—let alone being or becoming reflexive—does not come easily. In fact, people tend to avoid the deeper questions and to steer away from the feeling of unease caused by friction, disruptions, or dissonance (Barker 2003). Yet it is these tensions and inner conflicts that create the kind of energy and questioning needed to learn in terms of rethinking the way we think, and when the conditions are right, cocreating new ways of thinking, seeing, and doing (Mezirow 2000b; O'Sullivan, Morrell, and O'Connor 2002). This requires going deeper into our habits and assumptions to interrogate the foundations of our practices (Argyris and Schön 1978) and to enable participants in multi-stakeholder settings to redesign and cocreate new practices that, at least for the time being, are more sustainable than the ones they seek to replace (Pahl-Wostl et al. 2008).

"Boundary crossing," where people, ideas, and practices that transgress traditional boundaries come together to make a change, often enables this type of deeper learning (Star and Griesemer 1989; Crona and Parker 2012; Krasny and Dillon 2013). Civic ecology practices might represent a space for deeper learning, whereby everyday people set out to discover, understand, and address local problems through trial and error, often in partnership with NGOs and local, regional, or national governments (Krasny et al. 2013). However, we know little about both the nature of learning in civic ecology practices and the outcomes of such learning. Are citizens engaged in boundary crossing in multi-stakeholder environments able to transform and transgress resistant patterns and systems that contribute to local and global systemic dysfunction? What might be some levers and barriers for such learning and the possibilities for designing spaces, physical and social, that facilitate boundary crossing?

To address these questions we begin by exploring design principles for boundary crossing that contributes to transformative learning in civic ecology practices. Because these principles are expressed differently in diverse contexts, we contextualize them in specific civic ecology practices. We then explore the potential of regional *upscaling* of transformative civic ecology practices through promoting the design principles in a citywide network that includes organizations from the grassroots to the municipality. Finally, we focus on national *outscaling* or spreading of civic ecology practices across communities as a result of yearly gatherings that engage participants in communal reflection, diverse ways of learning, and the cocreation of shared visions and practices.

Design Principles for Transformative Learning

Transformative or deep engagement is foundational to boundary crossing and to changing our unsustainable habits. People are accustomed to being in their social, existential, and physical comfort zones, where they feel safe and in control. We normally will not leave this security unless we have a strong desire to experience something different, or if circumstances force us to. This is like being a tourist, traveling to an exotic place and experiencing what it has to offer but in the full knowledge that we can return to our home environment—our comfort zone. It could be visiting the family cabin in the mountains without electricity or running water, or watching a documentary about shamans in the Amazonian jungle who believe in spirits and the power of dreams. Although these experiences may provoke reflection, they do not necessarily empower individuals to change their frames of reference or question their worldviews, the ultimate goal of transformative learning (Moore 2005; Mezirow et al. 2000a). The question therefore is how to engage people in an ongoing transformative and cross-boundary experience in which they leave their comfort zone in a reflexive manner and deeply engage with sustainability challenges.

Based on our involvement in transformative civic ecology practices (Wals, van der Hoeven, and Blanken 2009; Wals and van der Waal 2014; Chaves et al. 2017), we offer the following principles for designing transformative spaces: experiencing a good or positive story, leading the story together, embracing organic processes, employing passions and emotions, and promoting plurality for change. As a means of validation, we shared these principles with the participants of the 2015 civic ecology workshop that launched this book (see introduction). Of the twenty-five ethnically diverse workshop participants, sixteen, with equal representation of practitioners and academics, responded to a survey where they were asked to rate the extent to which the principles resonated with their experiences and to provide feedback and critique through comments. The five principles resonated highly or somewhat, and there was no apparent difference in answers depending on respondents' background (figure 5.1). Next we describe the design principles, weaving in the respondents' comments and feedback.

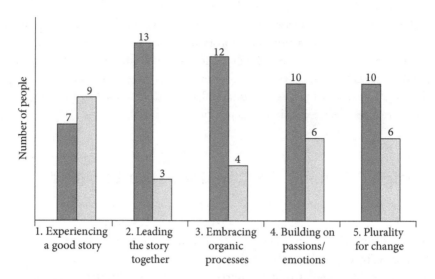

FIGURE 5.1 Resonance levels for the principles of transformative learning among practitioners and academics participating in the civic ecology workshop. Dark bars indicate principle "highly resonates" and light bars indicate principle "somewhat resonates" with respondents.

Experiencing a Good Story

People are more willing to leave their comfort zone if they are engaging in a cause they believe in. Throughout history, people and communities have come together across ethnic and cultural boundaries to fight against social injustice and eco-logical degradation. From the fight against apartheid in South Africa to the fight against deforestation of the Amazonian rain forest, such battles are often based on a narrative or "story," a fundamental way in which humans organize, store, and make meaning of information. Recently, stories of social injustice and environmental degradation have converged into the grand narrative of sustainability.

Krasny and Tidball (2015) argue that, in the context of local injustice and environmental degradation thresholds or "tipping points," coalitions led by civil society emerge to propose new ways of addressing these concerns. Their narratives come in many forms, from the global environmental and social justice movement described by Paul Hawken (2007) in *Blessed Unrest*, to community action groups addressing local issues such as food production or social isolation in community gardens (Lawson 2005; Reynolds and Cohen 2016), and the more extreme eco-militant views of those who seek to dismantle the industrial basis of society in order to save nature (Jensen, McBay, and Keith 2011).

What is interesting is that beyond adversarial stories of injustice creating "bad guy" antagonists against which to take a stand, unifying stories of "re-existence" and revitalization are emerging. Survey respondents talked about "finding a voice" and "uncovering those stories of past success that lead to present possibilities/opportunities." As one respondent expressed: "I also believe the energy in what mobilizes and unifies stories comes from places of empathy first, before the commonality of the 'bad guy.' When the unifying story finds the commonality of self-motivation for change, the antagonist takes a seat, and what unifies them becomes the power they share collectively, not the threat they each are under."

Importantly, the story needs to be *experienced* to create a change. As one respondent wrote, "I think what gives people the courage to step out is 'touching the fire.' When people live it directly or see the impact of it on someone they love, it is more real to them." With narratives such as sustainability and climate change taking on global significance, it can feel overwhelming to think about what one can do in one's own sphere of influence. For this reason, practical projects such as community gardening provide important arenas for bringing people together to interact and respond to a shared narrative, creating spaces for hope and transformation (see also discussion in chapter 8 of this book of Cox's [1998] spaces of dependence and engagement).

Leading the Story Together

A good story depends on leaders who envision a different world, break boundaries, and take action. Their role is to set the scene for new structures to evolve through the chaos and uncertainty of putting forward provocative ideas, thereby inspiring others who are not ready to leave their comfort zones. Thus leaders are critical to the success of new projects. As one respondent noted, "The problem of leadership burnout, and/or rigid control, or failure to delegate out of impatience with others, leaves an organization highly vulnerable, and ultimately, [to] fail."

Another respondent commented that beyond motivating and inspiring others into action, good leaders "recognize their obligation to build leadership in others and thus make room at the table for those beginning their journey." This, however, presents a challenge referred to as the founder's syndrome, where an organization's founders maintain disproportionate power and influence (often unintentionally), even after "stepping down" to let others lead (Christian 2003; Block and Rosenberg 2002; see also chapter 11). Such power can be realized through rank or how influential someone is in the group hierarchy (Brouwer et al. 2015), and by differences in experience and knowledge. As we have demonstrated through an eco-village case study in Colombia, the act of a leader coming to terms with her inherent rank and how it affects a project and its participants can be a transformative process of realizing who one really is and one's purpose in life (Chaves et al. 2015).

Sometimes leadership is collaboratively distributed within a group from the outset and expands and contracts as others join and leave the group. In this way, people can "lead the story together," as one respondent wrote, and "the leadership can come from a community organizing process that itself is cultivating leadership." This type of evolving collaborative leadership implies a high degree of commitment and self-discipline. Rather than one dominant leader giving directions or making space for others, evolving collaborative leadership is about creating conditions where actors across different domains and with different leadership styles, working rhythms, and levels of commitment are empowered to take responsibility and collaboratively tackle wicked or difficult issues by incorporating different perspectives.

Embracing Uncertainty and Organic Processes

We live in an accelerating world where change and uncertainty are constants. In trying to control this uncertainty, we tend to put what we know into neat little boxes and turn away from the complexity of social-ecological systems. Yet to face the deepening global crisis, we must recognize that systems are dynamic and to a large extent uncontrollable, acknowledge the embeddedness of all relations and how everything is connected, and be willing to cross boundaries of knowledge and certainty (Akkerman and Bakker 2011). This implies learning to be flexible and adaptive to evolving systems and processes (Diduck 2010).

One way of addressing this uncertainty is through promoting organic processes of change or self-organization. This involves continuously embarking in cycles of planning, action, evaluation or monitoring, and reflection that entails questioning practices and their underlying assumptions (Capra 2002; Chaves et al. 2015). Important to these feedback loops is a high tolerance for "failure," for as Brouwer et al. (2015, 62) note, "in the evolution of complex systems, there is much failure and just a few big successes that change the system." The important thing is to have the courage to experiment with something new and use failure as an opportunity to learn.

Although organic processes can boost cross-boundary and transformational learning, this is not an easy task. As one respondent commented, "We are individually and collectively starved for synthesis and discussion time; we don't know how to be nimble problem-solvers or we don't let ourselves; we prefer the ladder (one step at a time) to the web (throw it all out there and find your way)." Further, such organic processes can produce very slow change, and because of their complexity they are challenging to scale up. As one respondent noted, "Answers evolve from observations, and we have to be willing to learn, yet there is a mismatch of how quickly those observations will evolve into usable answers to benefit society." Despite these perspectives, we maintain that such smaller and slower processes may act to maintain enthusiasm among participants and a feeling of moving forward.

Using Passions and Emotions

Passions and emotions drive people to take action, pushing them out of their cognitive comfort zone and into what might seem like irrational situations. As one respondent wrote, "Our humanity, our neurobiology, seeks connection and belonging. We are at our strongest when we support this basic human need." By balancing our "head" with our "heart" understandings of the world, we have the possibility to break down barriers such as the human/nature divide, age and gender differences, and rationality versus intuition. Similarly, by opening oneself up to experiencing these emotions, we better connect with people and our surroundings. "People are drawn to passionate people who deliver stories and messages that resonate intellectually and emotionally. The ability to get fired up is alive but dormant in too many of us," as one survey respondent expressed. What we are looking for is what Capra (2002) conveys as an emotional and passionate climate conducive to emergence of new structures that promote mutual support, trust, and celebration, and a type of learning "from the heart."

Nevertheless, as a respondent noted, "emotions and passions can also have the opposite effect, causing people to resist innovation and to fall back on fear of change." Further, emotions may be directed at groups who are seen as the cause of the problem, resulting in an "us versus them" mentality and limiting our capacity to build alliances and find collective solutions. Thus, this principle also suggests avoiding fear-inducing passion to garner public engagement, as suggested by some environmentalists (Sterling 2009). To counter this, one respondent wrote, "we use intensive community engagement to entice people to feel more a part of the community first and then introduce innovative ideas into an atmosphere that already feels safer and more supportive." Through building these affective relations, people can experience a sense of community from the outset, feel supported, and in turn support others; a fellow volunteer becomes a friend, a place becomes a home, and the network becomes a family (cf. McMillan and Chavis 1986).

Plurality as a Driver for Change

"Expanding the boundaries of our own understanding is a critical step in changing the status quo." Consistent with this survey response, creating and facilitating plural environments helps push people to the edge of their reflexive boundaries.

This focus on difference and diversity for energizing people, pushing reflexivity, and unleashing creativity is supported by the social learning (Sterling 2009; Sol, Beers, and Wals 2013; Wals 2007; Chaves et al. 2015) and multi-stakeholder literature (Brouwer et al. 2015). What we want to emphasize here, however, is that beyond diversity, plurality implies the *engagement* of a society that includes a diversity of people (ethnicity, class, culture, worldviews); different beings (nature, spirits, entities); different knowledges (scientific, local, traditional); and different ways of learning (classroom, around the fire, artistic).

Plurality encourages us to move away from the idea that we live in a *uni*verse—where one truth and one sustainable way of living reign—toward the notion of a *pluri*verse, where different worlds coexist. Escobar (2011, 17) describes this as a world "ceaselessly in movement, an ever changing web of interrelations involving humans and non-humans." More simply, one survey respondent noted, "This broader definition of diversity is what we used to call open-mindedness. Our tendency to build and live in silos has shut this down considerably. We need to celebrate a convincible mind, so that information and emotion can indeed be transformative." A practitioner responding to the survey explained: "I have to do this [dealing with plurality] every day, and I'm a better, wiser person for it. Not always the easiest when you think you know all that you need to know about an issue/situation. However, when I'm humbled enough to open myself to the 'other,' new ways of thinking and being come into play."

Yet we must be careful not to romanticize plurality. It can be more aspirational than fact, and promoting and operationalizing it in practice can be challenging in terms of encountering misunderstandings and disagreements. How many of us, for example, would be comfortable having a conversation around a fire where spirits are invited guests? How seriously would we take what they have to "say"? Important for negotiating these tensions are what Wals (2011) describes as the "optimal dissonance," whereby a learner is far enough away from his or her comfort zone to be challenged, but not so far away as to be alienated.

Designing and Expanding Transboundary Spaces for Civic Ecology Practices

The five principles above can be used to design transboundary spaces to foster transformative learning in civic ecology. We next illustrate examples of civic ecology practices and describe bioregional and national networks that promote transboundary spaces for the emergence of novel relations between people and nature. By demonstrating the possibilities for bringing together diverse people and institutions in spaces for dialogue, capacity building, and action, we illustrate potential strategies to foster transformative learning and for upscaling and outscaling civic ecology practices.

A City in Transformation: The Emergence of Civil Society in Bogotá, Colombia

Described in the early 1990s as one of the most dangerous cities in the world, Bogotá, the capital of Colombia, with over ten million people, has undergone a dramatic transformation. Campaigning against violence, corruption, and nepotism, consecutive administrations starting in the mid-1990s set about transforming civic norms and habits through introducing bike lanes, effective public transport, and city parks. Although still a metropolis with grave problems of inequality and congestion, Bogotá is a "good story" of how it is possible to give a city back to its people, creating public spaces and civic pride.

Alongside these government-directed measures, grassroots civic ecology practices have emerged that encourage caring for nature and one's community through connecting people to their ancestral history and sacred natural sites in the city. For example, in the Eco Sembrando Barrio (Eco-planting Neighborhood) initiative, citizens varying in social and economic class use recycled materials to construct vertical and horizontal urban gardens (Eco Sembrando Barrio 2014). They cultivate edible, medicinal, and native plants as a form of memory retrieval of ancestral knowledge. Photographs of the person who sowed the plant are placed in the pots as a metaphor for planting and caring for oneself.

The NGO Naturaleza y Patrimonio (Nature and Patrimony) works with the local community to promote the connection between residents and nature through eco-tourism in Bogotá (Naturaleza y Patrimonio 2016). It has identified thirty-four nature sites in the city in danger of disappearing because of infrastructure development. To engage the community in helping preserve these sites, Naturaleza y Patrimonio worked with local authorities and community members to develop a bike tour that brings tourists to the sites, including Las Delicias ravine, which was a sacred site for indigenous Muisca people, and Santa María del Lago, one of the last remnants of the extended wetland that was once Bogotá. Together with the initiative Cantoalagua (Sing to the Water), Naturaleza y Patrimonio promotes conventional volunteer cleanup of the sites, as well as nonconventional cleansing activities where people go beyond rational boundaries dividing humans and nature to view nature as a living being that receives positive energy when people sing mantras to it (Cantoalagua 2017).

FIGURE 5.2 Members of Aula Viva marching in the streets of Bogotá in support of the protection of native seeds. Photo by Andres Boavida.

The Bogotá community-based stewardship practices illustrate the five principles of transformative learning, including the importance of plural knowledge (e.g., of elders and indigenous peoples) and experiencing a good or positive story by using passions and emotions in the artistic and spiritual activities of reconnection with ancestral ways and sacred sites. We turn next to how these and the other principles are expressed in regional and national networks of civic ecology practices.

Upscaling Civic Ecology Practices through Bioregional Networks

Urban gardening in eco-neighborhoods, the protection and propagation of ancestral seed varieties, and the restoration and conservation of natural sites in the city: where do all these initiatives meet? Apart from being civic ecology practices where local residents, activists, and institutions come together to protect local resources and promote community, these examples are connected by their shared participation in the Aulas Vivas Comunitarias Itinerantes de Bakatá (Itinerant Living Community Classrooms of Bakatá). Aulas Vivas are self-organized intercultural spaces where Bakatá (the ancestral name of Bogotá) residents, project leaders, and sometimes local authorities meet to network, share learning experiences from their respective projects, and carry out collective activities (Red Bakatá 2017).

Taking place at locations around Bogotá, Aulas Vivas are based on participatory methodologies such as *circulos de la palabra* (discussion circles) whereby the ancestral knowledge of the indigenous Muiscas is recognized and revived. Participants in ceremonies honor the sacred nature of Mother Earth and traditional crops such as maize and quinoa. Communal activities include cooking an *olla communal* (communal pot) of shared food to promote a sense of community, and dancing and singing to celebrate being together. Participants also seek to influence local politics by developing proposals to promote conservation of water, seeds, and biodiversity, and allocating 0.01 percent of local budgets and 0.1 percent of national budgets to strengthen cultural, artistic, permaculture, and digital community initiatives. They promote these proposals in strategic places such as the Climate Change Conference in the City Hall of Bogotá in 2015 and in public spaces such as libraries.

Bogotá's civic ecology practitioners recognize that their individual initiatives have limited possibilities for catalyzing systemic change. However, by working as the Aula Viva network, they are able to construct a more passionate and better articulated story of the need for reconnecting people to the ecological and cultural memory of ancestral Bakatá (transformative learning principles of "telling a good story" and "using passions and emotions"). Through becoming aware of the lost ecological wetland that was once their city, and through reviving the ancestral knowledge and places of the Muiscas, Aula Viva's diverse participants have gained transformative insights into their shared collective identity as descendants of the "water people" of Bakatá. This has involved organizing themselves as a bioregional and intercultural network that includes participants of different ages, ethnicities, social strata, and belief systems (design principles "leading the story together" and "plurality as a driver for change"), while allowing the network to evolve in its own time and directions (principle "embracing organic processes").

Recently, local authorities have recognized the importance of Aula Viva's work. On April 7, 2015, in conjunction with the Ministry of Culture, Recreation,

FIGURE 5.3 Exchange of native seeds during Aula Viva event. Photo by Andres Boavida.

and Sport and the District Board, and within the framework of the World Summit on Arts and Culture for Peace in Colombia, the organization carried out a living classroom focused on "walking toward peace-living community culture." As the bioregional network continues to grow and evolve, the hope is to increase its influence in proposing social and environmental policies that reflect and raise awareness of the city's ecological and cultural memories.

National Networks to Promote Outscaling
Civic Ecology Practices

In addition to *upscaling* through a bioregional network whose goal is to leverage grassroots movements for political impact, *outscaling* civic ecology practices across Colombia occurs through the annual intercultural gathering El Llamado de la Montaña (the Call of the Mountain). Here Aulas Vivas de Bakatá and other bioregional networks forge alliances, build leadership capacity, share methodological tools, and put into practice skills and knowledge through workshops and collective activities. Organized by the Council of Sustainable Settlements of America, El Llamado de la Montaña is a five-day workshop in sustainable living for peoples and initiatives from all over Colombia and beyond (El Llamado de la Montaña 2017). Participants meet in a host community and participate in social learning processes focused on how to cocreate sustainability visions and collective action (including civic ecology practices) in a plural society. Participants include Hare Krishna devotees, neo-rural eco-villagers, urban professionals, indigenous shamans, and local residents. Through opening up spaces for shared living and food preparation, and through engaging in intercultural discussions on shared concerns such as deforestation, food sovereignty, and mega-mining, the gathering promotes crossing boundaries and transformative learning.

Beyond acting as a social laboratory for sustainable living, El Llamado de la Montaña has developed a toolbox of approaches for generating sustainability actions and strengthening relations among participants, organizations, and regions. The approaches, which are practiced during the five-day co-living experience, seek to create learning spaces to promote reflexive learning. This includes cognitive learning through panel discussions and vision councils where participants collectively develop an agenda and reflect on hopes, expectations, and realities of the workshop, thus reflecting the learning principle of "embracing organic processes."

Other approaches encourage weaving social relations through experiencing the passion of a good story. To activate the heart and emotions while balancing the "head" focus on sustainability issues, El Llamado de la Montaña incorporates "dances of universal peace" that use sacred phrases, music, and movements from multiple spiritual traditions and create a sense of unity. At the *mambeo*, participants gather around a fire to listen to indigenous elders speak "from the heart" in a ceremonial conversation, inviting spirits to impart knowledge and wisdom. These approaches transcend the modern logic of individuality and rationality, challenging participants to leave their comfort zones and confront (if not embrace) emotion-laden ways of thinking and being.

Finally, participants in "hands" approaches apply what they have learned through activities like bio-construction and art. These and other hands-on activities like

FIGURE 5.4   Community leaders participating in panel discussion on *buen vivir* at Misak University during the event El Llamado de la Montaña, 2015. Photo by Andres Boavida.

preparing food, washing dishes, and cleaning compost toilets also bring out the "head" skills needed for self-organizing these activities, as well as "heart" feelings of contributing to the collective good of the community. During the *minga* (a Quechua word for collective work party), participants carry out a project for the local community such as building a playground, preparing a plot of land for planting,

FIGURE 5.5   Collective work party (*minga*) of tree planting on Misak land during El Llamado de la Montaña. Photo by Andres Boavida.

or working with local authorities and residents to replant a wetland damaged by cattle grazing. In the spirit of the "plurality as a driver for change" principle, the 2015 Llamado de la Montaña event was hosted by the indigenous Misak University, in the region of Guambia in southern Colombia. The wetland restoration *minga* connected action to the Misak people's cosmology, which describes the territory as a living organism made up of the relationships between people, animals, plants, and spirits. Several participants noted that the activity of planting trees within the context of Misak cosmology gave them an appreciation of the importance of a people's territory and the necessity of local stewardship (Chaves et al. 2017).

Beyond being a transformative space for individuals, El Llamado de la Montaña helps inspire and empower individuals to start regenerative practices in their own communities, especially in the cities from which most participants come. The event draws on the collaborative leadership model of sociocracy, which is a consensual form of decision making and distributed organizational structure (Romme and Van Witteloostuijn 1999). After *experiencing* a positive story of cocreating a more sustainable and intercultural world during the gathering, participants emerge from El Llamado de la Montaña to pollinate processes in their local spheres of influence.

Reflections on Designing and Expanding Transformative Learning and Civic Ecology

Civic ecology practices can be a source of social-ecological transformation when participants learn through small-scale experimentation and observation and collaborate with other sectors of society such as universities and NGOs in adaptive comanagement of local resources (see chapters 6 and 7). We have argued that one way of fostering the growth of civic ecology practices is through stepping out of one's comfort zone into situations that demand deep reflection on the assumptions that form the basis of our worlds. As reflected in the five principles of transformative learning, engaging in a meaningful story led by visionary leaders who enable collaborative and organic process to emerge is critical to this process. Plurality and emotions act as drivers of these deeper reflections and open up possibilities for deeper learning.

Related to these principles, civic ecology practices reflect local history, cultures, and aspects of the built and natural environment (Krasny and Tidball 2015). Aulas Vivas de Bakatá demonstrate how members of a regional network have articulated a shared vision of reconnecting people to places through the recognition and revival of Muisca ancestral practices. Participants upscale the impacts of their distinct practices through sharing and celebrating their visions and experiences in the network and advocating for changes in government policy. However, as one respondent noted, allowing for the organic development of collective processes means being patient and open to failure. While Aulas Vivas open up opportunities for upscaling activities through bringing together multiple actors, practices, and perspectives, a barrier to transformative learning is the slower pace of change taking place owing to negotiation among its members.

At the level of outscaling, El Llamado de la Montaña creates a space for transformative learning and for coalitions to develop among individuals and organizations that span cultural and institutional boundaries across Colombia. The gathering also builds leadership and shares approaches to addressing local sustainability issues that balance the domains of head, heart, and hands. Yet the dissonance created through incorporating diverse approaches risks alienating those who venture too far out of their comfort zones without a safety net. For example, a participant in a *mambeo* may simply not be able to connect to a night of elders speaking of and to spirits. Likewise, those connected at the spiritual level may not connect to the cognitive domain of critical thinking and planning and organizing. In the end, the transformative potential of civic ecology practices lies in the abilities of participants to find the right balance between comfort and disruption, to foster deep reflexivity, and to put the transformative learning principles into practice.

REFERENCES

Akkerman, S. F., and A. Bakker. 2011. "Boundary Crossing and Boundary Objects." *Review of Educational Research* 81 (2): 132–69. doi:10.3102/0034654311404435.

Argyris, C., and D. A. Schön. 1978. *Organizational Learning: A Theory of Action Perspective*. London: Wesley.

Barker, P. 2003. "Cognitive Dissonance." In *Beyond Intractability*, edited by G. Burgess and H. Burgess. Conflict Information Consortium, University of Colorado, Boulder. http://www.beyondintractability.org/essay/cognitive-dissonance.

Block, S. R., and S. Rosenberg. 2002. "Toward an Understanding of Founder's Syndrome: An Assessment of Power and Privilege among Founders of Nonprofit Organizations." *Nonprofit Management & Leadership* 12 (4): 353–68.

Brouwer, H., J. Woodhill, M. Hemmati, K. Verhoosel, and S. van Vugt. 2015. *The MSP Guide: How to Design and Facilitate Multi-stakeholder Partnerships*. Wageningen, Netherlands: Centre for Development and Innovation.

Brown, V. A., J. A. Harris, and J. Y. Russell, eds. 2010. *Tackling Wicked Problems through the Transdisciplinary Imagination*. London: Earthscan.

Cantoalagua. 2017. "Cantoalagua." http://www.cantoalagua.com.

Capra, F. 2002. *The Hidden Connections: A Science for Sustainable Living*. New York: Anchor Books.

Chaves, M., T. Macintyre, E. Riano, J. Calero, and A. E. J. Wals. 2015. "Death and Rebirth of Atlántida: The Role of Social Learning in Bringing about Transformative Sustainability Processes in an Ecovillage." *Southern African Journal of Environmental Education* 31:22–32.

Chaves, M., T. Macintyre, G. Verschoor, and A. E. J. Wals. 2017. "Towards Transgressive Learning through Ontological Politics: Answering the 'Call of the Mountain' in a Colombian Network of Sustainability." *Sustainability* 9 (1): 21.

Christian, D. L. 2003. *Creating a Life Together: Practical Tools to Grow Ecovillages and Intentional Communities*. Gabriola Island, BC: New Society.

Cox, K. 1998. "Spaces of Dependence, Spaces of Engagement and the Politics of Scale, or: Looking for Local Politics." *Political Geography* 17 (1): 1–23.

Crona, B. I., and J. N. Parker. 2012. "Learning in Support of Governance: Theories, Methods, and a Framework to Assess How Bridging Organizations Contribute to Adaptive Resource Governance." *Ecology and Society* 17 (1). doi:10.5751/ ES-04534-170132.

Diduck, A. P. 2010. "The Learning Dimension of Adaptive Capacity: Untangling the Multi-level Connections." In *Adaptive Capacity: Building Environmental Governance in an Age of Uncertainty*, edited by D. Armitage and R. Plummer, 199–222. Berlin: Springer-Verlag.

Dyke, M. 2009. "An Enabling Framework for Reflexive Learning: Experiential Learning and Reflexivity in Contemporary Modernity." *International Journal of Lifelong Education* 28 (3): 289–310. doi:10.1080/02601370902798913.

Eco Sembrando Barrio. 2014. "Eco Sembrando Barrio." https://sembrandobarrio. wordpress.com/.

El Llamado de la Montaña. 2017. "El Llamado de la Montaña." https://xn--llamad-odelamontaa-uxb.org/.

Escobar, A. 2011. *Encountering Development: The Making and Unmaking of the Third World*. Princeton, NJ: Princeton University Press.

Hawken, P. 2007. *Blessed Unrest: How the Largest Movement in the World Came into Being and Why No One Saw It Coming*. New York: Viking.

Jensen, D., A. McBay, and L. Keith. 2011. *Deep Green Resistance: Strategy to Save the Planet*. New York: Seven Stories.

Krasny, M. E., and J. Dillon. 2013. *Trading Zones in Environmental Education: Creating Transdisciplinary Dialogue*. New York: Peter Lang.

Krasny, M. E., C. Lundholm, E. Lee, S. Shava, and H. Kobori. 2013. "Urban Landscapes as Learning Arenas for Sustainable Management of Biodiversity and Ecosystem Services." In *Urbanization, Biodiversity and Ecosystem Services: Challenges and Opportunities*, edited by T. Elmqvist, M. Fragkias, J. Goodness, B. Güneralp, P. J. Marcotullio, R. I. McDonald, S. Parnell, et al., 629–64. New York: Springer.

Krasny, M. E., and K. G. Tidball. 2015. *Civic Ecology: Adaptation and Transformation from the Ground Up*. Cambridge, MA: MIT Press.

Lawson, L. J. 2005. *City Bountiful: A Century of Community Gardening in America*. Berkeley: University of California Press.

Lotz-Sisitka, H., A. E. J. Wals, D. Kronlid, and D. McGarry. 2015. "Transformative, Transgressive Social Learning: Rethinking Higher Education Pedagogy in Times of Systemic Global Dysfunction." *Current Opinion in Environmental Sustainability* 16:73–80. doi:http://dx.doi.org/10.1016/j.cosust.2015.07.018.

McMillan, D. W., and D. M. Chavis. 1986. "Sense of Community: A Definition and Theory." *Journal of Community Psychology* 14:6–23.

Mezirow, J., et al. 2000a. *Learning as Transformation: Critical Perspectives on a Theory in Progress*. San Francisco: Jossey-Bass.

———. 2000b. "Learning to Think Like an Adult: Core Concepts of Transformation Theory." In *Learning as Transformation: Critical Perspectives on a Theory in Practice*, by J. Mezirow et al., 3–33. San Francisco: Jossey-Bass.

Moore, J. 2005. "Is Higher Education Ready for Transformative Learning? A Question Explored in the Study of Sustainability." *Journal of Transformative Education* 3 (1): 76–91.

Naturaleza y Patrimonio. 2016. "Cultura viva comunitaria red Bakatá Colombia." May 5. https://www.youtube.com/watch?v=_TTWK-s0GLY&feature=youtu.be.

O'Sullivan, E., A. Morrell, and M. O'Connor, eds. 2002. *Expanding the Boundaries of Transformative Learning*. New York: Palgrave.

Pahl-Wostl, C., D. Tabara, R. Bouwen, M. Craps, A. Dewulf, E. Mostert, D. Ridder, and T. Tailleu. 2008. "The Importance of Social Learning and Culture for Sustainable Water Management." *Ecological Economics* 64:484–95.

Red Bakatá. 2017. "Aulas Vivas Comunitarias," accessed May 31, 2017. http://culturavivacomunitariabakata.org/aulas-vivas-comunitarias/.

Reynolds, K., and N. Cohen. 2016. *Beyond the Kale: Urban Agriculture and Social Justice Activism in New York City.* Edited by N. Cohen. Athens: University of Georgia Press.

Rittel, H. W. J., and M. M. Webber. 1973. "Dilemmas in a General Theory of Planning." *Policy Sciences* 4:155–69.

Romme, A. G. L., and A. Van Witteloostuijn. 1999. "Circular Organizing and Triple Loop Learning." *Journal of Organizational Change Management* 12 (5): 439–53.

Ryan, T. 2005. "When You Reflect Are You Also Being Reflexive?" *Ontario Action Researcher* 8 (1): 7–10.

Sol, J., P. J. Beers, and A. E. J. Wals. 2013. "Social Learning in Regional Innovation Networks: Trust, Commitment and Reframing as Emergent Properties of Interaction." *Journal of Cleaner Production* 49:35–43.

Star, S. L., and J. R. Griesemer. 1989. "Institutional Ecology, 'Translations' and Boundary Objects: Amateurs and Professionals in Berkeley's Museum of Vertebrate Zoology, 1907–39." *Social Studies of Science* 19 (3): 387–420.

Sterling, S. 2009. "Riding the Storm: Towards a Connective Cultural Consciousness." In *Social Learning towards a Sustainable World: Principles, Perspectives, and Praxis*, edited by A. E. J. Wals, 63–82. Wageningen, Netherlands: Wageningen Academic.

Wals, A. E. J., ed. 2007. *Social Learning towards a Sustainable World: Principles, Perspectives, and Praxis.* Wageningen, Netherlands: Wageningen Academic.

——. 2011. "Learning Our Way to Sustainability." *Journal of Education for Sustainable Development* 5 (2): 177–86.

——. 2015. "Beyond Unreasonable Doubt: Learning for Socio-ecological Sustainability in the Anthropocene." Inaugural Address, Wageningen, Netherlands.

Wals, A. E. J., N. van der Hoeven, and H. Blanken. 2009. *The Acoustics of Social Learning: Designing Learning Processes That Contribute to a More Sustainable World.* Wageningen, Netherlands: Wageningen Academic.

Wals, A. E. J., and Marlon E. van der Waal. 2014. "Sustainability-Oriented Social Learning in Multi-cultural Urban Areas: The Case of the Rotterdam Environmental Centre." In *Greening in the Red Zone: Disaster, Resilience and Community Greening*, edited by K. G. Tidball and M. E. Krasny, 379–96. New York: Springer.

Chapter 6

MAKING KNOWLEDGE IN CIVIC ECOLOGY PRACTICES
A Community Garden Case Study

Philip Silva and Rosalba Lopez Ramirez

Civic ecology practices often emerge in places struggling with deeply ingrained social, economic, and environmental challenges. Practitioners of civic ecology come together to foster hope and make meaningful and measurable changes in their communities. To make such changes, acting on knowledge that is created through their practice—by taking measurements, by observing, by sharing resources and ideas with peers, and by other means—is critical.

In this chapter, we explore how members of Kelly Street Garden, a community garden in the South Bronx in New York City, strive to produce, manage, and apply new knowledge in their work together, through measuring outcomes and by other means that are often overlooked in research on participatory forms of environmental management. We begin with an overview of the conceptual literature on knowledge making in practice and the social constructionist worldview that frame our insights. We continue with a short history of the social, economic, and environmental stresses that have characterized the South Bronx for the past fifty years and then focus on Kelly Street Community Garden and its various knowledge management practices. Finally, we highlight three insights into how knowledge management can strengthen a civic ecology practice, which we hope will prove useful to other civic ecology practitioners eager to be more reflexive about their work.

Knowledge Making

Urban planners and natural-resource managers sometimes use monitoring and data collection and analysis to adaptively improve routine practices in complex and emergent social-ecological systems. Efforts by professionals to strengthen their work through knowledge management also have been seen in smaller, mostly volunteer-led urban environmental stewardship initiatives, or civic ecology practices (Krasny and Tidball 2015; Silva and Krasny 2014). Although a comprehensive review of this cyclical approach to creating, testing, and refining useful knowledge is beyond the scope of this chapter, we offer a brief introduction to the literature to ground our observations from one community garden in the South Bronx within these broader academic traditions.

"Organizational learning involves the detection and correction of error," Argyris and Schön (1978, 2) wrote in their widely cited introduction to multiple-loop learning in organizations. Single-loop learning refers to changes in day-to-day practice that result from a critical appraisal of outcomes based on data derived from sustained outcomes monitoring. Double-loop learning deals with deeper modifications to "an organization's underlying norms, policies, and objectives" (3), which also can result from monitoring and analysis. These informational feedback loops function like a thermostat adjusting the temperature of a building in response to unpredictable weather patterns—they allow an organization to adapt to complex circumstances beyond its control and gradually strengthen its practices over time.

This concept of adaptive change based on perpetual knowledge-making-in-action found a welcome audience in the field of environmental management beginning in the 1970s. Around this time, the prevailing top-down, one-size-fits-all "command and control" approach to management proved increasingly incapable of dealing with the complexities and uncertainties of human-dominated ecosystems (Cundill and Rodela 2012). Walters and Holling (1990) dubbed the new approach "learning by doing," with scientists doing most of the "learning" through carefully designed and controlled field experiments (Layzer 2008). More recently, scholars have featured participatory forms of deliberation and knowledge creation with a variety of stakeholders—property owners, community members, and experts of all stripes—working together under the banner of adaptive *collaborative* management (Armitage et al. 2008; Charles 2008). Stakeholders in these cases work with scientists to develop knowledge about what works and what doesn't work for managing a resource over time, and they learn how to work together more inclusively and effectively to ensure better management outcomes (Cundill and Rodela 2012).

Most civic ecology practices find themselves in similar circumstances regarding the complexity of social-ecological systems and the need for adaptive knowledge-making processes. What was right yesterday may be wrong tomorrow (Nadasdy 2007), both in terms of which tomatoes grow best in the shady corners of a community garden *and* which community organizing practices bring the greatest number of volunteers out to turn the compost and weed the flower beds. To that end, civic ecology practices resemble "knowledge-intensive firms" (Starbuck 1992; Kärreman 2008; Blackler 1995), hungry for useful insights into the latest problem or puzzle that emerges from day-to-day practice.

Practitioners are not limited to formal scientific monitoring and field experimentation in their efforts to construct knowledge about the resources and ecosystems they manage. Although the pattern observations and causal explanations—in other words, the knowledge claims—that practitioners produce about biological, ecological, agricultural, and other biophysical phenomena may not be completely *scientific* in nature, they are nonetheless based on informal data collection, trial-by-error testing, and inductive reasoning, as scholars of traditional environmental knowledge have demonstrated in case studies of indigenous communities (Berkes, Colding, and Folke 2000; Dunbar 1996). Yet studies of knowledge production within environmental management practices often shift the focus from *biophysical* phenomena to *social* phenomena, such as managing group dynamics, facilitating stakeholder deliberation, building cross-scale linkages between social sectors, and achieving consensus in decision-making processes—phenomena that, taken together, add up to environmental *governance* (see chapter 8).

In this chapter, we focus on knowledge production around both biophysical and social phenomena within an environmental management practice—or, more specifically, a civic ecology practice—recognizing the interwoven nature of social-ecological systems (Berkes, Colding, and Folke 2003). Taking a view of learning-in-practice as synonymous with knowledge construction and discovery (Bruner 1996; Brown and Duguid 1991; Wenger 1998), we aim to build a clearer understanding of how civic ecology practitioners produce new and useful insights into their own practice. In doing so, we begin to create space for research into knowledge production within civic ecology practice that includes both biophysical and social phenomena.

A Constructivist Worldview

We situate ourselves within the traditions of *grounded theory* and *social constructivism* in our efforts to understand knowledge making in civic ecology practices.

Glaser and Strauss (1967) developed the methods of grounded theory as a reaction to decades of social research aimed at collecting data to either prove or disprove preexisting theories. To generate new theory, they argued, researchers must critically read through raw qualitative data on a particular subject and work to identify emergent categories and themes that appear consistently across similar cases of the same phenomenon. The theory that emerges, then, is *grounded* in the data. Charmaz (1990) further developed grounded theory from a social constructionist perspective, arguing that themes, categories, and theories don't passively emerge from a neutral reading of the data; rather, the researcher is an active participant in constructing a *particular* interpretation of patterns to make sense of what she sees in *particular* cases she investigates.

In taking a social constructivist grounded theory approach to developing this chapter, we make no claims to either objectivity in our methods or universal applicability in our findings (Guba and Lincoln 1989). Ours is a particular construction of events at Kelly Street Garden, crafted from interviews, focus groups, participatory workshops, and informal conversations with the garden leaders. This chapter is authored by a civic ecology practitioner (Rosalba Lopez Ramirez) and an academic researcher (Philip Silva). Yet these, too, are socially constructed categories with fuzzy boundaries. We both drew on our experiences as gardeners, gardening experts, and researchers, conscious of our biases but never so naïve as to assume that we could (or perhaps even should) push those biases away. Throughout our collaboration, Rosalba served as the garden's professional coordinator, compensated by the property owner in exchange for helping the garden get started. Rosalba also holds a master's degree in community development and is no stranger to social research. Philip was a doctoral candidate at Cornell University during the time he worked on this chapter, but he has also been both a community gardener and a technical assistance provider for gardens in New York City. The binary categories of "practitioner" and "academic" brought us together, but our collaboration blurred the lines between these two ways of making sense of the world.

Kelly Street Garden in the South Bronx

The South Bronx is a prime example of the economic disinvestment typically seen in postindustrial U.S. cities during the second half of the twentieth century (Beauregard 2003)—a prototypical "broken place" (Krasny and Tidball 2015) where civic ecology practices such as community gardening often emerge. "All of a sudden it broke apart and everybody started going into their own homes," one member of Kelly Street Garden recalled during a focus group discussion.

"People started moving and being displaced, so the neighborhoods got lost." In the Longwood neighborhood of the South Bronx, a tenacious coalition of activists and African American property owners worked to prevent the wave of building abandonment and arson that overtook much of the rest of the area in the 1970s and '80s (Gonzalez 2004). The Banana Kelly Community Improvement Association—earning its name from the prominent curve in the stretch of Kelly Street where the organization got its start—purchased and rehabilitated its first three apartment buildings in the neighborhood in 1977. It was one of the first groups to step into the local real estate economy during those challenging years, improving living conditions for hundreds of thousands of residents (Gonzalez 2004). By the 1990s, the community district that includes Longwood experienced the highest growth in repopulation of any neighborhood in the South Bronx, due in part to the early work of groups like the Banana Kelly Community Improvement Association (Banana Kelly).

The housing market in the South Bronx eventually achieved some stability through a combination of government programs and private investments in new affordable housing (Gonzalez 2004). Yet the South Bronx continues to have one of the greatest concentrations of poverty, unemployment, and crime in the United States. Prior to a 2013 redistricting, the South Bronx was home to the poorest congressional district in the country, with 38 percent of residents living at or below the federal poverty line (Sisk 2010). As New York City's fortunes rose in the late 1990s and into the twenty-first century, the gentrification of poor and working-class neighborhoods in other areas pushed low-income residents into the South Bronx (Institute for Children, Poverty, and Homelessness 2014).

He Left Us Alone—but Together

By Rosalba Lopez Ramirez

The sirens.
I did not hear the shot.
The shot that killed him
The shot that caused an earthquake on the block
The shot that murder him

. . . . . .

He left us—
He left us—
He left us—not alone BUT together.
Together.   (Cont.)

(Cont.) A few weeks passed after the murder of this young man known as Bam Bam. And one day we found ourselves huddled in a circle like a clan during a fall event in the garden that community members decided to call Grow Love. Young adults surrounded the perimeters, older adults sat on the inner ring, and a group of children sat in the middle caressing a dog, while other children sat on the couch that had been specially placed in the garden to create the feeling of a household living room. For thirty seconds my eyes remain closed. Many adults joined me in this act as we paid our respects to a young man who was murdered on the corner of the block late that summer. The children were as silent as they could be.

As my eyes are closed I feel a slight breeze caress my hair. I can hear the tears that are falling and the runny noses that accompany the tears. We open our eyes, and I come to find that the tears are being wiped away. They come from a young man with a gray hoodie whom I've seen on the block but whom I've never spoken to.

Grief is in the air, and this has been so as mothers had confided in me the sadness they carried as they joined me in the garden. And I know this is so as one child asked me what would happen to the garden after I die. With this in mind, I ask the people present to share some words to honor the life of the young man who died. For a moment there is a pause, and I decide that I, too, want to acknowledge that despite not knowing him well, our paths had crossed in the garden. I share with the group that Bam Bam stood in the garden one day, looking confused, almost in a daze but with a growing curiosity about the garden.

I know who will speak next, and he does. The young man in the gray hoodie speaks:

"Till this day I just can't believe he's gone, and like. I have a daughter. You feel me? That I have to worry about. I could have retaliated, you feel me? I think. Cuz that's like a brother, losing a brother, a brother. It hit me hard."

Poor urban areas like the South Bronx are often home to environmentally pernicious land uses such as power plants, highway interchanges, waste processing facilities, and truck depots (Sandler and Pezzullo 2007). The South Bronx is home to all these and more (City of New York 2007). Local air pollution may play a role in the area's inordinately high childhood asthma hospitalization rates. Poor air quality, coupled with limited access to open space, may also contribute to high childhood obesity rates in the area (Joseph 2010). To make matters worse, residents of the South Bronx often struggle to access fresh and affordable fruits and vegetables in local markets. The acute crises of the 1970s and 1980s have been replaced by a chronic "slow burn" or decline (Stedman and Ingalls 2013) related to social, economic, and environmental issues.

In the face of urban decline, community gardens can be a source of neighborhood revitalization (Lawson 2005) offering multiple social, public health, and environmental benefits (Cohen, Reynolds, and Sanghvi 2012; Okvat and Zautra 2014; Saldivar-Tanaka and Krasny 2004). Thus, it should come as no surprise to find that community gardening is one of many strategies employed by residents of the South Bronx to address the challenges they have faced for nearly half a century. Kelly Street Garden sprawls across the conjoined backyards of five four-story apartment

FIGURE 6.1 Neighbors come together in Kelly Street Garden in reaction to a local murder in the autumn of 2014. Photo by Rosalba Lopez Ramirez.

buildings, each with long histories of landlord neglect. Although the buildings were some of the few in Longwood maintained during the years of building arson and mismanagement, a change in ownership in 1987 brought on a twenty-year decline in basic upkeep. By 2007, the five properties were listed among the worst two hundred buildings in all of New York City by the municipal Housing Preservation and Development Agency (Perlman 2011; Ayres 2015). Workforce Housing Group, a company specializing in renovating and managing affordable housing in New York City, acquired the properties in 2011 and spent nearly two years refurbishing all eighty-one apartments in the complex (Wills 2013).

The new owners partnered with Banana Kelly to connect residents with social services and create a publicly accessible backyard community garden. Their aim was twofold: offering residents access to healthy food, while fostering community cohesion on a block that continues to struggle with crime, poverty, and short tenancies. The new garden harks back to an earlier effort at cultivating the same patch of land in the 1980s, when the "banana" portion of Kelly Street was an island of relative stability in the midst of a broken place. "I think this garden brings back a sense of community," one gardener reflected in a focus group. "It brings back a sense of the village, if you will, and it brings back a sense of 'I'm looking out for my neighbor as well as myself.'"

Residents and neighbors from other buildings on the block gained access to the garden in the spring of 2014. Six women quickly emerged as leaders, forming a small Gardening Committee with help from Rosalba and a resident and community services manager employed by Workforce Housing. With summer quickly approaching, the group moved to plant anything they could in the new raised beds, having little opportunity to think about ideal plant locations, companion planting, or any other horticultural rules of thumb. The simple goal was to get started and hope for the best in the first season.

Producing Knowledge at Kelly Street Garden

Early in the first season, Rosalba learned of a citywide project aimed at helping community gardeners and urban farmers collect data on the outcomes of their work. She assumed the building owners would want to see some proof that their investment had been worthwhile and that future funders would be more likely to support a project that could substantiate its successes. She signed up to attend a daylong training session for gardeners and farmers interested in using a toolkit of twenty measures for social, environmental, and health-related outcomes of urban agriculture. Both the toolkit and the training session were products of Five Borough Farm, a multiyear initiative sponsored by the local advocacy group Design Trust for Public Space to understand and interpret the benefits of growing food in urban areas (Cohen, Reynolds, and Sanghvi 2012). At the time, Philip was serving as an outreach fellow for the initiative, having coached a team of thirty community gardeners through the process of creating the different data-collection methods that went into the Five Borough Farm toolkit. Rosalba attended the daylong training in May and subsequently introduced the idea of data collection to the members of the Gardening Committee. The group agreed to use two methods from the kit during its inaugural season (measuring produce and volunteer hours).

FIGURE 6.2   Young people weighing produce grown at Kelly Street Garden. Photo by Rosalba Lopez Ramirez.

The gardeners kept a small kitchen scale provided by Five Borough Farm in a central location and used worksheets stored in a three-ring binder to track the weight of the different vegetables they harvested throughout the season. They quickly developed a habit of asking for "the binder" whenever they picked vegetables for themselves or for garden guests. One committee member stepped into the role of "data collector," recording volunteer hours contributed by regular gardeners and guests, exhorting them to sign in and sign out on a log-in sheet as they entered and left the garden. Rosalba worked with the resident and community services manager to periodically collect data worksheets from the gardeners and enter numbers into an online data tracking system hosted by Five Borough Farm. Together they discovered that Kelly Street Garden grew more than 350 pounds of food and generated nearly eight hundred hours of volunteer time by the end of its first year. The gardeners also hosted well-attended public workshops and neighborhood parties, making the garden a welcoming public space for nearby residents.

The Gardening Committee reconvened in the spring of 2015 to review its accomplishments and set goals and objectives for its second growing season. The process began in March when Philip facilitated an hour-long focus group that brought up the goals each committee member had for the garden. Philip recorded, transcribed, and analyzed the discussion, identifying themes of *hope, safety, happiness, health, social cohesion,* and *access to useful information* as committee members' goals. One month later, he returned to share his findings and use the six themes to kick off an objective-setting workshop with the committee. The group worked backward from their broad goals to name quantifiable proxy objectives for 2015, choosing data-collection methods from Five Borough Farm to measure their progress (table 6.1). In the case of *health*, the committee chose to collect data on the number of pounds of food harvested in the garden, relying on a standard logic modeling approach commonly used in nonprofit organizations (Knowlton and Phillips 2012) to infer that providing the neighborhood with access to free vegetables would have a positive impact on health. The committee set quantifiable objectives for pounds of food based on their data from the previous year, reasoning that with better gardening skills they could produce more food. However, they postponed naming quantitative objectives for measuring "good moods," "skills," and "knowledge" as proxy objectives for *hope, happiness,* and *access to useful information*. This was due in part to the lack of data from the previous year, which could have served as a baseline. "We would like more!" one gardener affirmed after reviewing the list of objectives posted on the wall in the workshop. "We always strive for more."

Yet collecting data for outcomes monitoring was not the only means of making new and useful knowledge at the Kelly Street Garden. Members of the Gardening

TABLE 6.1 Matching goals, objectives, Five Borough Farm measurement protocols (Design for Public Space 2015), and associated practices

GENERAL GOAL THEMES	QUANTIFIED OBJECTIVES FOR 2015	FIVE BOROUGH FARM MEASUREMENT PROTOCOLS	ASSOCIATED PRACTICES
Happiness and hope	"Good moods" generated from visiting the garden	Good moods in the garden	Keeping open hours; growing ornamental plants
Health	500 lbs. of food grown in the garden	Harvest count	Growing food in the garden
Safety and social cohesion	34 events 400 visitor hours 600 volunteer hours	Participation by task and reach of programs	Hosting workshops and events; providing volunteer work opportunities
Access to useful information	Skills shared in the garden; concepts shared in the garden	Skills and knowledge in the garden	Sharing knowledge and skills within the garden

Committee attended workshops on horticulture, fund-raising, and community organizing offered by technical assistance providers throughout New York City, such as the New York Botanical Garden and GreenThumb (a division of New York City Parks that supports community gardens). During their semi-regular meetings, committee members would report back on general themes from their workshops and make plans to apply new lessons in practice. The committee members also engaged in a constant stream of discussion and storytelling about what was and was not working in the garden, discovering their collective identity as gardeners at the same time that they grappled with challenges in their horticultural practices and group dynamics.

Knowledge Production in Civic Ecology Practices

Because of timing constraints, we find ourselves reflecting on just a portion Kelly Street's fledgling efforts to get in the habit of tracking outcomes for adapting practice. Although we do not know exactly how the group used the data it created to strengthen its practices in later seasons, we do have insights into the data-collection processes themselves. We offer three insights from Kelly Street Garden that may be useful to other civic ecology practices eager to be more reflexive in their data-collection practices as one step toward strengthening their work over time. We also hold out the observation that not all knowledge production efforts within a civic ecology practice are exclusively related to data collection for outcomes monitoring—that tacit knowledge produced as an outcome of daily practice or imported and reconstructed from sources *outside* a practice may not be scientific—but that doesn't make it any less useful.

First, although scientists and natural-resources managers argue that outcomes monitoring should specifically deal with tracking progress toward predetermined environmental management objectives (Hellawell 1991), some civic ecology practitioners may find that objective setting is difficult without baseline data to shape their expectations of what is (or isn't) accomplishable. Goals and objectives can drive an adaptive cycle of monitoring and testing described by Argyris and Schön (1978). However, practitioners new to a practice (or to data collection as a dimension of practice) may need to spend a season collecting baseline data before they can forecast and set meaningful, realistic milestones for their work. "The gardeners didn't know what they were capable of" in the first year, the resident and community services manager at Kelly Street recounted. Practitioners also may find motivations other than improving their practice to collect data. At first, Rosalba was motivated by a vague sense that both the garden's landlord and potential funders would want to see quantitative evidence of the garden's impact. Her hunch was proven correct when the garden secured small grants from local funders in its second year, using data about its previous harvest yields to prove the general value and viability of the gardeners' work.

Second, civic ecology practitioners look for knowledge from outside their practices to inform and improve their work, particularly during the early stages of a new initiative. Yet practitioners can struggle to apply new knowledge from other sources to their own day-to-day practices (Brown and Duguid 2000; Polanyi 2009). The Kelly Street gardeners brought back codified forms of explicit knowledge—pamphlets, tip sheets, how-to guides—and built an archive of reference material in a three-ring binder. On occasion, gardeners would "share back" what they learned from the workshops during their weekly meetings, recounting what they could remember from attending the workshops. Yet much of that explicit knowledge had yet to become a tacit part of the gardeners' repertoires, repurposed and reconstructed so as to make sense in the context of Kelly Street Garden. Although the "share back" binder was overflowing with literature on a wealth of subjects related to gardening, community organizing, and nonprofit management, gardeners readily admitted to not having transferred all that knowledge into practice. One notable exception had to do with a workshop on vegetable companion planting offered in a longer series of workshops on urban horticulture by the nearby New York Botanical Garden. After rushing to plant anywhere and everywhere in the first season, the gardeners were ready to apply new insights into planting strategies that could yield more produce in the second year. Their ability to transfer, reconstruct, and apply conceptual and skill-based knowledge on companion planting in their second season may be attributable to what adult education theorist Malcolm Knowles (1990) referred to as the *need to know* and the related principle of *immediacy* described by Jane Vella (2002) in her framework for adult learning. Having dealt with the challenges that resulted from unplanned crop layouts in their first season, the group faced a palpable *need to know* the details of crop arrangement in year two.

Third, transferring the skills and knowledge necessary for collecting data toward outcomes monitoring can be as challenging as transferring any other kind of knowledge about a practice. The gardeners at Kelly Street handily picked up the skills needed to track the weight of their harvests and log the hours they volunteered. Yet other protocols from the Five Borough Farm toolkit, such as leading an asset-mapping workshop to discover all the skills and knowledge gardeners bring to their community, proved more challenging to replicate at Kelly Street without help from outside—in this case, through a workshop facilitated by Philip at the start of the garden's second year. Sociologists of science and technology (Collins 1985) and of organizations (Orr 1996) have demonstrated that learning to replicate a complex research process or a technical practice is inherently a *social* process. Learning, in these cases, is not a matter of following codified instructions, but of entering into a sustained community of practice and of taking on the identity of a practitioner within that community (Wenger 1998; Bruner 1996). To that end, it may be that the practitioners at Kelly Street are still learning to see themselves not just as community gardeners, but also as gardeners who habitually strive to collect data on both the social and biophysical outcomes of their work to adapt and improve and to meet their goals and objectives for change over time.

Adaptive improvements based on formal data collection for outcomes monitoring may help civic ecology practitioners enhance the social and environmental outcomes of their work over time. At the same time, civic ecology practitioners face challenges in their efforts to monitor outcomes using formal data-collection protocols (Silva 2017; Silva and Krasny 2014). Yet these challenges are not insurmountable, and the benefits are both tangible and potentially transformative in communities hungry for social and environmental change. At Kelly Street, gardeners took on the task of formal data collection to evaluate their efforts and make a case to funders and other supporters about the value of their work. After just one year of measuring their harvests, they were able to critically reflect on the efficacy of their crop layouts and set a higher goal for food production through companion planting, drawing on qualitative observations of their successes and failures in their first year and importing and reconstructing knowledge about companion planting originating outside the garden. Importantly, knowledge production does not begin or end with scientific outcomes monitoring, and both the civic ecology and adaptive comanagement literature would benefit from a parallel focus on other forms of knowledge production in practice, as this case demonstrates.

Surfacing and transferring knowledge from one practice or setting to another is a common theme in the organizational knowledge management literature (Leonard 1998; Davenport and Prusak 2000). In the case of civic ecology practices, knowledge may be transferred through workshops and training sessions, reference documents, and site visits. In some cases, the tacit knowledge constructed in the daily work of a social practice is not easily decoupled, abstracted, and codified for transmission to other sites. Collins (2012, 1) describes tacit knowledge as "knowledge that is not explicated"—in other words, knowledge that is not made explicit in written or even verbal forms that are easily shared across social groups. For the philosopher of science Michael Polanyi (2009), tacit knowledge simply *cannot* be translated into an explicitly codified form—at least not with all its unspoken subtlety still intact (Collins 2012). Tacit knowledge exists holistically within the practices of a community that is perpetually constructing and reconstructing what it claims to know. Indeed, efforts to make the tacit knowledge encoded in one social practice explicit and available to other practices is prone to fail (Brown and Duguid 2001; Wenger 1998) unless practitioners thoroughly reconstruct and re-situate explicit knowledge to fit their context—a process of new knowledge construction in its own right (Nonaka 1994; Brown and Duguid 1991).

By the same token, knowledge of both social and biophysical phenomena can emerge *within* a practice as people puzzle through everyday challenges together and work to come up with innovative solutions to their problems (Orr 1996; Brown and Duguid 1991). The literature has grappled with biophysical knowledge production in daily management practice through the lens of indigenous or traditional ecological knowledge in rural settings (Berkes, Colding, and Folke 2000). This chapter points the way toward investigating practice-based knowledge production in *urban* practices. "There was a lot I didn't know, and I found out more about what I can do," one Kelly Street Gardening Committee member shared, reflecting on her growing sense of confidence in her development as a practicing gardener—and the knowledge she developed in daily practice.

As we have seen at Kelly Street Garden, knowledge production in a civic ecology practice is not just a matter of using data-collection protocols to monitor outcomes in an approximation of experimental field science. Instead, we find that knowledge production in environmental management practices like this one can be found in the daily work and observations of the practitioners themselves *and* in their efforts to transfer and reconstruct knowledge originating at other sites. We believe that drawing a more inclusive boundary around what "counts" as social-ecological knowledge produced in practice creates fertile new territory for scholarly research and for developing insights into strengthening civic ecology practices.

REFERENCES

Argyris, C., and D. A. Schön. 1978. *Organizational Learning: A Theory of Action Perspective*. Boston: Addison-Wesley.

Armitage, D. R., R. Plummer, F. Berkes, R. I. Arthur, A. T. Charles, I. J. Davidson-Hunt, A. P. Diduck, et al. 2008. "Adaptive Co-management for Social-Ecological Complexity." *Frontiers in Ecology and the Environment* 7 (2): 95–102. doi:10.1890/070089.

Ayres, A. 2015. "Watching the Block: Three Women Look Back—and Ahead—on Kelly Street." May 28. http://brie.hunter.cuny.edu/hpe/2015/05/28/watching-the-block-three-women-look-back-and-ahead-on-kelly-street-2/.

Beauregard, R. A. 2003. *Voices of Decline: The Postwar Fate of U.S. Cities*. Hove, East Sussex, UK: Psychology Press.

Berkes, F., J. Colding, and C. Folke. 2000. "Rediscovery of Traditional Ecological Knowledge as Adaptive Management." *Ecological Applications* 10 (5): 1251–62. doi:10.1890/1051-0761(2000)010[1251:ROTEKA]2.0.CO;2.

———. 2003. *Navigating Social-Ecological Systems: Building Resilience for Complexity and Change*. Cambridge: Cambridge University Press.

Blackler, F. 1995. "Knowledge, Knowledge Work and Organizations: An Overview and Interpretation." *Organization Studies* 16 (6): 1021–46. doi:10.1177/017084069501600605.

Brown, J. S., and P. Duguid. 1991. "Organizational Learning and Communities-of-Practice: Toward a Unified View of Working, Learning, and Innovation." *Organization Science* 2 (1): 40–57.

———. 2000. *The Social Life of Information*. Cambridge, MA: Harvard Business Press.

———. 2001. "Knowledge and Organization: A Social-Practice Perspective." *Organization Science* 12 (2): 198–213.

Bruner, J. S. 1996. *The Culture of Education*. Cambridge, MA: Harvard University Press.

Charles, A. 2008. "Adaptive Co-management for Resilient Resource Systems." In *Adaptive Co-management: Collaboration, Learning, and Multi-Level Governance*, edited by D. Armitage, F. Berkes, and N. Doubleday, 83–104. Vancouver: UBC Press.

Charmaz, K. 1990. "'Discovering' Chronic Illness: Using Grounded Theory." *Social Science & Medicine* 30 (11): 1161–72. doi:10.1016/0277-9536(90)90256-R.

City of New York. 2007. *plaNYC: A Greener, Greater New York*. New York: City of New York.

Cohen, N., K. Reynolds, and R. Sanghvi. 2012. *Five Borough Farm: Seeding the Future of Urban Agriculture in New York City*. New York: Design Trust for Public Space.

Collins, H. 1985. *Changing Order: Replication and Induction in Scientific Practice*. London: Sage.

———. 2012. *Tacit and Explicit Knowledge*. Reprint ed. Chicago: University Of Chicago Press.

Cundill, G., and R. Rodela. 2012. "A Review of Assertions about the Processes and Outcomes of Social Learning in Natural Resource Management." *Journal of Environmental Management* 113 (December): 7–14. doi:10.1016/j.jenvman.2012.08.021.

Davenport, T. H., and L. Prusak. 2000. "Working Knowledge: How Organizations Manage What They Know." *Ubiquity* 2000 (August). doi:10.1145/347634.348775.

Design for Public Space. 2015. Farming Concrete Data Collection Tool. New York: Design for Public Space.

Dunbar, R. I. M. 1996. *The Trouble with Science*. Cambridge, MA: Harvard University Press.

Glaser, B. G., and A. L. Strauss. 1967. *The Discovery of Grounded Theory: Strategies for Qualitative Research*. Piscataway, NJ: Transaction.

Gonzalez, E. D. 2004. *The Bronx*. New York: Columbia University Press.

Guba, E. G., and Y. S. Lincoln. 1989. *Fourth Generation Evaluation*. Newbury Park, CA: Sage.

Hellawell, J. M. 1991. "Development of a Rationale for Monitoring." In *Monitoring for Conservation and Ecology*, edited by F. B. Goldsmith, 1–14. London: Chapman and Hall.

Institute for Children, Poverty, and Homelessness. 2014. "The Process of Poverty Destabilization: How Gentrification Is Reshaping Upper Manhattan and the Bronx and Increasing Homelessness in New York City." New York: Institute for Children, Poverty, and Homelessness. http://www.icphusa.org/index.asp?page=16&report=120&pg=132.

Joseph, R. 2010. "Despite Promises, Asthma Still Plagues Hunts Point." *Hunts Point Express*, August 16. http://brie.hunter.cuny.edu/hpe/2010/08/16/asthma-an-express-news-analysis/.

Kärreman, D. 2008. "Knowledge-Intensive Firms." In *International Encyclopedia of Organization Studies*, by S. Clegg and J. Bailey. Thousand Oaks, CA: Sage. http://knowledge.sagepub.com/view/organization/n260.xml.

Knowles, M. S. 1990. *The Adult Learner: A Neglected Species*. Houston: Gulf Publishing.

Knowlton, L. W., and C. C. Phillips. 2012. *The Logic Model Guidebook: Better Strategies for Great Results*. Los Angeles: Sage.

Krasny, M. E., and K. G. Tidball. 2015. *Civic Ecology: Adaptation and Transformation from the Ground Up*. Cambridge, MA: MIT Press.

Lawson, L. J. 2005. *City Bountiful: A Century of Community Gardening in America*. Berkeley: University of California Press.

Layzer, J. A. 2008. *Natural Experiments: Ecosystem-Based Management and the Environment*. Cambridge, MA: MIT Press.

Leonard, D. 1998. *Wellsprings of Knowledge: Building and Sustaining the Sources of Innovation*. Boston: Harvard Business Review Press.

Nadasdy, P. 2007. "Adaptive Co-management and the Gospel of Resilience." In *Adaptive Co-management Collaboration, Learning, and Multi-Level Governance*, edited by F. Berkes, D. R. Armitage, and N. Doubleday, 19–37. Vancouver: UBC Press. http://site.ebrary.com/id/10203177.

Nonaka, I. 1994. "A Dynamic Theory of Organizational Knowledge Creation." *Organization Science* 5 (1): 14–37. doi:10.1287/orsc.5.1.14.

Okvat, H. A., and A. J. Zautra. 2014. "Sowing Seeds of Resilience: Community Gardening in a Post-Disaster Context." In *Greening in the Red Zone: Disaster, Resilience and Community Greening*, edited by K. G. Tidball and M. E. Krasny, 73–90. New York: Springer. doi:10.1007/978-90-481-9947-1_5.

Orr, J. E. 1996. *Talking about Machines: An Ethnography of a Modern Job*. Ithaca, NY: Cornell University Press.

Perlman, M. 2011. "Apartments Crumble on Kelly Street." *Hunts Point Express*, March 28. http://www.bkcianyc.org/docs/Apartments%20crumble.html.

Polanyi, M. 2009. *The Tacit Dimension*. Reissue ed. Chicago: University of Chicago Press.

Saldivar-Tanaka, L., and M. E. Krasny. 2004. "Culturing Community Development, Neighborhood Open Space, and Civic Agriculture: The Case of Latino Community Gardens in New York City." *Agriculture and Human Values* 21 (4): 399–412.

Sandler, R., and P. C. Pezzullo, eds. 2007. *Environmental Justice and Environmentalism: The Social Justice Challenge to the Environmental Movement*. Cambridge, MA: MIT Press.

Silva, P. 2017. "Knowledge from Data, Knowledge from Doing: The Inclusionary Production of Environmental Knowledge for Management." PhD diss., Cornell University.

Silva, P., and M. E. Krasny. 2014. "Parsing Participation: Models of Engagement for Outcomes Monitoring in Urban Stewardship." *Local Environment: The International Journal of Justice and Sustainability* 21 (2): 157–65. doi:10.1080/13549839 .2014.929094.

Sisk, R. 2010. "South Bronx Is Poorest District in Nation: 38% Live below Poverty Line." *New York Daily News*, September 29. http://www.nydailynews.com/new-york/south-bronx-poorest-district-nation-u-s-census-bureau-finds-38-live-poverty-line-article-1.438344.

Starbuck, W. H. 1992. "Learning by Knowledge-Intensive Firms." *Journal of Management Studies* 29 (6): 713–40. doi:10.1111/j.1467-6486.1992.tb00686.x.

Stedman, R. C., and M. Ingalls. 2013. "Topophilia, Biophilia, and Greening in the Red Zone." In *Greening in the Red Zone: Disaster, Resilience and Community Greening*, edited by K. G. Tidball and M. E. Krasny, 129–44. New York: Springer.

Vella, J. 2002. *Learning to Listen, Learning to Teach: The Power of Dialogue in Educating Adults*. Rev. ed. San Francisco: Jossey-Bass.

Walters, C. J., and C. S. Holling. 1990. "Large-Scale Management Experiments and Learning by Doing." *Ecology* 71 (6): 2060–68. doi:10.2307/1938620.

Wenger, É. 1998. *Communities of Practice: Learning, Meaning, and Identity*. Cambridge: Cambridge University Press.

Wills, K. 2013. "Kelly St. Rehabbed Buildings Officially Opened Thursday." *New York Daily News*, March 22. http://www.nydailynews.com/new-york/bronx/kelly-st-rehabbed-buildings-officially-opened-thursday-article-1.1295365.

Chapter 7

MAPPING THE ROUTE FROM CITIZEN SCIENCE TO ENVIRONMENTAL STEWARDSHIP

Integrating Adaptive Management and
Civic Ecology Practice

Rebecca Jordan

I enjoy asking questions and trying to find answers to them, and hope that as a group we can make an actual difference in our community.

(Collaborative Science participant, New Jersey)

Sitting around a table in a small, suburban New Jersey town, church members express concern about water quality in their building. Immediately the conversation turns from information gleaned from the Internet to water filtration and sustainability goals for the community. The group seems divided between individuals who have lived in town for a while and take pride in it, and younger transient students and newcomers.

> This community really has thought about environmental issues a lot and they've had . . . a long-standing deep commitment to the environment as a social justice issue. (female suburban New Jersey resident)

Whereas a newcomer comments

> [Becoming involved in this issue] would be a great opportunity for the kids to see me sort of struggle through and try to figure out . . . and in the process of becoming more involved, and I am only just recently involved. As somebody who is moving here, I am already having conversations with my wife about [water quality as parents]. This is a pretty imminent issue for us. (male suburban New Jersey resident)

A third resident expresses pessimism regarding whether factors beyond residents' control might impact their ability to attain township-level sustainability goals:

> I sense that part of the economic and racialized disparities in New Jersey are sort of bolstered by access to potable water and other resources . . . municipal wealth as being something that impacts everything. (male suburban New Jersey resident)

South of New Jersey, in West Baltimore, Maryland, neighborhood residents also talk about an environmental issue of concern. Here again pessimism regarding personal action is rampant:

> That trash pile in the same space has been there since I was six years old. . . . [I] called the city about it. [The] trash truck comes on Thursday morning, and it will be like that [filled with trash] by Thursday evening. The community sees it as normal. . . . The thing is: how do we start teaching people that this is not normal. . . . Do they not care, or is it just other things going on like murders and stuff that have more value? . . . At some point I decided to make an issue about that pile. Every day I call the city . . . and they have a system. . . . Then you will get an e-mail or call. [They say] "We see it, but you need to report it with the address." And I was like, I reported it and you know what I meant. . . . It is like they are playing a game. . . . I get worn down, every time I call. (male West Baltimore resident)

When asked who else in the group of seven residents has experienced this, all nod. However, when asked who continues to call, again all nod. The same resident asks: "Do the citizens even know it is a problem? We have a right [to not having trash], but it is just normal."

When the discussion moves to abandoned buildings and vacant lots, another group member states, "Vacancy is part of the culture of Baltimore City." Suggesting an emerging civic ecology practice, a fellow resident responds:

> This person . . . did an illegal act of beautifying [by a series of plantings in a park], but if we make a big deal, they will get cited, and then what will happen? (female West Baltimore resident)

Despite differences in concerns and a shared pessimism about the efficacy of their actions, the desire to take action among residents in suburban New Jersey and inner-city West Baltimore is clear. In both places, residents have volunteered to be part of Collaborative Science, a program that seeks to facilitate adaptive management of water, urban open space, and other resources. In this chapter,

I introduce Collaborative Science, the literature that frames it, and preliminary outcomes of the New Jersey and Baltimore cases. In so doing, I explore how by incorporating structured opportunities for participants to reflect on, question, and test their ideas about what leads to change in their communities, Collaborative Science seeks to overcome barriers to adaptive management and foster conservation outcomes in citizen science and civic ecology practices.

What Is Collaborative Science?

Collaborative Science integrates citizen science and participatory modeling with a goal of engaging citizens in local conservation action. Engaging residents in participatory modeling of a local resource issue in collaboration with scientists and environmental managers provides a means for going beyond the data-collection activities of citizen science to incorporate discussions about the implications of those data for a local resource (Jordan et al. 2016). Such structured learning allows knowledge, including local knowledge about a particular resource, to be shared among participants, who then develop hypotheses that they test through data collection. In some cases, participants go on to develop environmental management plans and commit to other forms of conservation action (Gray et al. 2017).

In their participatory modeling activities, residents use Mental Modeler, a software that facilitates "fuzzy" cognitive mapping in community resource management settings. A fuzzy cognitive map is a conceptual map with multiple components (e.g., stewardship actions, municipal water supplier, vacant lots) and lines between components indicating how strongly one component might influence another. Collaborative Science participants define the system of concern (e.g., town waste management), its components, the relationships between those components (what impacts what), and the strength of those relationships (weak, moderate, strong; see figure 7.1). For example, residents from the New Jersey project might create a model in which seasons, pollution, and managed and unmanaged portions of the environment are related to odor that is believed to be associated with drinking water and ill health effects. They then use the Mental Modeler software to run "what if" scenarios to determine how the system might react under a range of possible changes, including any actions that the participants themselves undertake. In short, Mental Modeler supports group decision making by allowing users to collaboratively represent and test their assumptions about interactions in a local social-ecological system and about impacts of management actions (Gray et al. 2013).

In addition to platforms for data collection and participatory modeling, Collaborative Science offers online instructional modules about ecosystem science,

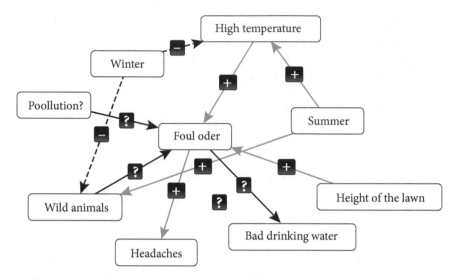

FIGURE 7.1   Church members' cognitive map of drinking water system. Credit: Rebecca Jordan.

data collection and analysis, representing and communicating data, advocacy, and how to support claims with evidence. Further, each local project is supported by a Collaborative Science facilitator, who brings scientific expertise and familiarity with the local context.

In sum, Collaborative Science is based on the hypothesis that by providing a platform for community members to jointly produce a representation of a local social-ecological system and collect data to test the validity of their representation, community members will engage in conservation action (Gray et al. 2017). In instances where community stakeholders create models and collect data around civic ecology practices, Collaborative Science could help facilitate adaptive comanagement in such practices.

Adaptive Comanagement, Social Learning, and Public Participation in Scientific Research

Collaborative Science builds on research and theory related to public participation in scientific research, adaptive management, and social learning. Public participation in scientific research can assume various forms, including participatory action research, citizen science, and community-based monitoring. Projects can be contributory, in which volunteers simply collect data for scientist-driven research, or co-created projects in which volunteers play a role in setting the research direction (Shirk et al. 2012; Bonney et al. 2009). Whereas multiple forms of public participation in scientific research have the potential to contribute to adaptive management, co-created projects provide greater opportunities for learning among participants.

Adaptive management involves monitoring outcomes of management interventions to improve environmental decision making (Holling 1978; see also chapters 6 and 8) and is necessarily iterative. Stakeholders repeatedly use tools to refine the information they gather over time and to refine their management practices. In the case of adaptive comanagement, learning and the responsibility for decision making and management are shared among stakeholders, who often hold diverse views about management issues (Armitage, Berkes, and Doubleday 2007; Olsson, Folke, and Berkes 2004; Plummer 2009). Such group or social learning can occur at three levels or "learning loops": information gathering to improve practice (first loop); questioning the assumptions underlying a practice (second loop); and challenging assumptions and established ideas about the processes that structure a system (third loop) (Keen, Brown, and Dyball 2005; Argyris and Schön 1978; Maarleveld and Dangbegnon 1999). This iterative process of group learning contributes to adaptive comanagement through ongoing input of information and stakeholder engagement in management decisions, or in the case of higher loop learning, challenging assumptions underlying management practices and governance structures (Berkes 2009). Wenger's (2003) notion of communities of practice is also useful in describing ongoing learning embedded in resource management practices. After 9/11 and Hurricane Katrina, civic ecology communities of practice emerged as social learning became part of citizen efforts to replant trees and create small living memorials (Tidball et al. 2010).

Adaptive comanagement can be seen as an "ideal" form of management when complex problems require ongoing data collection, adaptation, and stakeholder engagement. In reality, this ideal has proven difficult to realize. In the context of public lands management, institutional cultures that value command and control or engineering solutions to complex problems may preclude learning from past mistakes, and lack of trust among government managers and stakeholders may render collaboration problematic (Gunderson and Light 2006). In civic ecology practices, leaders' emotional investment in proving the worth of their efforts, as well as a need to demonstrate their value to funders, may present barriers to adaptive comanagement (Silva 2017). Further, in both large-scale and community-based efforts, public lands managers and volunteer stewards may lack resources, time, and skills needed for experimenting with different management strategies, data collection, and subsequent adaptation (see chapters 6 and 8).

In cases with ongoing and committed scientist engagement, adaptive coman-agement appears to have a greater chance of being implemented. For example, a university researcher helped facilitate varying degrees of adaptive comanage-ment of watersheds among stakeholder groups in Ontario, Canada (Plummer and FitzGibbon 2007); and in New York City, PhD student Megan Gregory worked intensively alongside community gardeners for several years in a pro-cess that integrated farmer field schools and participatory action research. Fol-lowing a co-created model of public participation in scientific research (Shirk et al. 2012), Gregory involved community gardeners in multiple stages of her research, including identifying priority management issues (gardeners identified soil fertility and structure), devising an intervention (cover crops), monitoring the results of different cover crop treatments, and applying what they learned in the gardens. Three types of outcomes were documented: for science, knowl-edge about cover crop treatments in urban soils; for individual gardeners, eco-system learning and adaptive management skills; and for the garden ecosystem, improved soil stewardship. Further, individual gardeners were motivated to share what they had learned with community members through workshops and gar-den demonstrations, leading to an emergent community of practice. Gregory went on to support this community of practice by providing garden instruction and accessible data-collection tools, and by helping gardeners as they assumed leadership and educational roles (Gregory 2016).

This soil management community of practice in New York City community gardens suggests how intensive scientist engagement with civic ecology stewards can lead to outcomes at multiple levels. However, realizing such outcomes is not without challenges, most notably how to structure meaningful practitioner engagement at all stages of the research and how to address community-defined goals within the constraints of university research expectations and limited gar-dener and researcher time. Silva (2017) identified additional constraints to adap-tive comanagement in civic ecology practices even when stewards were presented with accessible data-collection tools, including a disconnect between the goals of those who created the data-collection tools and of the civic ecology stewards. Despite relatively few instances of formal data collection, community gardeners and other stewards in Silva's (2017) study engaged in less formal experiential learning and reflection about their practices (see chapter 6).

Similar to what has been found for civic ecology and public participation in scientific research projects described above, a study of six cases of participa-tory modeling in Africa and Asia found that prolonged engagement of scien-tists, managers, and stakeholders along with skilled facilitation of the modeling process was critical to environmental decision-making outcomes (Sandker et al. 2010). Further, stakeholders valued the process of discussion, interpretation, and

consensus building despite holding varying views of the actual landscape outcomes of the modeling process. The authors conclude that the focus should not
be on models per se, or using models to predict and plan; rather participatory
models can be used as a tool or "boundary object" (Star and Griesemer 1989) to
help stakeholders understand resource management issues, explore options, generate new knowledge through consideration of multiple viewpoints and observations, and acquire capabilities useful beyond the modeling effort per se (Sandker
et al. 2010; Voinov et al. 2016). In short, participatory modeling can be viewed
as boundary work, where co-created cognitive maps are plastic enough to have
different meanings for different participants, but structured enough to reflect
areas of shared understanding and to generate debate (Voinov et al. 2016; Star
and Griesemer 1989).

Why Collaborative Science?

Despite the impressive growth of citizen science and the availability of data-
collection protocols designed for nonscientists, relatively few civic ecology practices engage in data collection and adaptive comanagement (Silva and Krasny
2014). At the same time, public participation in scientific research projects is
increasingly being used as a means to engage citizens in stewardship activities
in private yards, on rooftops, along beaches, and in other settings (Kobori et al.
2016; Haywood, Parrish, and Dolliver 2016; Wilderman 2004). One factor that
encourages such integration of participatory science and conservation outcomes
is sustained scientist engagement with local communities and recognition of the
knowledge and experience that local residents bring to management decisions.

Given this context, my colleagues and I sought means for deeper engagement
with community members with a goal of involving citizens in environmental
management and decision making. We turned to participatory modeling as a
means to complement citizen science data collection and, through encouraging
reflection and discussion, to foster conservation outcomes. Below I describe Collaborative Science projects in suburban New Jersey and Baltimore, Maryland.

Evidence of Change through Collaborative Science

Collaborative Science participants from New Jersey were members of the same
church and shared a concern about water quality in their township. Several advi-
sories to boil water had been posted in the previous year, calling into question
the quality of tap water used in meals at the church. The project began by participants producing a conceptual map of their water management issue. They

then collected data in area streams and a river that fed into their water supply. The group used these data in Mental Modeler to create a collaborative conceptual model of factors impacting their water quality issue. While this project initially focused on the church members' immediate needs, discussions around their co-created model led to collaboration with other organizations focused on water quality. These organizations included a local river management nonprofit, an organization established to help train homeless people and individuals transitioning from prison who live in towns along the river, and an environmental justice group.

Participants used their data not only to make a decision about the water they provide for their church, but also to start an ongoing monitoring project in their township. Characterizing her transition from a concerned individual to an environmental steward, one respondent shared how instead of just focusing on one of the stewardship options that emerged from the model-based decision-making process, "[this project] raised so many interesting things that I didn't realize. . . . I like the idea of thinking of particular stakeholders and how they view the world to have it make sense . . . then we might see some interesting points where there might be a win-win." This quote not only demonstrates how a participant is able to think at a higher level about the application of the project's tools (i.e., second-loop learning) but also reflects an optimism related to the ability of the group to work through differences and agree on courses of action.

In West Baltimore, residents engaged in Collaborative Science in a different manner. A colleague and I were already working in Baltimore with the Take Back the Block citizen science project in which residents collect data about mosquito habitat and annoyance. This project was developed by scientists in response to sightings of the tiger mosquito, which was new to Baltimore and poses health concerns (Jordan et al. 2016). A subset of volunteers in the mosquito project expressed interest in working on a new project related to their concerns about vacant homes, abandoned lots, and trash in their neighborhood. Residents connected the problem of uncollected trash to habitat for mosquitoes and rats.

Volunteers in the new project identified where trash, home abandonment, and vacant lots were important problems. They also characterized community assets and places in their neighborhoods that engender positive feelings. They then used data about mosquito habitat and trash, alongside information about community assets, to create a conceptual model of resource management in their community, and used Mental Modeler to structure discussions about ideas, additional data collection, and decision making about stewardship actions. Armed with data and empowered by their discussions, volunteers worked together as advocates and participants in cleanups and other neighborhood revitalization projects such as gardens and murals. Collaborative Science facilitators supported their efforts by encouraging residents to join with other groups to forge a collective voice and to plan strategically by focusing on realizing small successes while working toward a larger goal. For example, participants worked together to organize information sessions for neighborhood associations, gathered photos that were used in a local art show, and discussed specific target audiences for further education (e.g., asking local businesses to reduce the number of advertising flyers, which tend to blow from doorsteps and cause excess trash).

In the Baltimore case, group participation and community engagement afforded individuals a sense that they had learned something of value. Such learning can drive future changes, as more informed stakeholders with the capacity to assess the meaning of their data and success of implementation efforts become involved in decision making. The Baltimore group also accepted previously foreign labels of citizen scientist, community block leader, or even environmental steward as accurate characterizations of their newfound capacity to take meaningful action (Jordan et al. 2016). Further, they gained a sense of the way in which collective action compounds individual actions. For example, cleanup events involving individuals working together became part of ongoing initiatives in which members formalized a partnership. As partnerships transition to organizations, further training and credentials can be obtained and leveraged in the decision-making process.

"[How do we manage] where there are whole blocks of abandonment?" is a statement shared by a member of the group working in Baltimore. This statement reflects another vantage—namely, how the process of information gathering and data collection can be overwhelming, especially to those advocating for change. Yet, having gained a sense of accomplishment from the work they had completed, the Baltimore residents independently designed an experiment to test whether installing artwork on and conducting neighborhood watches around dumpsters might result in greater respect for trash containers. Should the group obtain the support of city officials and move ahead with their experiment, the results may challenge long-held assumptions about behavior and trash in low-income urban communities. Through this project, the Baltimore residents are engaging in second-loop and potentially third-loop learning—that is, challenging ideas about "what is normal" in their neighborhood.

The church group in New Jersey was similarly able to implement changes including streamside cleanups, establishing stream buffers, and an education plan for residents and town council members focusing on cleaning up the water that flows into the township's water filtration system. Individuals in this group continue to work with their environmental justice collaborators and have taken on new projects in other areas of their town. Additionally, one member of the environmental justice group has initiated his own Collaborative Science project to focus on land surrounding streams that flow into the river. This project will include initial data collection, cleanup, and ongoing stewardship.

In both the New Jersey and Baltimore projects, participants collected data that they used to establish an action plan. In New Jersey, the water quality database established in the project has been entered into a national database, and participants of the next iteration of the project are adding more data. In Baltimore, the data gathered about mosquito habitats have been given to biologists, who made recommendations to the city for mosquito control, and volunteers are engaging in larger-scale green-space cleanups in their neighborhoods. Additionally, several volunteers have offered to gather data post-cleanup to assess the effects of their action. These outcomes of participatory data collection leading to action in New Jersey and Baltimore are supported by a third Collaborative Science project in Virginia, where participants leveraged results of coliform monitoring to obtain government funding and to develop a management plan in collaboration with the Nature Conservancy (Gray et al. 2017).

Scientist's Reflections

Collaborative Science attempts to leverage citizen participation in data collection and modeling to influence resource management and local policy. In Baltimore, those management efforts included vacant lot cleanups, thus demonstrating how citizen science data collection and participatory modeling may lead to civic ecology stewardship efforts. In short, the Baltimore case suggests that rather than ongoing civic ecology practices incorporating data collection as a form of adaptive management, data collection may precede and lead to community stewardship efforts.

Regardless of whether data collection, participatory modeling, or stewardship practice comes first, ongoing scientist engagement is critical, which itself poses a number of challenges. Here I reflect on the challenges I faced as a scientist, while recognizing that residents in New Jersey and Baltimore faced their own challenges, not the least of which were finding common ground with stakeholders holding different values and overcoming a long history of feeling one's attempts at addressing neighborhood problems had been ignored by city officials.

Similar to how Collaborative Science participants model their local social-ecological system with reference to a specific local issue, I decided to use our software to model the Collaborative Science system. My conceptual map emerged out of a number of questions that arose as I engaged with the New Jersey and Baltimore communities. For example: How do we think the act of stewardship makes a change in the individual? What are these individuals thinking about in the face of gathering information or amending a resource? And most important,

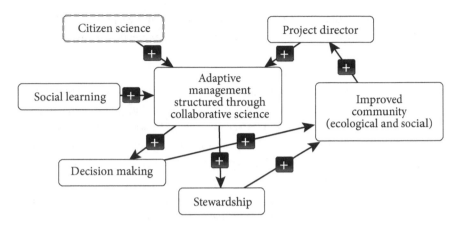

FIGURE 7.2   Cognitive map illustrating researcher's theory of change suggesting the impact of social learning, citizen science data collection, and skills of the project director on the adaptive comanagement process. Credit: Rebecca Jordan.

how can communities sustain a much-needed project director for Collaborative Science projects?

My research led me to believe that social learning, citizen science data collection, and project director skills would impact the adaptive comanagement process (figure 7.2). Constructing the model enabled me to more clearly articulate and reflect on my theory of change, and in so doing to identify the important Collaborative Science components and outcomes and the strength of the connections between them.

In order to test the ideas proposed in the model and to determine what, if any, elements are essential to improving community stewardship, I found that I needed to pay attention to all portions of the Collaborative Science project, including the residents, the data, the learning, the decisions, and the stewardship actions. This proved a difficult challenge because I was an outsider to the communities where I was working, and many aspects of a project are context specific. For example, in any one community, how do you balance the needs of the community with the needs of the research? While I argue that the highest-quality data will benefit the community, there certainly is a delay in gathering these data and therefore disseminating the results. Such data are essential to the adaptive management process, which in my model drives decision making and stewardship, both of which are essential for community gains. These competing demands required constant reflection about my role as researcher and activist trying to encourage an iterative but often ill-defined version of change. Defining what that change looks like is an ever-evolving process and varies with stakehold-ers' perspectives, with perhaps the least important perspective being mine as a community outsider.

Collaborative Science tackles head-on two barriers to adaptive comanagement in local data-collection and stewardship projects: scientist engagement and higher-order learning. First, in Collaborative Science, researchers are engaged with com-munities on an ongoing basis, which is an important factor in moving beyond simple data collection. Second, the participatory modeling activities provide a means for stakeholders to share their perspectives and seek commonalities vis-à-vis stewardship and policy goals, and to articulate, reflect on, and test their implicit theories of change. In short, Collaborative Science incorporates several elements to foster higher-order learning that encompasses hypothesis building, testing, and reflection in a manner consistent with adaptive comanagement.

Admittedly, any intervention attempting to address "wicked" social-ecological problems is an experiment in itself, whether it is focused on data collection, mod-eling, hands-on stewardship, or a combination of multiple approaches. That said, the engagement of Collaborative Science participants in local action and decision making is a promising outcome and suggests avenues by which civic ecology practices might expand their influence, perhaps starting with activities to make explicit their theory of change.

Acknowledgments

I would like to acknowledge my colleague Amanda Sorensen, who has been criti-cal to the work in Baltimore. I also acknowledge two National Science Founda-tion funding sources: IIS-1227550 and DEB-1211797.

REFERENCES

Argyris, C., and D. A. Schön. 1978. *Organizational Learning: A Theory of Action Per-spective*. London: Wesley.

Armitage, D., F. Berkes, and N. Doubleday, eds. 2007. *Adaptive Co-management: Col-laboration, Learning, and Multi-level Governance*. Vancouver: UBC Press.

Berkes, F. 2009. "Evolution of Co-management: Role of Knowledge Generation, Bridg-ing Organizations and Social Learning." *Journal of Environmental Management* 90 (5): 1692–1702. http://dx.doi.org/10.1016/j.jenvman.2008.12.001.

Bonney, R., H. Ballard, R. Jordan, E. McCallie, T. Phillips, J. Shirk, and C. C. Wilder-man. 2009. *Public Participation in Scientific Research: Defining the Field and Assessing Its Potential for Informal Science Education*. CAISE Inquiry Group Report. Washington, DC.

Gray, S., S. Gray, L. J. Cox, and S. Henly-Shepard. 2013. "Mental Modeler: A Fuzzy-Logic Cognitive Mapping Modeling Tool for Adaptive Environmental

Management." Forty-Sixth Hawaii International Conference on System Sciences, Wailea, Maui.

Gray, S., R. Jordan, A. Crall, G. Newman, C. Hmelo-Silver, J. Huang, W. Novak, et al. 2017. "Combining Participatory Modelling and Citizen Science to Support Volunteer Conservation Action." *Biological Conservation* 208:76–86. https://doi.org/10.1016/j.biocon.2016.07.037.

Gregory, M. 2016. "Enhancing Urban Food Production, Ecosystem Services, and Learning in Community Gardens through Cover Cropping and Participatory Action Research." eCommons, Cornell. https://ecommons.cornell.edu/handle/1813/47815.

Gunderson, L. H., and S. S. Light. 2006. "Adaptive Management and Adaptive Governance in the Everglades Ecosystem." *Policy Sciences* 39:323–34.

Haywood, B. K., J. K. Parrish, and J. Dolliver. 2016. "Place-Based and Data-Rich Citizen Science as a Precursor for Conservation Action." *Conservation Biology* 30 (3): 476–86. doi:10.1111/cobi.12702.

Holling, C. S. 1978. "The Spruce-Budworm/Forest-Management Problem." In *Adaptive Environmental Assessment and Management*, edited by C. S. Holling, 143–82. Hoboken, NJ: John Wiley & Sons.

Jordan, R., S. Gray, A. Sorensen, G. Newman, D. Mellor, G. Newman, C. Hmelo-Silver, S. LaDeau, D. Biehler, and A. Crall. 2016. "Studying Citizen Science through Adaptive Management and Learning Feedbacks as Mechanisms for Improving Conservation." *Conservation Biology* 30 (3): 487–95. doi:10.1111/cobi.12659.

Keen, M., V. A. Brown, and R. Dyball. 2005. *Social Learning in Environmental Management: Towards a Sustainable Future*. London: Earthscan.

Kobori, H., J. L. Dickinson, I. Washitani, R. Sakurai, T. Amano, N. Komatsu, W. Kitamura, et al. 2016. "Citizen Science: A New Approach to Advance Ecology, Education, and Conservation." *Ecological Research* 31 (1): 1–19. doi:10.1007/s11284-015-1314-y.

Maarleveld, M., and C. Dangbegnon. 1999. "Managing Natural Resources: A Social Learning Perspective." *Agriculture and Human Values* 16:267–80.

Olsson, P., C. Folke, and F. Berkes. 2004. "Adaptive Co-management for Building Resilience in Social-Ecological Systems." *Environmental Management* 34 (1): 75–90.

Plummer, R. 2009. "The Adaptive Co-management Process: An Initial Synthesis of Representative Models and Influential Variables." *Ecology and Society* 14 (2): 24.

Plummer, R., and J. FitzGibbon. 2007. "Connecting Adaptive Co-management, Social Learning, and Social Capital through Theory and Practice." In *Adaptive Co-management: Collaboration, Learning, and Multi-level Governance*, edited by D. Armitage, F. Berkes, and N. Doubleday, 38–61. Vancouver: UBC Press.

Sandker, M., B. M. Campbell, M. Ruiz-Pérez, J. A. Sayer, R. Cowling, H. Kassa, and A. T. Knight. 2010. "The Role of Participatory Modeling in Landscape Approaches to Reconcile Conservation and Development." *Ecology and Society* 15 (2): 13 (online).

Shirk, J., H. Ballard, C. Wilderman, T. Phillips, A. Wiggins, R. Jordan, E. McCallie, et al. 2012. "Public Participation in Scientific Research: A Framework for Deliberate Design." *Ecology and Society* 17 (2): 29.

Silva, P. 2017. "Knowledge from Data, Knowledge from Doing: The Inclusionary Production of Environmental Knowledge for Management." PhD diss., Cornell University.

Silva, P., and M. E. Krasny. 2014. "Parsing Participation: Models of Engagement for Outcomes Monitoring in Urban Stewardship." *Local Environment: The International Journal of Justice and Sustainability* 21 (2): 157–65. doi:10.1080/13549839.2014.929094.

Star, S. L., and J. R. Griesemer. 1989. "Institutional Ecology, 'Translations' and Boundary Objects: Amateurs and Professionals in Berkeley's Museum of Vertebrate Zoology, 1907–39." *Social Studies of Science* 19 (3): 387–420.

Tidball, K. G., M. E. Krasny, E. S. Svendsen, L. Campbell, and K. Helphand. 2010. "Stewardship, Learning, and Memory in Disaster Resilience." *Environmental Education Research* 16 (5–6): 591–609.

Voinov, A., N. Kolagani, M. K. McCall, P. D. Glynn, M. E. Kragt, F. O. Ostermann, S. A. Pierce, and P. Ramu. 2016. "Modelling with Stakeholders—Next Generation." *Environmental Modelling & Software* 77:196–220. http://dx.doi.org/10.1016/j.envsoft.2015.11.016.

Wenger, É. 2003. "Communities of Practice and Social Learning Systems." In *Knowing in Organizations: A Practice-Based Approach*, edited by D. Nicoline, S. Gherardi, and D. Yanow, 75–99. New York: M. E. Sharpe.

Wilderman, C. 2004. "The Realization of a Pipe Dream: Effective Partnerships in Community-Based Urban Stream Restoration: A Case Study of the Mully Grub, Letort Spring Run, Cumberland County, PA." Dickinson College Faculty Publications, Paper 430.

Part III
MOVEMENT BUILDING
Civic Ecology as Strategic Action Field

Chapter 8

ADAPTIVE MANAGEMENT, ADAPTIVE GOVERNANCE, AND CIVIC ECOLOGY

Lance Gunderson, Elizabeth Whiting Pierce, and Marianne E. Krasny

Wildfires are burning throughout the United States, and typhoons are causing massive destruction in the western Pacific. Yet we (the authors) go about our everyday lives, seemingly ignoring these large-scale environmental disasters. As we walk through our neighborhoods and local parks, change may not be so evident, making it easier to ignore. But we worry that accumulated human pressures over many years may have created irreversible change at larger scales—that we may have crossed irreversible thresholds, possibly at the scale of our planet. Yet sometimes when things seem to go utterly wrong at the local scale, we ourselves may cross a threshold of disengagement and decide to take action to reclaim a "broken" place—whether it be a neglected trail in the woods, a beach denuded of dunes or mangroves, or a tiny patch of open space that has become a magnet for dumping and even crime. Still, even as we engage in these local actions, we question their importance beyond the single trail, beach, or trashed lot.

From the plants that are cultivated in a garden to the mighty rivers of the world, the scale of human control over our environment has reached unprecedented levels, causing some to propose a new geologic epoch—the Anthropocene (Rockström et al. 2009; Steffen et al. 2011; Crutzen and Stoermer 2000). The Anthropocene acknowledges the scale at which humans are transforming the planet, including land-use changes (Turner, Lambin, and Reenberg 2007) and alterations of water, carbon, and nitrogen cycles (Vitousek et al. 1997; Steffen et al. 2011). More than half the human population now resides in cities and urban areas (Steffen et al. 2011), and humans have co-opted the bulk of our planet's biological productivity (Vitousek et al. 1997). We have transformed much of the arable land to provide food, fiber, and other ecosystem goods (MEA 2005) and have mined and burned fossil fuels that have accumulated for millennia to the point where increased concentrations of carbon-based greenhouse gases are impacting our climate (Steffen et al. 2011; IPCC 2014).

So what's new? We have heard these scenarios before to the point of exhaustion, of helplessness, even hopelessness. Yet, however dire the observed and projected changes to our environment, there is still room for optimism and hope— hope that these undesirable trajectories can be altered. Much of civic ecology is about exploring alternative trajectories and futures. In short, we propose that the field of civic ecology is emerging as a positive human endeavor in response to the undesirable social and ecological transformations of the Anthropocene.

The value of civic ecology practices lies in their ability to nurture positive social and ecological changes at multiple scales. This chapter explains how civic ecology practices can have this multi-scale effect by introducing readers to three closely related bodies of theory and practice: "panarchy," a theory of how social-ecological systems change, which is grounded in the field of environmental science; "adaptive management," a mode of natural resource management that draws heavily on panarchy and notions of change; and "adaptive governance," a model of governing in which collective decision-making among multiple actors has the capacity to support ongoing change.

Panarchy: Change in Social-Ecological Systems

Over the last four decades, scientists have come to recognize the surprising and unpredictable nature of change in ecosystems (Gunderson and Holling 2002; Gunderson, Holling, and Light 1995). Studies have generated four general observations about how ecosystems and social-ecological systems change over time:

> *Systems are complex.* The number of factors that influence change is large, leading to inherent unpredictability.
>
> *Systems vary greatly over space.* This is true in terms of both system structures and processes. Further, variations in structure create spatial variations in system processes. For instance, bioswales, dirt ditches, and concrete canals are structures that affect how quickly dirty water runs off highways and infiltrates ground or surface waters. The rate of infiltration—a process—differs from spot to spot, according to structure.

Systems are nested. For example, the carbon cycle in a small community garden is part of a larger citywide and even global carbon cycle.

Systems change over time. This includes changes that we can predict, as well as unpredictable changes that occur as systems develop (Gunderson and Holling 2002).

Over time, social-ecological systems change in ways that are not continuous or linear (Holling 1973, 1986). But neither is such change random, chaotic, or totally unpredictable. Rather, change can be slow and expected, and sudden and episodic. Ecological systems such as forests undergo predictable patterns of succession over time. Such succession is characterized by slow accumulation of biological materials like the biomass of trees and other forms of natural capital. Similar changes occur in urban areas; for example, structural complexity increases as houses and buildings replace farms. As systems such as forests and cities develop over time, they become more vulnerable to external shocks or disturbances. Disturbances, including hurricanes, floods, and fires, occur at various intervals and can lead to sudden and dramatic changes to cities as well as remote forested systems.

Holling (1986) proposed that ecological systems undergo four sequential phases over time, in what he called the adaptive cycle (figure 8.1). More recently scholars have applied Holling's thinking to social-ecological systems, including cities. The first two phases of the adaptive cycle, growth and conservation, correspond to patterns inherent to ecological succession. As systems begin to form, for example new cities, they exhibit a phase of rapid growth. The growth phase is characterized by accumulation of structure and an increase in complexity, such as more and different types of buildings and roads. As systems accumulate structure and become more diverse, they also become more connected. In cities, roads, sewers, and electricity connect buildings, parks, and rivers. Gradually, system net growth slows as more resources and energy are allocated to system maintenance (maintaining roads and sewers) rather than building new structure. Because the energy that drives this second phase goes into conserving rather than building new structure, Holling (1986) calls this the conservation phase. During a conservation phase, the system becomes even more connected, but also less flexible and more vulnerable to external disturbances (Holling 1986; Ernstson et al. 2010). A failed subway station or train has broader impacts on a highly connected transportation system than on a younger, simpler system.

As systems mature and persist in a conservation phase, they become increasingly vulnerable to external forces. External disturbances—whether they be a terrorist attack or a superstorm—can generate a sudden release of accumulated

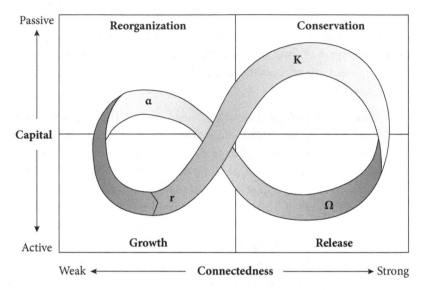

FIGURE 8.1   Adaptive cycle. The growth phase is labeled r (rate) and refers to a period of fast growth, whereas the conservation phase is labeled K, which comes from the German word for capacity and refers to the carrying capacity or capacity limit of an ecosystem. The release phase is symbolized by omega, the last letter in the Greek alphabet, whereas the reorganization phase is denoted by the first letter in the Greek alphabet, alpha (Holling and Gunderson 2002). Copyright 2002 Island Press. Reproduced by permission of Island Press, Washington, DC.

capital or structure. This phase is called a period of creative destruction, or the omega (end) phase. In forest systems, for example, fuel in the form of trees slowly accumulates after a fire. As fuel accumulates, the system becomes more vulnerable to disturbance, like a lightning strike, leading to an increasing probability of fire. In cities, fires, disease outbreaks, or tornadoes are all examples of the omega phase, in which existing structure, like hospitals, transport systems, and the electrical grid, can become quickly overwhelmed.

The collapse or release during the omega phase is quickly followed by a reorganization (alpha) phase, where a new system emerges, eventually leading to the growth phase of a new cycle. The new growth phase may lead the system in a trajectory similar to what it was before a disturbance, say a mature forest or a prosperous city dependent on fossil fuel. Or it may lead to something quite different, as when drought limits forest regeneration, or a city converts to renewable energy and human-powered transportation. This pattern of rapid and then slowing growth, and swift destruction followed by reorganization, has been observed in many systems with varying levels of human influence, including temperate

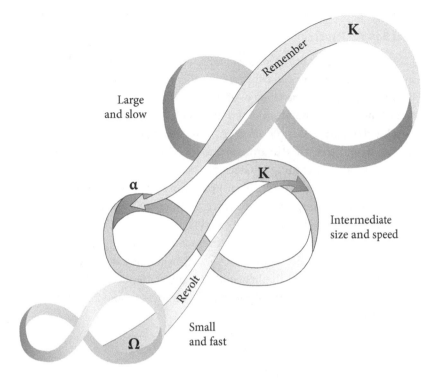

FIGURE 8.2 Panarchy model, showing how adaptive cycles link across scales (Gunderson and Holling 2002). Copyright 2002 Island Press. Reproduced by permission of Island Press, Washington, DC.

forests subject to pest outbreaks and fires (Holling 1986), the Everglades and surrounding agricultural systems (Light, Gunderson, and Holling 1995), and the Great Barrier Reef (Olsson, Folke, and Hughes 2008), among others (Walker and Salt 2006).

In the early 2000s, it occurred to scientists that studies of the four phases of the adaptive cycle had been limited to a single geographic scale. Yet it was becoming increasingly apparent that what happens at one scale—for example, a city—can impact what happens at smaller scales—let's say a neighborhood or even a vacant lot. It can also impact what happens at larger scales—like a state or country. Scientists searched for a term and a theory that would help them understand how adaptive cycles at various scales interact. They hit on the term *panarchy* (text box 1).

Panarchy theory helps explain how civic ecology practices may influence more than one scale at a time. It shows how cleaning up and planting one vacant lot or stretch of streambank can play a role in the adaptive cycles of neighborhoods, cities, and regions. Below we discuss how such cross-scale interactions happen.

Text Box 1   Panarchy

Ecosystem scientists Buzz Holling and Lance Gunderson struggled to come up with a term that would capture how adaptive cycles at different scales interact. "Hierarchy" was one possibility, but the term was burdened by its rigid, top-down connotation. Then the scientists happened upon Pan, the Greek god of nature. With "horns, legs, and tail of a goat, a thick beard, snub nose, and pointed ears," Pan arouses feelings of panic as he roams the Arcadian Mountains. According to Greek mythology, Pan destroys and creates, transforming fleeing nymphs into mountain pine trees or reeds that he shapes into pipes, or simply into a voice left to repeat Pan's mountain cries forever. Holling and Gunderson decided that the images evoked by Pan— of unpredictable change and transformation—were fitting for the notion of change and transformation among adaptive cycles at different scales. The scientists combined the image of Pan and the notion of hierarchy to come up with a new term—"panarchy" (Gunderson and Holling 2002; Theoi Project 2017).

Cross-Scale Interactions

A panarchy has three ingredients that reflect notions of ecological complexity and scales of time and space (Gunderson and Holling 2002). The first panarchy ingredient is *multiple systems*, each of which occupies a specific geographic area (Gibson, Ostrom, and Ahn 2000). Because the smaller systems, like a city block, are nested in larger systems, like the neighborhood and city, we can think of these multiple systems as a hierarchy. It is important to note that things happen faster in a city block than they do in a metropolitan region—it's easier for residents on one block to decide to water and provide fences to protect street trees than it is to implement a citywide street tree stewardship program. For this reason, systems at the bottom of the hierarchy are referred to as smaller and faster, whereas those at the top are considered to be larger and slower.

The second panarchy ingredient is *adaptive cycles*, which represent change within each of these systems occupying different levels. We have already seen how the phases of growth, conservation, collapse, and reorganization can occur in a forest. These same phases can occur in a community garden or a city.

The third ingredient, which distinguishes a panarchy from a hierarchy, is *interactions among the individual systems across the different scales*. Two cross-scale interactions are possible in a panarchy—*revolt* and *remember*. Revolt occurs when interactions move from smaller, faster systems lower down in the panarchy to larger, slower levels higher up in the panarchy. Because some disturbances, such as fires or disease outbreaks, can rapidly grow from a single individual tree or person to a forest or city, these upward-moving processes are called revolt. Relative to civic ecology, the question becomes whether a small-scale, community-based stewardship activity, like caring for trees on a single block, can "revolt" up the panarchy to impact urban forestry adaptive cycles at the level of the neighborhood, city, or even region. The downward-moving interactions in a panarchy are captured by the word "remember." Once a catastrophe is triggered at a lower level, opportunities for renewal at that level are constrained by conserved structures and processes at the larger level. After a fire, for example, options for renewal depend on resources and related processes accumulated in the form of surviving mature trees and a healthy understory that slow nutrient leakage from scorched vegetation. Options for renewal also depend on biotic legacies—or "memories"—that have accumulated during the growth of the forest (Gunderson and Holling 2002). These include the seed bank (seeds that survived the fire), physical structures (surviving trees that provide shade for young seedlings), and surviving clonal material (sprouting trees and shrubs). Applying the notion of "remember" to a civic ecology practice such as oyster restoration (Krasny et al. 2014), one might ask: Are there genetic sources of oysters remaining that oyster stewards can draw on to restore oyster populations in an estuary? Do state government policies constrain the ability of oyster stewards to install artificial oyster reefs in estuaries?

In addition to its three ingredients, panarchy theory describes at least three categories of change in social-ecological systems: gradual or incremental change, adaptive change, and transformative change. Incremental changes occur slowly and predictably, as systems mature and develop. Adaptive change occurs after disturbances, when self-organized processes return the system to a pre-disturbance state. For example, following a tropical cyclone, mangrove forests regrow, or cities rebuild damaged highways and other structures. Over time, systems adapt to disturbances and develop resilience, or the ability to absorb a disturbance without undergoing a dramatic shift into a different system (Holling 1973; Ernstson et al. 2010). However, sometimes an ecosystem can lose resilience and undergo shifts in ecosystem structure and function, such as the transition from grasses to shrubs in semiarid rangelands (Walker et al. 2002); forests decimated by pest outbreaks (Ludwig, Jones, and Holling 1978); shifts from clear water to turbid, shallow lakes (Scheffer et al. 1993); and transitions from coral to algae-dominated reefs (Gunderson and Pritchard 2002; Folke et al. 2004). Transformational change occurs when new social-ecological systems appear across multiple levels of the panarchy.

Resilience thinking and panarchy theory are frameworks that arose from empirical studies of ecosystem change over time and space. They are based on systems perspectives that contrast factors that stabilize a system with those that destabilize.

The concepts of thresholds, cross-scale interactions, and abrupt, transformational change embodied in resilience thinking have large implications for the way in which humans intervene in and manage such systems, the topic of the next section.

Stewardship and Adaptive Management

How can humans manage systems to ensure desirable change? Adaptive management integrates the insight from ecological resilience theory that ecosystems are dynamic and unpredictable. Adaptive management also integrates natural resource managers' experiences of watching ecosystems become vulnerable to destructive changes (e.g., forest fires) as a result of management decisions that seek to maximize short-term production of a resource (e.g., lumber). As an approach to natural resources management, adaptive management acknowledges that natural resources constantly change; therefore humans must adjust their approach—or adapt—to shifting conditions on the ground (Holling 1978). Learning about conditions and how they change is a critical aspect of adaptive management (Chapin, Kofinas, and Folke 2009; Gunderson 2000; Walters 1986). Learning in formal adaptive management has focused on structured experimental trials rather than trial-and-error learning as might occur in civic ecology practices (see also chapters 6 and 7).

As employed by government agencies, adaptive management is a highly structured, scientific approach that begins with a formal assessment of the problem, followed by stakeholder meetings to identify agreed-on management objectives. Managers then develop models for how different management actions might reach these objectives and conduct management experiments to test the models. Scientists monitor the impact of such experiments and use the results to suggest future management actions, which in turn are viewed as new experiments in an iterative process. Experiments to test the effect of massive water releases on sediment accumulation and fish populations in the Grand Canyon provide an example of adaptive management (Gunderson and Light 2006).

However, it turns out that the Grand Canyon is one of only a handful of cases where formal adaptive management experiments were actually implemented. More commonly, adaptive management is hampered by the costs and risks of experimentation (e.g., experiments that involve endangered species), concerns associated with a manager's or policy maker's reputation, long-standing feuds among stakeholders such as farmers and environmentalists, and lack of trust between stakeholders and government officials (Gunderson and Light 2006; Walters and Gunderson 1994).

Similarly, a study of civic ecology practices in New York City and Newark, New Jersey, revealed that only a small number of practices monitored the results of their management actions (e.g., measuring survival of recently planted urban trees), whereas only one practice conducted formal experiments (small trials of the impact of different nutrient management schemes in community gardens) (Silva and Krasny 2014; see also chapter 6). Some factors hindering monitoring and experimentation may be similar to those present in larger-scale resource management, including resistance to experimentation that might suggest a leader is not "correct" in his or her knowledge and management actions. This can be especially true for struggling community-based organizations, which need to exude a command of solutions to problems in order to garner support from funders. Other constraining factors may be more specific to civic ecology practices, like a lack of scientific expertise and capacity.

Despite the paucity of examples of monitoring and formal experimentation in community-based resource management, civic ecology stewards constantly adapt their practices based on informal observations, participation in workshops, and social learning among stewards and between stewards and government and other partners who share different types of knowledge (see chapters 5 and 6). They also develop informal means of data collection, such as before-and-after photos of spot fixes posted on the Ugly Indian Facebook group (see chapter 12). Further, citizen science and other projects involving citizen-collected data may lead to community-based stewardship efforts (Olsson and Folke 2001; see also chapter 7). In addition to learning about the practice (e.g., which plants survive in an urban environment), learning and adaptation in civic ecology practices focus on social processes, such as how to create trust, how to form social norms related to acceptable pesticide use in a community garden, or how to garner support of municipal authorities in a manner that does not constrain volunteer enthusiasm.

By focusing on informal observations and on social processes rather than ecosystem experiments, civic ecology practices demonstrate limited aspects of formal adaptive management as described by Gunderson and Light (2006). In fact, adaptive governance may provide a more useful perspective to examine the broader impacts of civic ecology practices. Adaptive governance in natural resource settings encompasses the roles people and institutions play in setting policies and how social norms drive human interactions with land, water, and other resources. We turn next to an overview of adaptive governance and the role civic ecology practices can play in these governance systems.

Adaptive Governance

Similar to adaptive management, adaptive governance incorporates notions of change and learning into social-ecological systems management. However, adaptive governance differs from adaptive management in paying greater attention to social system processes across scales (Gunderson and Light 2006; Dietz, Ostrom, and Stern 2003; Bruner et al. 2005). Adaptive governance suggests that not just management actions but also governance systems must adapt to changing conditions (Chaffin, Gosnell, and Cosens 2014).

Governance systems consist of formal government agencies, NGOs, the private sector, and informal institutions that try to influence collective-action problems, including those focused on social and environmental issues (Ostrom 1990). Whereas *government* refers exclusively to state actors or agencies that make, execute, and amend laws and policies, *governance* extends beyond government or state actors to encompass multiple public and private-sector organizations. Rules and norms designed by the array of governance actors to organize individual and collective actions include formal laws but also informal shared expectations.

Governance systems exhibit polycentricity, literally having "multiple centers" of power, including state and non-state actors (Ostrom 2010). Ideally, these centers of power partner to form governance networks that facilitate communication, integrate scientific and local knowledge, and mobilize social capital across multiple levels (Klijn and Koppenjan 2012). Because polycentric or network governance systems incorporate diverse institutions, they enable multiple policy options in the face of change; different actors have different ideas, and where one fails, others may succeed (Dietz, Ostrom, and Stern 2003). In this way, polycentric or network governance systems enable adaptive governance—governance that experiments with various formal and informal rules and rule-making systems and learns from these experiments.

Ideally, adaptive governance networks link actors across multiple scales (Olsson, Folke, and Hahn 2004), making it possible to coordinate local, regional, and even global natural resource management by transmitting lessons learned. Learning across organizational levels and physical resource scales enables transformations in management and governance that would not be possible in the absence of polycentric governance systems (Ostrom 2010). In short, adaptive governance entails finding the right configuration of actors working at different scales and in different sectors that enables adaptation to and innovation in the face of change.

An example of cross-scale governance linkages comes from a wetland ecosystem in southern Sweden, where local stewardship efforts ignited changes involving higher levels of governance. The Swedish initiative started when a scientist working at a county museum joined with others concerned about degradation of the local wetland, including loss of flooded grasslands leading to declines in bird populations. The scientist, who began by monitoring water quality, eventually became the director of the wetland initiative and formed strategic partnerships with multiple sectors and at multiple levels of governance, including bird watchers, local farmers and environmental groups, a local hotel director and former local tourism board president, universities, conservation NGOs, and Sweden's national natural history museum. Together these individuals and organizations developed a shared vision of wetland management that encompassed the multiple ecosystem services the wetland provided to the region. The director also worked with local municipal officials, who saw the potential of the project for regional economic and environmental revitalization. Eventually links were forged with the Swedish environmental protection agency, which led to the wetland ecosystem being designated as a UNESCO Man and Biosphere Reserve. Through this process of expanding networks and accompanying information exchange, as well as ongoing negotiations with municipal and national government officials, the original water monitoring project undertaken by a county museum scientist and concerned citizens was transformed into an adaptive governance network with broad influence on the wetland social-ecological system (Olsson, Folke, and Hahn 2004).

Recognizing that the Swedish wetland adaptive governance system was not static, Hahn (2011) used the lens of panarchy and nested adaptive cycles to examine change in this system. After a period of substantive growth, the local governance network had reached the conservation phase, with support coming from local and national government. Then, in 2008, the global financial crisis led municipal officials to scrutinize the costs associated with managing the wetlands for multiple ecosystem services. This, alongside the election of conservative politicians who engaged in public criticism of the initiative's leader, led to a crisis that threatened municipal support. However, by this point the initiative had garnered support at higher levels of governance (the Swedish environmental protection agency and UNESCO), which exerted pressure on lower levels of governance to "stay the (conservation) course." In short, resources and recognition at upper levels of the panarchy provided a "memory" of the importance of the wetlands initiative, which helped the local governance system move from crisis to reorganization encompassing conservation values.

Similar to how adaptive management has limitations (e.g., institutional cultures that feel threatened by experimentation, lack of organizational capacity for authentic stakeholder participation), adaptive governance faces challenges. In particular, scholars have raised issues of fairness and equity—who is included and excluded—when non-state actors, including civil society and the private sector, take on roles traditionally assumed by representative government. While extolling the potential for flexibility and innovative governance options, Hahn (2011) raises the specter of a loss of accountability to the citizenry in self-organized governance networks where grassroots efforts grow to assume functions normally associated with government. In the Swedish wetlands governance network described above, local and national government made the final decisions about resources, thus ensuring accountability to citizens. In addition, by starting with small management actions in collaboration with key stakeholders, the Swedish initiative built trust and legitimacy, which helped to bridge adaptability with accountability (Hahn 2011).

The difficulty of balancing flexibility and accountability is also illustrated by the Landcare governance network in Australia. The National Landcare Program was initiated by the Australian government in 1988, with the goal to engage local communities in sustainable farm and forest management (Tennent and Lockie 2013; Prager 2010). Initially, monetary incentives allowed farmers flexibility in deciding on sustainability practices and encouraged them to work with peers to generate new ideas and implement new practices. In so doing, the farmers built social capital that empowered them and their organizations to engage in collective action, which had the unintended consequence of maintaining the status quo of intensive land use (Compton and Beeton 2012). Responding to political change, in 2008 the national government deemphasized community engagement and local institutional capacity building in favor of accountability in measuring soil and water management outcomes. Because the new regional groups or "organizational collaboratives" had a mandate to coordinate management and policy across a larger area, the local groups ("action collaboratives") that were focused on local stewardship action felt their interests were no longer being addressed (Prager 2010). This and other factors eventually led to a decline in local engagement and social networking in some groups, and an overall decline in Landcare activities (Tennent and Lockie 2013). In short, issues of flexibility, scale, and social capital came up against issues of accountability, leading to a "crisis" or omega phase in the Landcare governance adaptive cycle.

Panarchy, Scale, and Adaptive Governance in Civic Ecology Practices

So what do civic ecology practices have to do with adaptive governance? Civic ecology stewardship and restoration groups tend to collaborate around narrowly defined projects, and thus their organizational structure may be described as an "adhocracy" (Hahn 2011). In contrast, governance networks formulate and create meaning around visions and policies, solve conflicts, and develop links across agencies and other organizations for gaining political, legal, and financial support (Olsson et al. 2007). Compared to local stewardship practices, governance systems are concerned with larger geographic areas and include not only community-based stewardship groups, but also more powerful government, NGO, and private-sector actors. Thus, governance systems incorporate geographic scale as well as a range of organizational scales. Nevertheless, environmental governance systems often incorporate, or even depend on, civic ecology practitioners. Here we use the history of community gardening in New York City to show these relationships. The processes inherent in adaptive cycles and panarchy impact governance systems that involve civic ecology practitioners alongside other actors. Those processes—including crisis, reorganization, growth, and conservation followed by another crisis—can result in creation of meaningful places and linkages across civic ecology practitioners and other actors in the governance system.

Multiple waves of community gardening have arisen during crises in the United States, including the Liberty and Victory Gardens in response to concerns about food security in World Wars I and II (Lawson 2005). Similarly, the guerrilla gardening movement in New York City emerged during the disruptions of the 1970s (Smith and Kurtz 2003; see chapter 6) and contributed to the reorganization phase of the adaptive cycle. In the 1970s, middle-class residents fled to the suburbs, leaving behind abandoned buildings and vacant lots in the midst of a city tottering on bankruptcy; in some neighborhoods in the Bronx over 97 percent of the buildings were burned or abandoned (Flood 2010). "Guerrilla gardeners," who lobbed "seed grenades" (water balloons filled with water, compost, and seeds that exploded on impact) over a fence in the Bowery district of Manhattan, are credited with sparking a community gardening movement in the devastation of the 1970s. After a period of growth in the late 1980s, New York City counted over one thousand gardens. In New York and other cities, community gardens are credited with playing a role in transforming city neighborhoods from sites of decay and violence to places where people gather to do physical and civic work in green spaces (NYC Parks 2014).

As early as 1978, grassroots community gardeners in New York City reached out to municipal government and thus started to develop a community gardening governance network. In response to gardeners' lobbying efforts, the city created GreenThumb, which provided fences and garden construction materials and horticultural training. Nonprofit organizations, such as Trust for Public Land and Green Guerillas, became part of the governance network in the growth period for community gardens from the late 1970s to the late 1990s. However, as the city, having recovered from the 1970s crisis, entered the rapid economic growth phase in its adaptive cycle, Mayor Giuliani looked to the lots occupied by community garden "squatters" for commercial development. This created a crisis for the committed and passionate gardeners, who set about to "reorganize" not just their neighborhoods but also political priorities in city governance (NYC Parks 2014).

In tracing the history of New York's community gardening movement, Smith and Kurtz (2003) draw on Cox's (1998) notions of "spaces of dependence" and "spaces of engagement." Community gardens are spaces of dependence in that they provide emotional and material sustenance. The community gardening *movement* during the late 1990s was a space of engagement, in which actors worked to preserve and protect the spaces of dependence—the community gardens. These larger, advocacy spaces of engagement encompassed multiple efforts drawing in different levels of governance and governance actors. For example, previously isolated community gardens (described as individual "little outposts") formed small local associations to mobilize quickly to defend individual gardens. They also created citywide advocacy groups to track the mayor's actions and help preserve gardens across the city. Community garden activists joined with other movements to symbolically broaden the spaces of engagement to include parallel struggles like those focused on environmental quality and antiprivatization. Finally, the activists successfully lobbied the New York state government, convincing Attorney General Eliot Spitzer to file a lawsuit against the city for failure to perform required environmental reviews. In the end, money raised by the gardeners and by several nonprofit groups helped to purchase and provide long-term legal protection for community gardens (Eizenberg 2012). Viewed from a social science lens, the community gardeners "jumped scales" from spaces of dependence to spaces of engagement, in part by forming networks of different institutions (Cox 1998). Viewed through a panarchy lens, the community garden adaptive cycle responded to a crisis created by the city governance adaptive cycle that attempted to constrain community gardening in a "remembrance" process; community gardens also formed governance networks that helped transform city governance policy to incorporate green spaces as integral to the health of the city and its residents in a "revolt" process. Importantly, the spaces of engagement were able to bridge interests among multiple gardens and garden organizations (cf. Olsson et al. 2007). This bridging ability helps explain why community gardening did not decline, in contrast to the decline in local Landcare activity once the regional organizational collaboratives formed in the case mentioned earlier (Prager 2010).

Going beyond scales of dependence and scales of engagement, Smith and Kurtz (2003, 193) describe the effort to save the community gardens as a "politics of scales" in which garden "advocates contested the fragmentation of social urban space wrought by the application of neoliberal policies." Drawing on earlier work demonstrating how scales can be constructed for political purposes, Smith and Kurtz (2003, 199) contend that "'politics of scale' refers to the ways in which social actors draw on relationships at different geographical scales to press for advantage in a given political situation. Although geographers have traditionally taken 'scale' to refer to scales of analysis—such as urban, regional, national, or global—recent work on the political construction of scale calls attention to the processes that reify familiar geographical scales, suggesting that their constitution is fluid." The geographer Swyngedouw (2004, 131–32) goes a step further in claiming that "starting analysis from a given geographical scale . . . [is] deeply antagonistic to apprehending the world in a dynamic, process-based manner. . . . Scalar configurations [are] the outcome of sociospatial processes that regulate and organize social power relations. As a geographical construction, scales become arenas around which sociospatial power choreographies are enacted and performed."

In short, whereas ecosystem scientists refer to spatial or temporal scales measured in hectares or years, social scientists recognize that scales are constructed by humans, in part to influence others and exert power (Reed and Bruyneel 2010). Because scale involves "framing conceptions of reality" (Delaney and Leitner 1997) for political purposes, it can be both symbolic and involve organizational networks (Cox 1998). This work suggests an expansion of the way in which scale is depicted in panarchy and related social-ecological processes.

In the New York City community gardening case, Mayor Giuliani's attempt to bypass community boards, which had traditionally served as venues for citizen input into decisions about city property development, triggered the creation of new scale boundaries. Through forming coalitions among gardens and between gardens, NGOs, and state government, and through protest politics that extended beyond gardens to include advocacy against privatization of public space, the community garden activists expanded the scale of urban green-space governance networks. Further, they linked issues of social equity to control of and access to green spaces, and thus expanded the symbolic scale of community garden activism (Smith and Kurtz 2003). More recently, community gardening has helped spur and become part of a global food security movement, again expanding symbolic scales through joining forces with farmers' markets, faith-based institutions, university agriculture extension services, and national institutions such as the U.S. Department of Agriculture and the American Community Gardening Association. In short, governance networks and symbolic scales shape community gardens, but community gardens also play a role in shaping governance networks and symbolic discourse at multiple scales. In this way, human-constructed notions of scale interact up and down levels within a panarchy. Regardless of whether scale can be measured in acres, as suggested by social-ecological systems scholars, or is a creation of political actors trying to exert control over other actors, as claimed by political geographers, we can see interactions similar to revolt and remember across scales.

As we have used community gardening to illustrate notions of panarchy and scale and the role of civic ecology practices in adaptive governance, we contend that similar processes of scaling up could occur in other civic ecology practices. Additional examples lending themselves to such analyses include community tree-planting efforts, which have taken flight in cities across the United States (Fisher, Svendsen, and Connolly 2015; see chapter 11), and networks of litter cleanup efforts that influence municipal governments in one or multiple cities (see chapter 12).

In response to resilience thinking that emerged in the early 2000s, including notions of change, scale, and interactions across scales, scientists embraced adaptive management. Although the formal experimental nature of adaptive management causes barriers to its implementation in the field, the notion of management as learning from experience and adapting to change has persisted. Adaptive governance attempts to address weaknesses of adaptive management, by encompassing less formal learning about social in addition to ecosystem processes. In civic ecology, adaptive governance is a means to expand the impact of individual isolated practices. In short, it appears that civic ecology practices reflect insights from adaptive governance even if they do not often employ the scientific methods of adaptive management. This may be because the skill set of civic ecology stewards is in leadership, relationship building, and other social competencies (Krasny et al. 2015), rather than in ecosystem sciences and formal research.

Panarchy provides a lens for understanding both adaptive management and adaptive governance. It encourages us to think about various scales and the interaction among scales. Scholars have expanded the notion of scale to include organizational and symbolic dimensions. Further, they have demonstrated that citizens' needs may be met at one scale (the scale of dependence), while citizens may wield political influence at another (scale of political engagement). In so doing, they have sharpened panarchy's account of how processes at different scales influence each other socially as well as ecologically. Applied to civic ecology, these notions suggest that civic ecology practices operate in a space of dependence, but through expanding their organizational networks and symbolic meanings, they can impact governance systems, or spaces of engagement. These advocacy-oriented spaces of engagement provide opportunities for civic ecology practices to grow in influence. Focusing on cross-scale interactions, the potential for memories and social and natural capital built through civic ecology practices can be "stored" at higher levels in the panarchy and can be drawn on in times of crisis.

Finally, notions of place, practice, and scale are contested. We see numerous conflicts over place and practice, not just in community gardens in New York

City. The Ugly Indian has contested Indian citizens' and municipal governments' inability to see public spaces as anything other than dumping grounds (see chapter 12), and the Landcare example illustrates how progress may be gained and lost as stewardship action is incorporated into regional collaborations or governance networks. Determining the right configuration of geographic, symbolic, and governance scale is critical to expanding the influence of civic ecology practices while maintaining local stewards' commitment and a social-ecological context that sparks grassroots innovations.

REFERENCES

Bruner, R., T. A. Steelman, L. Coe-Juell, C. Cromley, C. Edwards, and C. Tucker. 2005. *Adaptive Governance: Integrating Science, Policy, and Decision Making.* New York: Columbia University Press.

Chaffin, B. C., H. Gosnell, and B. A. Cosens. 2014. "A Decade of Adaptive Governance Scholarship: Synthesis and Future Directions." *Ecology and Society* 19 (3): 56.

Chapin, F., III, G. Kofinas, and C. Folke, eds. 2009. *Principles of Ecosystem Stewardship: Resilience-Based Natural Resource Management in a Changing World.* New York: Springer.

Compton, E., and R. J. S. Beeton. 2012. "An Accidental Outcome: Social Capital and Its Implications for Landcare and the 'Status Quo.'" *Journal of Rural Studies* 28:149–60. doi:10.1016/j.jrurstud.2011.12.004.

Cox, K. 1998. "Spaces of Dependence, Spaces of Engagement and the Politics of Scale, or: Looking for Local Politics." *Political Geography* 17 (1): 1–23.

Crutzen, P. J., and E. F. Stoermer. 2000. "The Anthropocene." *Global Change Newsletter* 41:17–18.

Delaney, G., and H. Leitner. 1997. "The Political Construction of Scale." *Political Geography* 16 (2): 93–97.

Dietz, T., E. Ostrom, and P. C. Stern. 2003. "The Struggle to Govern the Commons." *Science* 302 (5652): 1907–12. doi:10.1126/science.1091015.

Eizenberg, E. 2012. "The Changing Meaning of Community Space: Two Models of NGO Management of Community Gardens in New York City." *International Journal of Urban and Regional Research* 36 (1): 106–20. doi:10.1111/j.1468-2427.2011.01065.x.

Ernstson, H., S. E. van der Leeuw, C. L. Redman, D. J. Meffert, G. Davis, C. Alfsen, and T. Elmqvist. 2010. "Urban Transitions: On Urban Resilience and Human-Dominated Ecosystems." *Ambio* 39 (8): 531–45.

Fisher, D. R., E. S. Svendsen, and J. J. Connolly. 2015. *Urban Environmental Stewardship and Civic Engagement: How Planting Trees Strengthens the Roots of Democracy.* New York: Routledge.

Flood, J. 2010. "Why the Bronx Burned." *New York Post*, May 16. http://nypost.com/2010/05/16/why-the-bronx-burned/.

Folke, C., S. R. Carpenter, B. H. Walker, M. Scheffer, T. Elmqvist, L. H. Gunderson, and C. S. Holling. 2004. "Regime Shifts, Resilience, and Biodiversity in Ecosystem Management." *Annual Review of Ecology Evolution and Systematics* 35:557–81.

Gibson, C. C., E. Ostrom, and T. K. Ahn. 2000. "The Concept of Scale and the Human Dimensions of Global Change: A Survey." *Ecological Economics* 32 (2): 217–39.

Gunderson, L. H. 2000. "Ecological Resilience: Theory to Practice." *Annual Review of Ecology and Systematics* 31:421–39.

Gunderson, L. H., and C. S. Holling, eds. 2002. *Panarchy: Understanding Transforma-tions in Human and Natural Systems*. Washington, DC: Island Press.

Gunderson, L. H., C. S. Holling, and S. S. Light. 1995. *Barriers and Bridges to the Renewal of Ecosystems and Institutions*. New York: Columbia University Press.

Gunderson, L. H., and S. S. Light. 2006. "Adaptive Management and Adaptive Gover-nance in the Everglades Ecosystem." *Policy Sciences* 39:323–34.

Gunderson, L. H., and L. Pritchard, eds. 2002. *Resilience and the Behavior of Large-Scale Systems*. Washington, DC: Island Press.

Hahn, T. 2011. "Self-Organized Governance Networks for Ecosystem Management: Who Is Accountable?" *Ecology & Society* 16 (2): 18.

Holling, C. S. 1973. "Resilience and Stability of Ecological Systems." *Annual Review of Ecology, Evolution, and Systematics* 4:1–23.

——. 1978. "The Spruce-Budworm/Forest-Management Problem." In *Adaptive Envi-ronmental Assessment and Management*, edited by C. S. Holling, 143–82. Hobo-ken, NJ: John Wiley & Sons.

——. 1986. "The Resilience of Terrestrial Ecosystems: Local Surprise and Global Change." In *Sustainable Development of the Biosphere*, edited by W. C. Clark and R. E. Munn, 292–317. Cambridge: Cambridge University Press.

Holling, C. S., and L. H. Gunderson. 2002. "Resilience and Adaptive Cycles." In *Panar-chy: Understanding Transformations in Human and Natural Systems*, edited by L. H. Gunderson and C. S. Holling, 25–62. Washington, DC: Island Press.

IPCC (Intergovernmental Panel on Climate Change). 2014. *Climate Change 2014: Impacts, Adaptation, and Vulnerability. Part A: Global and Sectoral Aspects. Contribution of Working Group II to the Fifth Assessment Report of the Inter-governmental Panel on Climate Change*. Edited by C. B. Field, V. R. Barros, D. J. Dokken, K. J. Mach, M. D. Mastrandrea, T. E. Bilir, M. Chatterjee, et al. New York: Cambridge University Press.

Klijn, E., and J. Koppenjan. 2012. "Governance Network Theory: Past, Present and Future." *Policy & Politics* 40 (4): 587–606. http://dx.doi.org/10.1332/030557312X 655431.

Krasny, M. E., S. R Crestol, K. G. Tidball, and R. C. Stedman. 2014. "New York City's Oyster Gardeners: Memories, Meanings, and Motivations of Volunteer Envi-ronmental Stewards." *Landscape and Urban Planning* 132:16–25. doi:10.1016/j. landurbplan.2014.08.003.

Krasny, M. E., P. Silva, C. W. Barr, Z. Golshani, E. Lee, R. Ligas, E. Mosher, and A. Reynosa. 2015. "Civic Ecology Practices: Insights from Practice Theory." *Ecology and Society* 20 (2): 12.

Lawson, L. J. 2005. *City Bountiful: A Century of Community Gardening in America*. Berkeley: University of California Press.

Light, S. S., L. H. Gunderson, and C. S. Holling. 1995. "The Everglades: Evolution of Management in a Turbulent Ecosystem." In *Barriers and Bridges to the Renewal of Ecosystems and Institutions*, edited by L. C. Gunderson, C. S. Holling, and S. S. Light, 103–68. New York: Columbia University Press.

Ludwig, D., D. D. Jones, and C. S. Holling. 1978. "Qualitative Analysis of Insect Out-break Systems: The Spruce Budworm and Forest." *Journal of Animal Ecology* 47:315–32.

MEA (Millennium Ecosystem Assessment). 2005. *Ecosystems and Human Well-Being: Synthesis*. Washington, DC: Island Press.

NYC Parks. 2014. "History of the Community Garden Movement: Green Guerril-las Gain Ground." http://www.nycgovparks.org/about/history/community-gardens/movement.

Olsson, P., and C. Folke. 2001. "Local Ecological Knowledge and Institutional Dynamics for Ecosystem Management: A Study of Lake Racken Watershed, Sweden."
Ecosystems 4 (2): 85–104.

Olsson, P., C. Folke, V. Galaz, T. Hahn, and L. Schultz. 2007. "Enhancing the Fit
through Adaptive Comanagement: Creating and Maintaining Bridging Functions for Matching Scales in the Kristianstads Vattenrike Biosphere Reserve
Sweden." *Ecology and Society* 12 (1): 28.

Olsson, P., C. Folke, and T. Hahn. 2004. "Social-Ecological Transformation for Ecosystem Management: The Development of Adaptive Co-management of a Wetland
Landscape in Southern Sweden." *Ecology & Society* 9 (4): 2.

Olsson, P., C. Folke, and T. P. Hughes. 2008. "Navigating the Transition to Ecosystem-
Based Management of the Great Barrier Reef, Australia." *Proceedings of the
National Academy of Sciences* 105 (28): 9489–94.

Ostrom, E. 1990. *Governing the Commons: The Evolution of Institutions for Collective
Action*. New York: Cambridge University Press.

———. 2010. "Polycentric Systems for Coping with Collective Action and Global Environmental Change." *Global Environmental Change* 20:550–57.

Prager, K. 2010. "Local and Regional Partnerships in Natural Resource Management:
The Challenge of Bridging Institutional Levels." *Environmental Management*
46:711–24. doi:10.1007/s00267-010-9560-9.

Reed, M. G., and S. Bruyneel. 2010. "Rescaling Environmental Governance, Rethinking
the State: A Three-Dimensional Review." *Progress in Human Geography* 34 (5):
646–53. doi:10.1177/0309132509354836.

Rockström, J., W. Steffen, K. Noone, Å. Persson, F. S. Chapin, E. Lambin, T. M. Len-
ton, et al. 2009. "Planetary Boundaries: Exploring the Safe Operating Space for
Humanity." *Ecology and Society* 14 (2): 32.

Scheffer, M., S. H. Hosper, M.-L. Meijer, B. Moss, and E. Jeppesen. 1993. "Alternative
Equilibria in Shallow Lakes." *Trends in Evolutionary Ecology* 8:275–79.

Silva, P., and M. E. Krasny. 2014. "Parsing Participation: Models of Engagement for
Outcomes Monitoring in Urban Stewardship." *Local Environment: The International Journal of Justice and Sustainability* 21 (2): 157–65. doi:10.1080/13549839
.2014.929094.

Smith, C. M., and H. E. Kurtz. 2003. "Community Gardens and Politics of Scale in
New York City." *Geographical Review* 93 (2): 193–212.

Steffen, W., Å. Persson, L. Deutsch, J. Zalasiewicz, M. Williams, K. Richardson, C.
Crumley, et al. 2011. "The Anthropocene: From Global Change to Planetary
Stewardship." *Ambio* 40 (7): 739–61. doi:10.1007/s13280-011-0185-x.

Swyngedouw, E. 2004. "Scaled Geographies: Nature, Place, and the Politics of Scale."
In *Scale and Geographic Inquiry: Nature, Society, and Method*, edited by
E. Sheppard and R. B. McMaster, 129–53. Oxford: Blackwell.

Tennent, R., and S. Lockie. 2013. "Vale Landcare: The Rise and Decline of Community-
Based Natural Resource Management in Rural Australia." *Journal of Environmental Planning and Management* 56 (4): 572–87. doi:10.1080/09640568.2012.
689617.

Theoi Project. 2017. "Pan." http://www.theoi.com/Georgikos/Pan.html.

Turner, B. L., E. Lambin, and A. Reenberg. 2007. "Land Change Science Special Feature: The Emergence of Land Change Science for Global Environmental Change
and Sustainability." *Proceedings of the National Academy of Sciences of the United
States of America* 104 (52): 20666–71. doi:10.1073/pnas.0704119104.

Vitousek, P. M., H. A. Mooney, J. Lubchenco, and J. M. Melillo. 1997. "Human Domi-
nation of Earth's Ecosystems." *Science* 277:494–99.

Walker, B. H., S. R. Carpenter, J. Anderies, N. Abel, G. S. Cumming, M. Janssen,
    L. Lebel, J. Norberg, G. D. Peterson, and R. Pritchard. 2002. "Resilience Manage-
    ment in Social-Ecological Systems: A Working Hypothesis for a Participatory
    Approach." *Conservation Ecology* 6 (1): 14.
Walker, B. H., and D. Salt. 2006. *Resilience Thinking: Sustaining Ecosystems and People
    in a Changing World*. Washington, DC: Island Press.
Walters, C. J. 1986. *Adaptive Management of Renewable Resources*. New York:
    McGraw-Hill.
Walters, C. J., and L. H. Gunderson. 1994. "A Screening of Water Policy Alternatives
    for Ecological Restoration in the Everglades." In *Everglades: The Ecosystem and
    Its Restoration*, edited by S. M. Davis and J. Ogden, 757–67. Delray Beach, FL:
    St. Lucie Press.

Chapter 9

THE HEALING POWERS OF NATURE IN JOPLIN'S CUNNINGHAM PARK

Coupling Design-Build and Civic Ecology

*Keith E. Hedges, Traci Sooter, Nancy Chikaraishi,
and Marianne E. Krasny*

May 22, 2011, was supposed to be a day to celebrate, as high school graduates in Joplin, Missouri, tossed their caps into the air. But the Sunday graduation ceremony quickly turned to tragedy when a tornado barreled down through the middle of the city, killing 161 residents (SPC-NOAA 2015; *Kansas City Star* 2011). The entire community felt the impact of the tornado's destructive path (Letner 2011). Yet after the tragedy, Joplin community members, along with a flood of volunteers from nearby Drury University and beyond, generated multiple "civic waves" of recovery.

This chapter describes Drury University's design-build of historic Cunningham Park, whose trees and infrastructure were decimated by the tornado. Whereas we focus on the greening aspects of recovery, Joplin's post-disaster efforts also encompassed building new homes for tornado victims, an initiative of the network television show *Extreme Makeover: Home Edition*. Other actors included TKF Foundation's Open Spaces Sacred Places program, which funded Drury and Cornell universities and the U.S. Forest Service to explore the healing outcomes of one greening initiative. As a result of these efforts, Joplin's Volunteer Tribute garden provides an environment to support group healing, while its Butterfly Garden and Overlook offers private moments for individual recovery.

The creation of the Joplin healing spaces illustrates a foundational tenet of civic ecology—that people often turn to stewarding nature after disaster or conflict, in what has been labeled "greening in red zones" (Tidball and Krasny 2014). Such greening actions may be spurred by humans' innate need to connect with nature, or bio-philia (Kellert and Wilson 1993; Wilson 1984). For some people, this need becomes more powerful during trying times (Okvat and Zautra 2014; Helphand 2006), in a phenomenon referred to as "urgent biophilia" (Tidball 2014c; Tidball 2012b). Post-disaster stewardship actions also may be motivated by a desire to restore places where people have spent their lives and to which they have become attached—what has been called "restorative topophilia" (Tidball and Stedman 2013).

While illustrating some tenets of civic ecology, the Joplin case also pushes the boundaries of previously described community-driven civic ecology initiatives. Not only did the Joplin greening efforts involve significant expertise and leader-ship from students and faculty at a university seventy miles away from Joplin; they also engaged volunteers and researchers from across the country, a national television show, and a national funder. In so doing, the Joplin case raises issues we have observed in volunteer greening efforts more broadly, most notably the bal-ance between the engagement of local actors and more powerful outside actors in design of community space (Eizenberg 2012), the importance of short-term vol-unteers (Fisher, Svendsen, and Connolly 2015), and the engagement of univer-sity students in stewardship through service learning and student clubs (Sooter, Chikaraishi, and Hedges 2013; Krasny and Delia 2014). In this chapter we first describe the creation of two gardens after the tornado and then discuss the Joplin case within the context of scholarship in civic ecology and volunteer stewardship.

Joplin's Cunningham Park

Cunningham Park, Joplin's first city park, is deeply rooted in the city's history and its residents' sense of place, and reflects ongoing efforts of private, civil soci-ety, and local government actors. The park takes its name from Thomas Cun-ningham, a miner, farmer, grocer, and Civil War volunteer, who is best known for founding the Bank of Joplin and becoming the city's first mayor in 1897. Cunningham donated seven acres to Joplin in 1899, which the City Council des-ignated as a park, vowing "to make it a place second to no park in the state." The Joplin Women's Park Association then used a tax levy to develop the park, installing a fountain with a waterfall. Subsequently, the city added flower beds, a bandstand, a shelter, a playground, a refreshment stand, a swimming pool, and a bathhouse. By the Great Depression in the 1930s, the park was a vital Joplin land-mark, known for its concentric circular gardens. The majestic Carl Owen house, built around 1911, overlooked the park. In addition to being used for commu-nity gatherings, Cunningham Park carried special meaning for Joplin residents because of its history, amenities, and over two hundred beautiful, centuries-old trees (Simpson 2011).

The Tornado

Federal Emergency Management Agency (FEMA) director Craig Fugate described the situation after the tornado: "We're talking thousands of families impacted, hundreds of deaths, the trauma to the community alone was overwhelming" (Lieb 2012). The tornado destroyed or damaged over 7,500 homes and 550 businesses and left in its wake over three million cubic yards of debris. Over 40 percent of the city's fifty thousand residents were directly impacted, and ninety-two

FIGURE 9.1   Cunningham Park, with Saint John's Hospital in background. Image from video by Jeremy Scherle, Jeremy Scherle Entertainment.

hundred people were displaced, with losses estimated at more than $100,000 per impacted resident (Onstot 2013; U.S. Census Bureau 2015). Although the Carl Owen house had saved the lives of three residents sheltering in its basement, its first floor collapsed, and the second floor toppled into the street.

The tornado also created an environmental disaster. The bark of all trees left standing had been stripped, and the earth was scoured along the tornado's path. The cleanup entailed scraping the earth multiple times to remove debris, leaving miles of cheerless gray landscape. Cunningham Park, along with its more than two hundred mature trees, was destroyed, leaving no vertical landmarks, as was common throughout the tornado's direct path.

Two Waves of Community Support

After the storm, the Joplin City Council expanded Cunningham Park by purchasing six vacant lots whose homes had been destroyed, including the Carl Owen house. The city also planted 161 trees, one in memory of each victim. Then, after an initial convergence of volunteers from across the United States and other countries, Drury University's Design-Build team designed and helped create two living memorials (cf. McMillen et al. 2016; Svendsen and Campbell 2006)—the Volunteer Tribute, and the Butterfly Garden and Overlook. Supporting Drury University students and faculty in these efforts were community volunteers, Cornell University and U.S. Forest Service researchers, and national for-profit, nonprofit, and government partners.

Volunteer Tribute

Extreme Makeover: Home Edition (*EM:HE*) was an Emmy Award–winning, reality television show that remodeled or built new homes for families suffering from the loss of a loved one, managing a long-term illness, or having experienced a natural disaster. The show aired for nine seasons and two hundred episodes, with the Joplin episode being its biggest and final home build (Kimball 2011). Although *EM:HE*'s stated purpose was to provide entertainment to a mass audience, its creators included many caring individuals who intended to use the show's celebrity status to create a second wave of voluntarism months after the disaster, by engaging the community in rebuilding the houses of seven Joplin families who had lost their homes. With each episode, *EM:HE* also built a special project for the families or communities they served, which in Joplin was rebuilding Cunningham Park.

In addition to installing a new playground and basketball court in the park, *EM:HE* supported the creation of a garden that pays tribute to the more than

170,000 volunteers who came to the aid of Joplin immediately after the tornado. Joplin city manager Mark Rohr referred to the initial rise to action after the destruction as the "miracle of the human spirit" (Rohr 2012), and the Volunteer Tribute garden would honor that spirit.

Drury University professor and Design-Build director Traci Sooter, who had worked on three previous *EM:HE* projects, led the university rebuild efforts in Joplin. During a walk through Cunningham Park, city parks director Chris Cotten told Sooter about the horrific night he had endured in the aftermath of the storm. The bond forged between Cotten and Sooter then and during the Volunteer Tribute design process played a significant role in Drury University's subsequent involvement in the second project—the Butterfly Garden and Overlook.

Students in a third-year architectural studio course met with tornado survivors to elicit design ideas for the Volunteer Tribute. They learned about the depths of loss and how to respond with design sensitivity and empathy. The design featured four rings of stone walls, four bronzed tools, and stainless steel pedestals representing the four processes of search and rescue, debris removal, demolition, and rebirth of Joplin. The concentric circles followed an original design element of the Cunningham Park gardens from a century earlier. At the center of the ring, a mosaic butterfly symbolized residents' stories of butterflies protecting children during the storm (Real-McKeighan 2011). Parks director Cotten provided the volunteers with special wristbands, replicating the six-foot stainless steel ring and inscribed with "The Miracle of the Human Spirit." He gave one band from his own wrist directly to Sooter. In designing a garden space rather than a building to honor the volunteers, the architecture students respected input from community members while venturing outside their comfort zone. Their final Volunteer Tribute garden design would allow visitors to connect with and become aware of nature as part of the healing process.

Once the design was completed, Drury University volunteers, including 370 students, faculty, staff, administrators, and their families, worked alongside 13,000 local volunteers, the Joplin Parks Department, and a team from *EM:HE* to build the twelve-thousand-plus-square-foot Volunteer Tribute in 168 hours on a continuous 24/7 job site (Sooter, Chikaraishi, and Hedges 2013). (*EM:HE* required that construction be completed within a specific seven-day window.) *EM:HE* captured 168 hours of camera footage at the Volunteer Tribute, and filmed scenes at the park with survivors and the host for its television audience. The university volunteers, following a whole school design-build transdisciplinary philosophy (Sooter, Chikaraishi, and Hedges 2014), laid concrete block walls, poured and stamped concrete, planted plants, and built wooden benches, picnic tables, and a trellis. They also walked the tornado path, collecting shards to incorporate into mosaics, ran errands to hardware stores and lumberyards, and delivered food for other volunteers. A Spanish-language professor led Girl Scout volunteers helping to create the butterfly mosaic. University administrators exhibited strong support by participating in the planning meetings and construction activities and lending vehicles, but their most significant action was offering scholarships to all graduating high school students and children of families in the seven *EM:HE* homes. Local builders and suppliers also volunteered time and equipment and donated construction materials, including the stainless steel ring valued at $35,000.

FIGURE 9.2   The Volunteer Tribute. Photo by Evan Melgren, Drury University.

A formal student group calling itself the Drury University SmartMob! emerged out of the Volunteer Tribute rebuild effort. The SmartMob! is a flash mob whose purpose is to provide an opportunity for any university student, faculty, staff, or community member to participate in community design-build and service projects. During the Volunteer Tribute build, more than 120 students, faculty, staff, and administrators joined the SmartMob! to lay nearly twelve thousand square feet of sod in a "hyper-regreening" effort that took only forty-five minutes. The SmartMob! also was to play a role in building Joplin's second Living Memorial.

Butterfly Garden and Overlook

Similar to the Volunteer Tribute, the Butterfly Garden and Overlook project enlisted both well-resourced outsiders and local volunteers. Shortly after the tornado, researchers from Cornell University (Keith Tidball) and the U.S. Forest Service (Erika Svendsen, Lindsay Campbell, and Nancy Falxa Sonti) approached the Joplin Parks and Recreation Department to collaborate on an Open Spaces Sacred Places (OSSP) proposal to TKF Foundation. An OSSP is a space designed to help those who have experienced personal hardship owing to poverty, loss, or natural disaster heal within nature. Since its founding in 1996, TKF Foundation has identified passionate and persevering partners, whom they call Firesouls, to create more than one hundred OSSPs (Stoner and Rapp 2008).

Joplin parks director Cotten became the Firesoul for the OSSP in Cunningham Park. When first approached by the Cornell University researcher, Cotten said that he was "not in" unless Drury was participating, and immediately contacted Sooter. The eventual Landscapes of Resilience grant team included Cornell, the U.S. Forest Service, Drury University, Forest ReLeaf of Missouri, Great River Associates, and Joplin Parks and Recreation. Drury University served as the design-builder, with a multidisciplinary team including architecture, music therapy, and psychology professors.

TKF Foundation required that the design have four distinct elements: portal, path, destination, and surround. These elements offer a "comforting enclosure, complemented by a well-defined portal that marks the transition from the hectic city to the quiet enclave" (Mueller 2008, 12). As opposed to the entertainment value and honoring of outside volunteers inherent to the *EM:HE* Volunteer Tribute rebuild effort, the goals for the OSSP garden were healing among local Joplin survivors. Further, the Cornell and U.S. Forest Service researchers sought to understand processes involved in creating healing gardens and to disseminate this information to influence future post-disaster greening efforts.

Drury students involved in the Butterfly Garden and Overlook project sought to create a place within nature to help individuals heal from the loss of a loved one, a home, or a job, and which would provide a sense of security and community. Inspired by the work of students in the English Department who collected, transcribed, and archived survivor stories, two architecture students worked with tornado survivors and professors to develop the healing garden concept. Third-year architecture students then designed and built five elements within the garden, including an outline of three homes erased by the tornado, a pavilion, water

FIGURE 9.3 Butterfly Garden and Overlook. Photo by Evan Melgren, Drury University.

features, educational storyboards, and a butterfly garden incorporating four sacred spaces, each with a bench and a journal.

The final design for the Butterfly Garden and Overlook weaves together concepts from Worden's four tasks of mourning (Worden 1991) reflected in the OSSP-required design elements. Worden recognizes the mourning process as accepting loss, managing the pain of grief, adjusting to the new environment, and making an enduring connection with the deceased. Accepting loss is reflected in the OSSP portal, which is the front door of the destroyed Carl Owen home. The OSSP path takes the visitor on a journey through the site, allowing for processing the pain of grief and promoting reflection. As it surrounds the visitor, the space permits the user to adjust to a world marked by the death of loved ones and other losses. Eleven native Missouri shade trees, additional native plantings, the "outlines" of the homes, and the unifying circle of the Butterfly Garden provide an encompassing sense of boundary, safety, and enclosure. Plaques tell the story of the tornado, thus providing visitors insight into the destruction, acts of heroism, survival, and the "Miracle of the Human Spirit." In short, the garden elements communicate "We move on but do not forget."

Using a blitz-build approach, thirteen architecture students and sixty Smart-Mob! students, faculty, and staff aided by community volunteers constructed the Butterfly Garden and Overlook in one week. Reflecting the design-build transdisciplinary philosophy (Sooter, Chikaraishi, and Hedges 2014), music therapy students played uplifting music at a rejuvenation station during the build. Civic actors, including middle school children, garden clubs, and families, planted the garden four months later. These efforts were supported by Joplin Parks and Recreation staff, including tornado survivors who participated in the volunteer days.

Joplin and Civic Ecology: Healing, Expertise, and Volunteers

The Volunteer Tribute and Butterfly gardens both incorporate design elements that use nature to promote a sense of well-being and healing. These include written narratives on storyboards, a circular journey with destinations, and a sense of surround. However, the two sites diverge in their relation to the availability of public and private encounters in the outdoor spaces. The scale and intent of the Volunteer Tribute create a gathering place for larger groups, while the Butterfly Garden and Overlook is meant to provide a sense of security and comfort for individual healing. Both projects used a whole-school transdisciplinary approach to the design and realization of the project, and both have become sacred spaces to the people of Joplin (Sooter, Chikaraishi, and Hedges 2014).

The garden projects reinforce some elements of earlier writing about civic ecology, while expanding on others. Both of the Joplin initiatives provide yet another example of the importance of greening as part of the recovery process. Krasny and Tidball (2015) originally observed how refugees talked about community gardens as sources of resilience in the face of the emotional hardships they had endured, and Tidball (2014b) recorded how residents of New Orleans used tree planting as a means of personal recovery following Hurricane Katrina. Similarly, living memorials planted by survivors of the 9/11 terrorist attacks helped to commemorate those who had been lost and helped communities heal from the tragedy (McMillen et al. 2016; Svendsen and Campbell 2005, 2006). In their preliminary content analysis of journal entries by visitors to OSSP gardens in multiple cities, Tidball, Svendsen, et al. (2012) identified nature as a central theme in the writings, connected to other themes such as love, bench, and walk. They also identified two important theme subclusters. The first subcluster, "sacredness," included the themes God, life, time, love, heart, and someone, thus reflecting key notions of remembrance. The second subcluster, "spatial-temporal," included the themes walk, day, spot, bench, and drawing, alluding to design elements in OSSPs. These themes are consistent with the intent and design of Joplin's Butterfly Garden and Overlook. In short, Joplin's OSSP site reflects Tidball's scholarship on civic ecology practices emerging in post-disaster settings and the importance of nature in the recovery process (Tidball 2009, 2012a, 2014a; Tidball and Krasny 2008; Tidball, Krasny, et al. 2011).

The Joplin case also reflects civic ecology's focus on social-ecological memories and topophilia, by including Joplin residents' memories of and attachment to Cunningham Park as an important place in the city's history. Further, the engagement of multiple private and public-sector actors reflects civic ecology's emphasis on governance and civic environmentalism (Sirianni 2009; Krasny and Tidball 2015; see also chapter 8). However, the Joplin case, and in particular the Volunteer Tribute garden, challenge earlier writing about civic ecology. Perhaps most notable is the large role played by outsiders, including a national television show. In deciding to focus on Joplin, *EM:HE* had multiple purposes: rebuilding to help tornado survivors, creating a second wave of voluntarism, and attracting a national audience of television viewers. However, *EM:HE* did not dictate the design of the Volunteer Tribute, which was determined by Drury University students and faculty who integrated local input alongside their expertise in design, psychological resilience, and other fields. The design for the Butterfly Garden and Overlook followed a similar process of students incorporating local concerns, including survivor testimonials recorded by fellow university students, with expertise drawing from multiple disciplines.

Although largely ignored in previous writing, professional design plays an important role in some civic ecology practices. In Joplin, the university designers incorporated the concerns of community members as well as historic elements unique to Cunningham Park (e.g., concentric circle gardens) into the Butterfly Garden design. In contrast, a well-resourced and well-meaning nonprofit organization brought in professional landscape designers and corporate funders to enhance community gardens in New York City, leading to feelings of exclusion among the previous gardeners living in neighborhoods surrounding the gardens (Eizenberg 2013). Design experts have been more sensitive to local needs in the case of spot fixes (short-term cleanups of degraded public space in cities) conducted by the Ugly Indian organization in Bangalore (see chapter 12). For example, design experts have designed no-smell urinals, thus addressing the issue of urination in public spaces, and determined culturally sensitive colors for walls in the newly created pocket parks. Although designers and other experts make critical contributions in some civic ecology practices, they may be largely absent from simpler streamside or park cleanups and grassroots community gardens.

Another important issue raised by the Joplin case is the role of short-term volunteers in urban greening efforts. In researching New York City's Million Trees initiative, Fisher, Svendsen, and Connolly (2015) distinguished between novice volunteers who come out for a single event, and committed volunteers who engage in long-term and multiple forms of environmental stewardship and civic activism. Committed volunteers recruit their friends and colleagues to participate in short-term events as novice volunteers; contribute technical expertise; help plan, monitor, and manage urban forests; and influence urban green-space policy. Both types of volunteers are crucial for large-scale ongoing efforts like citywide tree planting, and in short-term, labor-intensive events like the Joplin greening initiatives. Further, volunteering in one sector can lead to civic activism in other sectors, and longer-term volunteers may be recruited from first-time volunteers (Fisher, Svendsen, and Connolly 2015). The formation of the Drury University SmartMob! is an example of how helping with the Volunteer Tribute led to engagement in the Butterfly Garden and to the creation of an institutional structure that fosters further university engagement in community design efforts.

Finally, the Joplin case demonstrates how universities in particular can contribute to local stewardship efforts, not just through novice voluntarism, but also through service learning and related committed volunteer efforts that draw on student and faculty expertise (Sooter, Chikaraishi, and Hedges 2013). We have observed similar university student novice voluntarism in mangrove restoration in China (Abigail 2016) and litter cleanups on the Cornell campus. In instances of expert-driven voluntarism, Cornell architecture students bring expertise in gravestone restoration to civic ecology practices in a historic city cemetery in Ithaca, New York (Deen 2016), and CEU San Pablo University architecture students applied their design expertise to plan for the restoration of abandoned military dumps near Madrid, Spain (Gálvez Pérez 2016). In another effort, committed members of a Cornell University student club engaged in trail restoration in campus natural areas and influenced campus natural area policy, bringing their passion for the outdoors but no particular academic expertise (Krasny and Delia 2014). In short, whether utilizing short-term university volunteers who may go on to additional civic action (cf. Fisher, Svendsen, and Connolly 2015) or longer-term and expert volunteers who help design restoration projects, form SmartMobs!, and may even influence university policy, consideration of the engagement of university students and faculty in civic ecology practices merits further consideration.

Healing is a matter of time, but it is sometimes also a matter of opportunity.

—Hippocrates

Hippocrates was aware that healing may not take place unless appropriate conditions present themselves. The success of the Volunteer Tribute and the Butterfly Garden and Overlook projects is attributable to involvement of the private, university, civil society, and government actors, and to the relationships that were forged early in the process through participation in the network television show rebuild and the TKF Foundation research grant. From outward to inward, the first wave of support recognized the efforts of the outsiders who helped Joplin, whereas the second wave was to help the Joplin community heal themselves. Strong emotional ties were formed between the government and the university participants, Joplin and Drury, who were proximate to the tornado and can be said to have ridden, but not created, the waves of support.

Partly owing to the severity of the disaster, the Joplin efforts were initiated by outsiders and do not reflect the conventional self-organized nature of civic ecology practices. In this way, they expand our thinking about the diversity of volunteer engagement in urban greening, including the role of design and other types of expertise, of novice and committed volunteers, and of city government and private-sector actors who see the value of greening in urban and post-disaster settings.

Although the initial volunteer builds have been completed, the Volunteer Tribute and Butterfly gardens continue to provide opportunities for tourists to understand the role of nature in healing and for further healing of Joplin residents. Local and outside visitors to Cunningham Park learn about the tornado

FIGURE 9.4   An individual preparing a journal entry. Photo by Evan Melgren, Drury University.

FIGURE 9.5 Walk of Unity, gathering at the Volunteer Tribute, 2012. Photo by Jared Hoffpauir, J. Design Studios.

and the community's responses through the storyboards and write in the journals in the Butterfly Garden. And on the tornado's one-year anniversary, over ten thousand people participated in the Walk of Unity, re-creating the tornado's destructive path in reverse and ending at Cunningham Park. The reverse direction represented the healing process for individuals and families, while the gathering at ground zero in Cunningham Park helped build community strength.

Acknowledgments

We would like to thank the countless hundreds of volunteers and donors for the two projects, which without your assistance would have never come to fruition.

REFERENCES

Abigail, J. 2016. "Cultivating Mangroves." In *Civic Ecology: Stories about Love of Life, Love of Place*, edited by M. E. Krasny and K. Snyder, 1–5. Ithaca, NY: Civic Ecology Lab, Cornell University.

Deen, S. 2016. "Friends of Ithaca City Cemetery." In *Civic Ecology: Stories about Love of Life, Love of Place*, edited by M. E. Krasny and K. Snyder, 43–51. Ithaca, NY: Civic Ecology Lab, Cornell University.

Eizenberg, E. 2012. "The Changing Meaning of Community Space: Two Models of NGO Management of Community Gardens in New York City." *International Journal of Urban and Regional Research* 36 (1): 106–20. doi:10.1111/j.1468-2427.2011.01065.x.

——. 2013. *From the Ground Up: Community Gardens in New York City and the Politics of Spatial Transformation*. Farnham, Surrey, UK: Ashgate.

Fisher, D. R., E. S. Svendsen, and J. J. Connolly. 2015. *Urban Environmental Stewardship and Civic Engagement: How Planting Trees Strengthens the Roots of Democracy*. New York: Routledge.

Gálvez Pérez, M. A. 2016. "Civic Ecology Practices in the 'Waste Grounds' Network of Madrid." In *Civic Ecology: Stories about Love of Life, Love of Place*, edited by M. E. Krasny and K. Snyder, 110–20. Ithaca, NY: Civic Ecology Lab, Cornell University.

Helphand, K. 2006. *Defiant Gardens: Making Gardens in Wartime*. San Antonio, TX: Trinity University Press.

Kansas City Star. 2011. *Joplin 5:41: When a Monster Storm Shattered a Missouri Town but Didn't Break Its Spirit*. Kansas City, MO: Kansas City Star Books.

Kellert, S. R., and E. O. Wilson, eds. 1993. *The Biophilia Hypothesis*. Washington, DC: Island Press.

Kimball, T. 2011. "*Extreme Makeover: Home Edition*: Cancelled, No Season 10 but . . ." TV Series Finale, December 15. http://tvseriesfinale.com/tv-show/extreme-makeover-home-edition-canceled-season-nine-21618/.

Krasny, M. E., and J. Delia. 2014. "Natural Area Stewardship as Part of Campus Sustainability." *Journal of Cleaner Production* 106:87–96. http://dx.doi.org/10.1016/j.jclepro.2014.04.019.

Krasny, M. E., and K. G. Tidball. 2015. *Civic Ecology: Adaptation and Transformation from the Ground Up*. Cambridge, MA: MIT Press.

Letner, J. 2011. "A Fist Coming out of the Sky: Six Miles of Terror." *Joplin Globe*, May 29.

Lieb, D. A. 2012. "Records Show Joplin Twister Was Costliest since 1950." *Rome (GA) News Tribune*, May 20. http://www.northwestgeorgianews.com/rome/records-joplin-twister-was-costliest-since/article_3542db84-fade-5754-9af2-097ac257660d.html.

McMillen, H., L. Campbell, E. S. Svendsen, and R. Reynolds. 2016. "Recognizing Stewardship Practices as Indicators of Social Resilience: In Living Memorials and in a Community Garden." *Sustainability* 8 (8): 775.

Mueller, G. M., Jr. 2008. Foreword to *Open Spaces Sacred Places*, edited by T. Stoner and C. Rapp, 9–13. Annapolis, MD: TKF Foundation.

Okvat, H., and A. Zautra. 2014. "Sowing Seeds of Resilience: Community Gardening in a Post-disaster Context." In *Greening in the Red Zone: Disaster, Resilience and Community Greening*, edited by K. G. Tidball and M. E. Krasny, 73–90. New York: Springer.

Onstot, L. 2013. "Joplin, Missouri Hit by EF-5 Tornado on May 22, 2011." Joplin, MO: City of Joplin.

Real-McKeighan, T. 2011. "Fremonters Hear Amazing Stories while on Mission Trip to Joplin." *Fremont (NE) Tribune*, June 14.

Rohr, M. 2012. *Miracle of the Human Spirit*. Mustang, OK: Tate Publishing and Enterprises.

Simpson, L. 2011. "Chapters Erased from Joplin's Architectural History." Historic Joplin. http://www.historicjoplin.org/?tag=blendville.

Sirianni, C. 2009. *Investing in Democracy: Engaging Citizens in Collaborative Governance*. Washington, DC: Brookings Institution Press.

Sooter, T. D., N. Chikaraishi, and K. Hedges. 2013. "Extreme Service-Learning: Engaging a University Design-Build Course with a Broadcast Network Television Show in the Aftermath of the Joplin Tornado." In *New Developments in Structural Engineering and Construction*, edited by S. Yazdani and A. Singh, 1463–68. Singapore: Research Publishing.

——. 2014. "Whole School Design-Build in the Liberal Arts Tradition." In *Working Out: Thinking While Building*, edited by T. Cavanagh, U. Hartig, and S. Pallerino, 546–54. Washington, DC: ACSA.

SPC-NOAA (Storm Prediction Center–National Oceanic and Atmospheric Administration). 2015. "The 25 Deadliest U.S. Tornadoes." http://www.spc.noaa.gov/faq/tornado/killers.html.

Stoner, T., and C. Rapp, eds. 2008. *Open Spaces Sacred Places*. Annapolis, MD: TKF Foundation.

Svendsen, E. S., and L. Campbell. 2005. "Living Memorials Project: Year 1 Social and Site Assessment." *US Forest Service General Technical Report NE-333*. Newtown Square, PA: U.S. Department of Agriculture, Forest Service, Northern Research Station.

——. 2006. "Land-Markings: 12 Journeys through 9/11 Living Memorials." Newtown Square, PA: U.S. Department of Agriculture, Forest Service, Northern Research Station.

Tidball, K. G. 2009. "Trees and Rebirth: Ritual and Symbol in Community-Based Urban Reforestation Recovery Efforts in Post-Katrina New Orleans." Philadelphia: American Anthropological Association.

——. 2012a. "Greening in the Red Zone: Valuing Community-Based Ecological Restoration in Human Vulnerability Contexts." PhD diss., Cornell University.

——. 2012b. "Urgent Biophilia: Human-Nature Interactions and Biological Attractions in Disaster Resilience." *Ecology and Society* 17 (2): 5. http://dx.doi.org/10.5751/ES-04596-170205.

——. 2014a. "Peace Research and Greening in the Red Zone: Community-Based Ecological Restoration to Enhance Resilience and Transitions toward Peace." In *Expanding Peace Ecology: Peace, Security, Sustainability, Equity and Gender: Perspectives of IPRA's Ecology and Peace Commission*, edited by U. O. Spring, H. G. Brauch, and K. G. Tidball, 63–83. Berlin: Springer-Verlag.

——. 2014b. "Trees and Rebirth: Social-Ecological Symbols and Rituals in the Resilience of Post-Katrina New Orleans." In *Greening in the Red Zone: Disaster, Resilience and Community Greening*, edited by K. G. Tidball and M. E. Krasny, 257–96. New York: Springer.

——. 2014c. "Urgent Biophilia: Human-Nature Interactions in Red Zone Recovery and Resilience." In *Greening in the Red Zone: Disaster, Resilience and Community Greening*, edited by K. G. Tidball and M. E. Krasny, 53–73. New York: Springer.

Tidball, K. G., and M. E. Krasny. 2008. "'Raising' Urban Resilience: Community Forestry and Greening in Cities Post-disaster/conflict." Resilience, Adaptation and Transformation in Turbulent Times, Resilience Alliance Conference, Stockholm, Sweden, April 14–17.

——, eds. 2014. *Greening in the Red Zone: Disaster, Resilience and Community Greening*. New York: Springer.

Tidball, K. G., M. E. Krasny, E. S. Svendsen, L. Campbell, and K. Helphand. 2011. "Stewardship, Learning, and Memory in Disaster Resilience." In *Resilience in Social-Ecological Systems: The Role of Learning and Education*, edited by M. E. Krasny, C. Lundholm, and R. Plummer, 120–37. New York: Routledge.

Tidball, K. G., and R. C. Stedman. 2013. "Positive Dependency and Virtuous Cycles: From Resource Dependence to Resilience in Urban Social-Ecological Systems." *Ecological Economics* 86:292–99. http://dx.doi.org/10.1016/j.ecolecon.2012.10.004.

Tidball, K. G., E. S. Svendsen, L. K. Campbell, N. Falxa-Raymond, and K. L. Wolf. 2012. "Preliminary Analysis of TKF 'Book & Bench' Texts Using Unsupervised Semantic Mapping of Natural Language with Leximancer Concept Mapping." Ithaca, NY: Civic Ecology Lab, Cornell University.

U.S. Census Bureau. 2015. "Joplin, Missouri EF-5 Tornado: May 22, 2011." Emergency Preparedness. https://www.census.gov/topics/preparedness/events/tornadoes/2011-missouri.html.

Wilson, E. O. 1984. *Biophilia*. Cambridge, MA: Harvard University Press.

Worden, J. W. 1991. *Grief Counseling and Grief Therapy: A Handbook for the Mental Health Practitioner*. 2nd ed. London: Springer.

Chapter 10

COUNTERING ENVIRONMENTAL GENTRIFICATION THROUGH ECONOMIC, CULTURAL, AND POLITICAL EQUITY

The 11th Street Bridge Park

Dennis Chestnut and Marianne E. Krasny

The Anacostia Freeway went up the same year as the Berlin Wall. It meant about the same thing.

(Washington, DC, blues musician Nap Turner, quoted in Williams 2001, 420)

Olin partner Hallie Boyce said the design would encourage interaction between both sides of the river and become a destination for people from around the city. "We knew it had to be both connector and place," she said.

(O'Connell 2014)

Even before the Navy Yard was constructed along the west shore of the Anacostia River in 1799, tobacco farmers had cleared much of the native forest in the surrounding watershed. Rain washed soil off farm fields, clogging up the river and reducing its navigability (Haynes 2013). By 1883, modern warships could no longer wend their way up the river, so the Navy Yard abandoned ship manufacturing and began producing guns and ammunition. As it expanded to meet the demand for armaments during World War II, the Navy Yard displaced hundreds of Anacostia residents and spewed chemical effluent into the river, eventually leading to the Navy Yard's designation as a Superfund site (Wennersten 2008). Today, manufacturing has ceased, and the Navy Yard site has been cleaned up and converted to housing and office space for government, nonprofits, and private incubator firms.

The Anacostia River is often referred to as Washington's "other river," bordered by the city's "forgotten neighborhoods." As wealthier and whiter neighborhoods along the more prominent Potomac River received the bulk of the public's attention, Anacostia neighborhoods were neglected. Although the abolition-ist Frederick Douglass bought a home in Anacostia in 1877, it wasn't until after World War II that many African Americans moved into and eventually became the majority of residents in the area. The construction of a freeway in the 1960s cut off Anacostia residents from the river, which at the time had become so polluted as to be avoided in any case. Yet in the face of exclusion and environmental deteriora-tion, African Americans attempted to reclaim the river starting in the 1940s. Today kayakers can enjoy a leisurely paddle along the river. But as the river transforms from an eyesore to an amenity, it carries with it the threat of environmental gen-trification and of changing the face—and faces—of Anacostia's neighborhoods.

How have Anacostia's African American stewards, more recently joined by environmental nonprofits, helped transform the river and its neighborhoods? And what might be done to avert displacement of low-income African American residents living in a gentrifying Anacostia? We begin with the black Seafarers Yacht Club in the 1940s, and follow the story of stewardship and cleanup in what is now considered "green-space-rich" Anacostia. We end with a look at the 11th Street Bridge Park—an initiative that from the beginning set out to tie the green-ing of derelict infrastructure with equitable urban development, and thus avoid the environmental gentrification that has accompanied other greening efforts, ranging from community gardening to New York City's High Line.

As we trace the history of environmental stewardship and activism along the Anacostia River and its tributaries, we demonstrate how communities excluded from the river created their own ways to access and to care for the river and its humans, fish, birds, and other inhabitants. We also explore how communi-ties negatively impacted by the river's use as an industrial, defense, and sew-age dumping ground and as a transportation corridor have joined forces with environmental organizations and government agencies to transform pockets of the watershed and its neighborhoods. In this way, we examine environmental justice issues of "inclusion" in environmental degradation and "exclusion" from environmental goods, as well as how nonprofits, government, and community members respond to these issues. Finally, we explore efforts to thwart physical displacement of long-term lower-income residents. We use the case of the 11th Street Bridge Park and how it is creating new strategies to ensure housing, cul-tural, and political equity.

In addressing the issue of environmental gentrification, this chapter adds a cau-tionary tale about civic ecology practices and larger-scale urban greening. The fact that an urban neighborhood, still pockmarked by vacant properties and stricken by industrial contamination, is becoming a desirable place for people to live reflects how civic ecology practices can be one factor among others in revitalizing U.S.

cities. Partly as a result of the cleanup of the river and consistent with national demographic trends, young professionals are moving to Anacostia, creating impetus for further green development and environmental gentrification. This chapter also offers hope for countering a trend toward exclusion of long-term, low-income residents—the same residents who often initiate civic ecology practices—in neighborhoods that have become desirable to newer and wealthier residents.

Green Space and Stewardship in DC's Forgotten Neighborhoods

Before there was Earth Justice or Friends of the Earth there were black yachtsmen who loved the Anacostia. Yes, they admitted, it was a tired old river, but there was also delight to be found in the sound of fish jumping on a summer's eve, and gentle breezes offered refuge from Washington's intense summer heat. Moreover, the river was theirs—beyond the purview of haughty whites whose expensive boats seldom ventured farther than Haines Point.

(Wennersten 2008, 224)

In one sense, Anacostia's residents are blessed with "environmental goods." Green space is abundant, and the river and its tributaries flow gently through neighborhoods. Along the shores of the Anacostia are the Kenilworth Aquatic Gardens—a preserved wetland that boasts expanses of lily pads inhabited by frogs, egrets, and great blue herons. The Anacostia Riverwalk Trail runs along both sides of the river, and Anacostia Park, operated by the National Park Service, offers inline skating, picnicking, golfing, and a swimming pool. But Anacostia's African American residents have historically faced hurdles to accessing these environmental goods—including social exclusion, pollution, and even life-threatening dangers.

Like much of Anacostia, the swimming pool—just a few short miles from the U.S. Capitol Building—has a history steeped in racial segregation. A June 29, 1949, newspaper article titled "Police Called in Washington Race Fighting: Pool Segregation Is Cause of Rows" starts out,

> More than 20 policemen were called out to halt a series of fights between Negroes and whites in the vicinity of Anacostia park swimming pool today in the latest flare-up over racial segregation at the city's pools. . . .
> Last Sunday, six Negro youths were booed and forced by white bathers to leave a pool which the Negro youngsters attempted to enter. Each

day for about a week larger groups of Negroes have been appearing at pools customarily patronized only by whites. . . .

The situation has developed into a row between the Interior department, which insists there be no segregation in the pools; the District of Columbia recreation board, which served an ultimatum that Negroes and whites must use separate pools, and various civic groups which are split on the issue. (*Chicago Daily Tribune* 1949, 2)

For children growing up when pools were segregated, the Anacostia River and its tributaries offered a welcome, albeit less protected, alternative for swimming during Washington's sultry summers. Another open space that children frequented was the Kenilworth dump; such outings were curtailed after 1968, when a seven-year-old boy perished in one of the dump's persistent trash fires. The hilltop forts encircling the city as part of the Civil War defenses of Washington, which had once offered sanctuary for fleeing slaves, provided additional open space (Williams 2002). And despite river siltation and rampant dumping, black men continued to enjoy the quiet waters of the Anacostia in their small skiffs (Wennersten 2008).

Unfortunately, these black boaters could not find a place to dock their boats at the whites-only boat clubs. During the 1940s, the Department of Interior refused to rent slips to black residents along the Anacostia. So the black boaters enlisted the help of Mary McLeod Bethune, a member of Franklin Roosevelt's "Black Cabinet" and a friend of Eleanor Roosevelt. Mrs. Roosevelt in turn called on Interior Secretary Harold Ickes, who granted permission for the Seafarers Yacht Club. Built in 1945 and thought to be the oldest African American yacht club in the United States, the Seafarers Yacht Club is part of a long tradition of black sailors that started before the American Revolution and continued during slave times when seafaring offered a chance to escape the bonds of plantation life (Wennersten 2008).

From the beginning, the Seafarers Yacht Club was not just a recreational boating club. Its members and their families embodied Anacostia's sprit of civic engagement through offering emergency assistance to flood victims, helping to feed needy neighbors, and, starting in 1985, conducting annual riverside cleanups. The Seafarers' cleanups were eventually subsumed into the annual Anacostia Watershed Society's Anacostia River Cleanup Day, which today enlists nearly two thousand volunteers each year (Williams 2001; Anacostia Watershed Society 2014).

In addition to cleaning up the river, Anacostia residents cared for small public spaces. Retired schoolteacher Frieda Murray cofounded the Anacostia Garden Club in the 1990s, and persuaded her fellow gardeners to plant flowers and cherry trees in a tiny triangle park at a busy Anacostia intersection. "I want those commuters sitting there waiting for the light to see how lovely this neighborhood is," Mrs. Murray told a *Washington Post* news reporter. "I want them to know the people of this neighborhood care" (Wheeler 1998).

At around the same time that Murray enlisted gardeners to demonstrate care for their neighborhood, Anacostia resident Dennis Chestnut organized his neighbors to pick up trash on their block. From there he ventured into a leadership role with the nonprofit Washington Parks and People, and helped convert a derelict strip along Watts Branch tributary into a vibrant walkway and green space called Marvin Gaye Park, its name commemorating a local boy who became a Motown singing and songwriting star, only to die tragically in gun violence. Similar to how the Seafarers Yacht Club began to expand its stewardship activities in partnership with the Anacostia Watershed Society, Dennis, in his next position as director of Groundwork Anacostia River DC, linked up with local environmental organizations to bring about multiple changes in the Anacostia River and community.

Dennis grew up in Anacostia and remembers exploring its creeks, green spaces, river, and landfill as a child, and being excluded from the neighborhood whites-only swimming pool. He describes his work and recent changes in Anacostia, a place he has lived his entire life.

> Before assuming the leadership at Groundwork Anacostia, I was a master carpenter and vocational educator. The combination of these skills and my love for the outdoors led me to develop programs that include environmental youth leadership and green workforce development. One such initiative is Groundwork's Bandalong Litter Trap program, which reduces trash and floatable debris entering the Anacostia River. Partnering with DC's Department of Energy and Environment and Anacostia RiverKeeper, Groundwork Anacostia hires youth to manage four Bandalong litter traps and utilizes the program for workforce development, environmental stewardship, and creating the next generation of conservation leaders.
>
> I believe that to increase access to and use of Anacostia's many green spaces and waterfront, these natural assets must be clean, safe, and well maintained. I also believe that the residents must be involved in the entire revitalization process. I see how the recent confluence of pedestrian and bike trails connected to the waterfront and Anacostia Park corridor will serve as an economic engine, help fuel revitalization and green infrastructure improvements, and create an opportunity for residents to gain the skills required to install and maintain these green infrastructure projects—all of which are greatly needed in Anacostia's poor, African American neighborhoods. Just as participation of local residents in civic

and green revitalization is crucial to green-space use and access, participation in this economic renaissance by existing residents is critical in order to build the needed resilience to potential gentrification.

I have seen the number of civic and environmental organizations in Anacostia grow. Groundwork Anacostia is now a member of a newly formed network of local nonprofits, the Anacostia Park and Community

FIGURE 10.1 Author Dennis Chestnut gives directions to Earth Conservation Corps stewardship interns at Marvin Gaye Park. Photo by Alex Russ.

Collaborative, which is a project of the Anacostia Waterfront Trust. The Anacostia Waterfront Trust is a newly formed, citizen-led nonprofit organization committed to transforming the Anacostia River corridor into a place that unites the nation's capital. The centerpiece of this effort will be a vibrant, twenty-first-century civic space on a healthy river, providing enormous benefits to the entire region, but especially the communities nearby. In the words of former DC mayor and chairman of the Anacostia Waterfront Trust Anthony A. Williams, "It's time for Anacostia Park to become Washington's twenty-first century waterfront—the model for other urban parks across the nation."

A Changing River

Through the years, Anacostia residents have attributed different meanings to their river: a place to fish and swim, a putrid place to avoid at all costs, a place to restore and revitalize, and a place that divides the rich from the poor, the white from the black (Williams 2001). Realizing that residents who viewed the river as a dangerous, filthy, smelly place would never join efforts to clean it up, starting in the late 1980s the Anacostia Watershed Society, the Seafarers Yacht Club, and other organizations began a conscious effort to have people experience the river in canoes and kayaks. As the river quality improved, other groups joined in, like the Anacostia River Rowing Center just below the 11th Street Bridge. The Rowing Center started offering free lessons and use of boats to youth living in Anacostia, and eventually was joined by the Capital Rowing Club, which relocated to the Anacostia River from Washington's larger and more celebrated Potomac (Anacostia Community Boathouse, n.d.). In the words of Robert Boone, founder of the Anacostia Watershed Society, "If you remove the visible blight, people will come back. We did river cleanups, road side cleanups. The message was simple: Clean it up!" (Anacostia Watershed Society 2014, 4).

Today, an ethic of caring for the river is visible throughout Anacostia. Rowers and canoers glide by recently returned bald eagles and great blue herons, and interns install wetland fences to thwart the ever-present Canada geese from decimating native wild rice (Haynes 2013). Groups embedded in African American communities like Groundwork Anacostia River DC, and groups with white leadership like Anacostia RiverKeeper and the Anacostia Watershed Society, are working together toward environmental restoration linked to community revitalization. The Navy Yard no longer spews toxic wastes into the river; rather, it houses a vibrant community of businesses, nonprofits, and residents, often newcomers to the city attracted by its walkability, green space, and jobs.

FIGURE 10.2 Enjoying peaceful nature alongside the Anacostia River. Photo by Alex Russ.

Today, a critical piece of this restoration and revitalization puzzle is the 11th Street Bridge Park. The park is envisioned as "Washington, D.C.'s first elevated public park located on the piers of the old 11th Street Bridge spanning the Anacostia River: a new venue for healthy recreation, environmental education and the arts" (11th Street Bridge Park, n.d.-a). And referring to how the river has historically divided the rich white and poor black neighborhoods, the American Society of Landscape Architects states, "The 11th Street Bridge Park will be the first of its kind. This landscape will be a vibrant destination park which reuses aged infrastructure to connect. . . . [It] will bring the citizens of Washington together, and to the edges of the Anacostia River. . . . When complete, the bridge park will span the length of three football fields" (Myers 2016).

As long-term residents of low-income, African American neighborhoods on the east side of the river are "brought together" with newer, whiter, and richer residents at the former Navy Yard, how will the 11th Street Bridge Park avert environmental gentrification accompanied by burgeoning rents that force out Anacostia's poorer residents? Do recent housing and office building development in the former Navy Yard, and rebranding of the Anacostia River from a filthy, smelly, dangerous place to an urban recreation way, portend a wave of "sustainable" or "green" development that creates new social and environmental injustices (Checker 2011; Agyeman and Evans 2004)? After providing an overview of environmental gentrification, we explore ways residents, government, and the nonprofit and private sectors have sought to foster equity in the face of rising housing costs that accompany urban greening in U.S. cities.

Environmental Gentrification

Gentrification can be characterized as "a rapid increase in property values and rents, improvements to the housing stock, and the replacement of lower-income residents with middle- to upper-class households," which often leads to "displacement, financial burden, and loss of political influence for long-time residents" (Pearsall 2012, 1014). Urban sustainability initiatives, including civic ecology practices, create amenities in a neighborhood and thus can be a driver of gentrification as new, wealthier residents move into neighborhoods that have become greener and safer. Thus, despite the health, community, and environmental benefits of converting derelict industrial and transportation infrastructure and vacant lots to parks, community gardens, and other "green" amenities, such improvements can lead to displacement of longtime, lower-income residents—or, more simply, efforts to provide access to environmental goods can lead to exclusion from these same goods (Marche 2015; Anguelovski 2016; Wolch, Byrne, and Newell 2014).

Based on a study of homeless people's use of public green space in Seattle, Dooling (2009, 630) defined ecological gentrification as "the implementation of an environmental planning agenda related to public green spaces that leads to the displacement or exclusion of the most economically vulnerable human population—homeless people—while espousing an environmental ethic." Checker (2011, 212, 216) expanded beyond homeless people to include low-income residents and residents of color in her definition of environmental gentrification—"the convergence of urban redevelopment, ecologically-minded initiatives and environmental justice activism in an era of advanced capitalism," or simply, "greening and whitening" of neighborhoods. Environmental gentrification has been taken up by the environmental justice movement, which has expanded from its original fight against inequitable exposure to toxics ("brown" environmental justice) to advocating for access to green space and against displacement of low-income and homeless residents in the face of urban greening ("green" environmental justice: Anguelovski 2013; Marche 2015).

A classic example of how converting derelict transportation and industrial infrastructure to green amenities can lead to increased property values is Manhattan's High Line. The High Line was built on a derelict elevated rail line that in the early 1900s delivered goods to and from Manhattan's meat processing plants. It is a stunning transformation of abandoned infrastructure to a landscape whose design synthesizes natural and human history, and has become one of the top tourist destinations in New York City, with more than seven million visitors annually (Dunphy 2016). In an article called "Disney World on the Hudson," the High Line was described as "a tourist-clogged catwalk and a catalyst for some of the most rapid gentrification in the city's history" (Moss 2012). Tourists come and go, but apartment dwellers stay . . . provided they can. Like weeds that invaded the railroad bed when it was abandoned in the 1930s, in recent years luxury apartments have sprouted on both sides of the High Line, replacing moderately priced housing and abandoned warehouses. With the median price of condos along the High Line topping $6 million, the Meatpacking District is a far cry from its pre–High Line days. The High Line's so-called halo effect has become a crown of thorns for old-time residents who depended on affordable housing (Barbanel 2016).

At the other end of the meticulously designed, well-heeled spectrum of urban sustainability represented by the High Line are vacant-lot community gardens. Yet these tiny, citizen-managed green spaces also add green amenities and may even reduce crime (Branas et al. 2011; Hurley 2004) and contribute to environmental gentrification. At the same time, residents who take the initiative to create something of value in neighborhoods neglected by municipal governments may become empowered to resist commercial development and gentrification (Marche 2015; Anguelovski 2013). Thus, while civic ecology practices can be a driver of environmental gentrification, civic ecology stewards often fight desperately to hold on to these practices and the green space they create, including in low-income neighborhoods and communities of color (Smith and Kurtz 2003; Schmelzkopf 1995; Anguelovski 2013; Newman 2008; Reynolds and Cohen 2016).

Countering Environmental Gentrification

Countering environmental gentrification entails actions to ensure that long-term residents are able to remain in their neighborhood and that the neighborhood reflects aspects of place valued by those residents. Residents, municipal governments, and the nonprofit and private sectors all play a role.

"Equitable revitalization" refers to efforts to avoid displacement of residents, ensure long-term affordable housing, and create economic opportunities, thus helping residents to remain in a neighborhood when housing prices rise. Municipal governments and nonprofit strategies to counter displacement include providing homeowners with information on how to avoid predatory lending and foreclosure and providing tenants right of first refusal and assistance in buying homes. Governments and nonprofits also can maintain and expand affordable housing through rent control; grants, loans, or tax abatements to landlords; inclusionary zoning (requiring developers to set aside low-income housing in exchange for expedited building permits and other compensation); and acquiring and rehabilitating privately owned properties as affordable housing (Dooling 2009; Center for Community Progress, n.d.). Strategies deployed by residents in New York City neighborhoods undergoing brownfield cleanup and redevelopment included leveraging social networks (e.g., finding roommates to share apartment costs) and seeking out rent-stabilized apartments, public housing, or housing assistance (Pearsall 2012, 2013).

Residents and their allies also use political strategies to maintain affordable housing and valued green space, ranging from speaking out at community board meetings, to seeking historic area designation, to large-scale, highly visible protests (Pearsall 2012, 2013; Center for Community Progress, n.d.). In New York City in the 1990s, community gardeners, attempting to preserve their gardens in the face of development pressure and hostility stemming from Mayor Giuliani's administration, captured media attention by chaining themselves to fences bordering their gardens. Their protests also captured the attention of the state attorney general, who intervened by designating park status to community gardens that fulfilled public access and other requirements (Smith and Kurtz 2003). At around the same time, the NGO Trust for Public Land purchased nearly seventy New York City garden properties, eventually transferring them to community land trusts created to help preserve the gardens (TPL 2011; Eizenberg 2012). Although the New York Restoration Project also bought up community gardens, it converted them to professionally landscaped gardens sponsored by major corporations. This new nonprofit saw its work as cleaning up uncared-for eyesores, but the earlier community gardeners felt unwelcome in gardens that appeared "gentrified" (Eizenberg 2012). Such varied efforts to preserve community gardens provide evidence of how countering environmental gentrification encompasses not just maintaining housing but also holding on to aspects of local "place" that are created and valued by residents (Anguelovski and Martínez Alier 2014; Anguelovski 2013; Curran and Hamilton 2012).

Initiatives to convert vacant and derelict urban properties to urban gardens and farms represent a second movement in U.S. land trusts, following on the footsteps of the original 1960s land trust movement organized to help rural African American farmers secure land (Hachmyer 2013; Baldwin et al., n.d.; Davis 2014; DSNI 2016). The Dudley Street Neighborhood Initiative in Boston represents a third community land-trust movement focused on securing land to thwart gentrification. This comprehensive effort began in 1988 in a neighborhood where one-third of the property was vacant. Over time, the Dudley Street Neighborhood Initiative has converted vacant properties to affordable housing and open space, including a community greenhouse, small parks, and community gardens. It also helped launch additional community land trusts in Chinatown and other Boston neighborhoods. As housing prices in Boston have risen, the Boston community land trusts have assumed new importance as a means to enable home ownership for low-income residents.

In Philadelphia, community land trusts are working with municipal land banks to retain affordable housing, establish communal property rights, and encourage urban agriculture, community gardening, and other types of green space stewardship (Baldwin et al., n.d.; Hachmyer 2013). Under pressure from a coalition of community, labor, and faith groups, the City of Philadelphia established a municipal land bank in 2014, which seeks to assume ownership and facilitate community control over the city's thousands of vacant parcels, and to ensure that the properties are "developed with the long-term interests of the community in mind" (Alexander 2005). The land bank is partnering with the Neighborhood Garden Trust to identify, establish long-term leases for, and transfer ownership of community garden properties to ensure they are managed for the collective benefit of residents (Loh 2015; Campaign to Take Back the Vacant Land, n.d.).

In some cases, low-income residents facing the threat of gentrification have advocated for preserving spaces that appear derelict to outsiders but have meaning for long-term residents (Checker 2011). These residents use "just green enough" strategies to fight for a "just sustainability" (Agyeman and Evans 2004) as an alternative to the high-end "parks, cafés, and a riverwalk" model of urban sustainability. The cleanup of Newtown Creek in the Greenpoint neighborhood of Brooklyn illustrates how "just green enough" strategies can "improve the health and quality of life of existing residents, but not so literally green as to attract upscale 'sustainable' LEED-certified residential developments that drive out working-class residents and industrial businesses" (Curran and Hamilton 2012, 1028). One factor contributing to Greenpoint's ability to slow gentrification was that both long-term working-class residents and younger newcomers with previous activism experience shared a common vision for incorporating green and historic industrial features into development. Further, the area was designated as a Superfund site, which required active participation of residents in planning and enabled access to state funds for local government and community-led brownfield redevelopment efforts. The residents chose to maintain an industrial corridor and a working waterfront that would provide an alternative to market-led commercial and residential development and would encourage boat transport as an alternative to trucks (Curran and Hamilton 2012). Superfund designation can also thwart private development and thus counter gentrification because of so called "place stigmatization" (Pearsall 2013).

Anacostia's 11th Street Bridge Park

"Anacostia Crossing," the proposal for the 11th Street Bridge Park, does not describe plans to simply convert pilings remaining from an earlier car bridge into a pedestrian bridge. It proposes a pedestrian bridge with a central plaza, a café, and interactive art and theater, along with hammocks and nets that allow people to dangle out over the river. Also proposed are a waterfall, an environmental education center, rain gardens, urban agriculture, and, harking back to the black Seafarers Yacht Club, a boat launch. The project, which aims to "create economic development, improve public health, connect communities on either side of the river and re-engage residents with the river itself," is envisioned "as a defining feature for a river typically characterized by the pollution it endures and a yawning gap in economic fortunes between residents on its two banks" (O'Connell 2014).

As an innovative use of outdated infrastructure not unlike Manhattan's High Line, the 11th Street Bridge Park has already incited concerns about—and action to counter—environmental gentrification. As one resident who wants to help African American residents build equity and receive preference for upcoming business opportunities remarked, "If you look at the city in recent years, you can see it: If you can pay, you can stay" (O'Connell 2016).

Learning from the mistakes of past green infrastructure projects, 11th Street Bridge Park project director Scott Kratz has committed to a series of efforts to avert environmental gentrification. Prior to thinking about park design, he and his colleagues facilitated more than two hundred public planning meetings to engage neighborhood residents and business owners alongside government officials, policy experts, and nonprofit partners. Residents expressed enthusiasm for the proposed park but wanted to see it coupled with community spaces for social services, health, and cultural programs, alongside the creation of jobs, workforce development, affordable housing, and opportunities for local businesses. Once the decision was made to go forward with the park, community members participated in a series of design charrettes, and through community meetings, design oversight committees, and voting, helped choose the architectural firm to proceed with their designs.

Kratz then decided to align the 11th Street Bridge Park with an east-of-the-river nonprofit, Building Bridges Across the River, which helps provide educational, health, cultural, recreation, and workforce development programs for Anacostia residents, and will take the lead in moving forward with park construction. The 11th Street Bridge Park also joined forces with the DC Office of the Local Initiatives Support Corporation (LISC) to conduct a yearlong equitable-development planning process involving multiple meetings on both sides of the river. This led to the Equitable Development Plan, whose goal is to ensure that the park is a driver of inclusive development for low-income communities of color in the vicinity of the park and becomes an example of how "public and private sectors can invest in and create world-class public space in an equitable manner" (11th Street Bridge Park, n.d.-b, 5). Strategies to support affordable housing include creating a home-buyers' club working in partnership with nonprofit housing developers and efforts to launch a community land trust to acquire vacant and blighted properties for future housing. Support for small business enterprise and workforce development will come through a network of local businesses and setting local hiring goals for construction and operations (O'Connell 2016). In 2016, LISC put money on the table by launching its $50 million Elevating Equity initiative to "foster equity, inclusiveness, and an improved quality of life in the neighborhoods surrounding the future 11th Street Bridge Park." It uses a combination of loans, grants, and technical expertise to build and preserve affordable housing, as well as support community-serving nonprofits and programs that assist lower-income families and improve the quality of life in the neighborhood.

But the 11th Street Bridge Park did not stop with housing and economic development. Kratz and his LISC colleagues also wanted to ensure cultural, social, and political equity. LISC's Elevating Equity initiative has supported organizations working to promote residents' mental health, access to green space and healthy foods, cultural and music festivals, and historic preservation (LISC 2015). And to help build the next generation of civic and political leaders, Kratz is working to develop a series of workshops for community members on how to forge consensus and develop other policy-making skills.

Drawing from the experience of other gentrifying neighborhoods, Kratz (2017) shared four principles to follow in order to avoid the economic and cultural isolation that drives long-term residents to relocate. First, use green infrastructure projects as a platform for long-term residents to tell their stories, and to show how "newcomers can join rather than supersede the existing community." Second, define quantifiable goals and benchmarks for agreements with the private sector and government for housing and jobs, and include consequences for not meeting those goals. Third, begin early with steps like homebuyers' clubs and community land trusts before housing prices make such efforts prohibitive. Finally, support local organizations, provide training, and include all residents in planning to avert cultural and political displacement. According to Kratz (2017),

> Hopefully, by learning from [past gentrification], Anacostia will be a more vibrant, equitable, and inclusive community when it gets its new bridge-park in a few years. Acknowledging that the project simply will not be a success if longtime residents can't live near it or don't feel welcome to use it shows the 11th Street Bridge Park is starting off on the right foot. Thinking about political and cultural displacement, and finding positive ways to respect and lift up the neighborhood's history, can make sure [the project] remains on the right track moving forward.

Because gentrification often accompanies the green transformation of derelict properties and industrial and transportation infrastructure, the sustainable-cities movement has been criticized for focusing on environment and economic development, while failing to address social and economic equity (Agyeman and Evans 2004). Although smaller in scale than large green infrastructure projects like the High Line and the 11th Street Bridge Park, civic ecology practices often form networks with other civic and environmental groups that collectively transform neighborhoods and thus contribute to gentrification. When civic ecology practices and large green infrastructure projects are integrated into initiatives that address housing and jobs, and seek to maintain the cultural and political fabric of a community, the potential for more equitable development exists. As illustrated by the 11th Street Bridge Park, committing to long-term and meaningful citizen engagement from the time a new greening initiative is just a vague idea is critical to honoring the efforts of previous local stewards like the members of Seafarers Yacht Club, and to ensuring that their descendants can maintain their homes, find employment, and carry on their unique cultures.

FIGURE 10.3   Architectural drawings for the planned 11th Street Bridge Park. Image courtesy of OMA+OLIN.

Acknowledgments

The authors thank Adam Kent from LISC and Scott Kratz and Jessica Smith from 11th Street Bridge Park for sharing their work in Anacostia and for providing feedback on this chapter. We also thank Bjorn Whitmore for critical comments on the chapter.

REFERENCES

Agyeman, J., and B. Evans. 2004. "'Just Sustainability': The Emerging Discourse of Environmental Justice in Britain?" *Geographical Journal* 170 (2): 155–64. doi:10.1111/j.0016-7398.2004.00117.x.

Alexander, F. S. 2005. *Land Bank Authorities: A Guide for the Creation and Operation of Local Land Banks*. New York: Local Initiatives Support Corporation.

Anacostia Community Boathouse. n.d. "History: Two Decades of Non-motorized Recreational Boating on the Anacostia." http://www.anacostiaboathouse.org/about/history.

Anacostia Watershed Society. 2014. *What Does It Take to Clean a River? The Anacostia*. Bladensburg, MD: Anacostia Watershed Society.

Anguelovski, I. 2013. "New Directions in Urban Environmental Justice: Rebuilding Community, Addressing Trauma, and Remaking Place." *Journal of Planning Education and Research* 33 (2): 160–75.

——. 2016. "From Toxic Sites to Parks as (Green) LULUs? New Challenges of Inequity, Privilege, Gentrification, and Exclusion for Urban Environmental Justice." *Journal of Planning Literature* 31 (1): 1–14. doi:10.1177/0885412215610491.

Anguelovski, I., and J. M. Alier. 2014. "The 'Environmentalism of the Poor' Revisited: Territory and Place in Disconnected Glocal Struggles." *Ecological Economics* 102:167–76. http://dx.doi.org/10.1016/j.ecolecon.2014.04.005.

Baldwin, B., M. Gay, R. Nagin, V. Kulwicki, and J. Wool. n.d. *Development without Displacement: The Case for Community Land Trusts.* Medford, MA: Tufts University.

Barbanel, J. 2016. "The High Line's 'Halo Effect' on Property: Residential Values along the Park Appreciate Faster Than Those Farther Away." *Wall Street Journal* (online), August 7. http://search.proquest.com/docview/1809530445?pq-origsite=summon.

Branas, C. C., R. A. Cheney, J. M. MacDonald, V. W. Tam, T. D. Jackson, and T. R. Ten Have. 2011. "A Difference-in-Differences Analysis of Health, Safety, and Greening Vacant Urban Space." *American Journal of Epidemiology* 174 (11): 1296–1306. doi:10.1093/aje/kwr273.

Campaign to Take Back the Vacant Land. n.d. "Partnership Potential: Land Banks and Community Land Trusts." http://takebackvacantland.org/?page_id=253.

Center for Community Progress. n.d. "Preventing Involuntary Displacement of the Neighborhood's Lower-Income Residents." Accessed September 16, 2016. http://www.communityprogress.net/preventing-involuntary-displacement-of-the-neighborhood-s-lower-income-residents-pages-243.php.

Checker, M. 2011. "Wiped Out by the 'Greenwave': Environmental Gentrification and the Paradoxical Politics of Urban Sustainability." *City & Society* 23 (2): 210–29. doi:10.1111/j.1548-744X.2011.01063.x.

Chicago Daily Tribune. 1949. "Police Called in Washington Race Fighting: Pool Segregation Is Cause of Rows." June 29. http://archives.chicagotribune.com/1949/06/29/page/2/article/police-called-in-washington-race-fighting.

Curran, W., and T. Hamilton. 2012. "Just Green Enough: Contesting Environmental Gentrification in Greenpoint, Brooklyn." *Local Environment* 17 (9): 1027–42.

Davis, J. E. 2014. "Origins and Evolution of the Community Land Trust in the United States." Community-Wealth.org.

Dooling, S. 2009. "Ecological Gentrification: A Research Agenda Exploring Justice in the City." *International Journal of Urban and Regional Research* 33 (3): 621–39. doi:10.1111/j.1468-2427.2009.00860.x.

DSNI (Dudley Street Neighborhood Initiative). 2016. "Dudley Street Neighborhood Initiative Historic Timeline." http://www.dsni.org/dsni-historic-timeline/.

Dunphy, M. 2016. "Secrets of the High Line in New York City." *NewYork.Com*, August 16, online only. http://www.newyork.com/articles/attractions/secrets-of-the-high-line-in-new-york-city-13926/.

Eizenberg, E. 2012. "The Changing Meaning of Community Space: Two Models of NGO Management of Community Gardens in New York City." *International Journal of Urban and Regional Research* 36 (1): 106–20. doi:10.1111/j.1468-2427.2011.01065.x.

11th Street Bridge Park. n.d.-a. "About the 11th Street Bridge Park." Accessed September 15, 2016. http://www.bridgepark.org/about-11th-st-bridge-park.

——. n.d.-b. "Equitable Development Plan." https://indd.adobe.com/view/f22c1340-3bc2-4fff-94da-cde1395bef99.

Freed, B. 2013. "How Navy Yard Built Up One of DC's Fastest-Growing Neighbor-
    hoods." September 18. https://www.washingtonian.com/2013/09/18/how-navy-
    yard-built-up-one-of-dcs-fastest-growing-neighborhoods/.
Hachmyer, C. 2013. "The Institutionalization of Food Movement Projects and the
    Role of Land Rights in Social Transformation: Stories from Boston, Detroit and
    Philadelphia." Medford, MA: Tufts University.
Haynes, E. C. 2013. "Currents of Change: An Urban and Environmental History of
    the Anacostia River and Near Southeast Waterfront in Washington, D.C." Pitzer
    Senior Thesis, Pitzer College (36).
Hurley, D. 2004. "Scientist at Work—Felton Earls; On Crime as Science (a Neighbor at
    a Time)." *New York Times*, January 6. http://query.nytimes.com/gst/fullpage.htm
    l?res=9405E6D61531F935A35752C0A9629C8B63.
Kratz, S. 2017. "Building Political & Cultural Equity." 11th Street Bridge Park. http://
    www.bridgepark.org/blog/building-political-cultural-equity.
LISC (Local Initiatives Support Corporation, District of Columbia). 2015. "Elevating
    Equity Initiative." http://www.liscdc.org/elevatingequity/.
Loh, P. 2015. "How One Boston Neighborhood Stopped Gentrification in Its Tracks."
    YES! Magazine, January 28, online.
Marche, G. 2015. "What Can Urban Gardening Really Do about Gentrification? A
    Case-Study of Three San Francisco Community Gardens." *European Journal of
    American Studies* 10 (3): 1–10.
Moss, J. 2012. "Disney World on the Hudson." *New York Times*, August 22, 2012. http://
    www.nytimes.com/2012/08/22/opinion/in-the-shadows-of-the-high-line.html.
Myers, C. 2016. "Bridge Park as Community Gateway." *The Field: ASLA Professional
    Practice Networks' Blog*. https://thefield.asla.org/2016/03/10/bridge-park-as-
    community-gateway/.
Newman, A. 2008. "Inclusive Planning of Urban Nature." *Ecological Restoration* 26 (3):
    229–34.
O'Connell, J. 2014. "Architects OMA and Olin Studio Selected to Design 11th Street
    Bridge Park." *Washington Post*, October 15. https://www.washingtonpost.com/
    news/digger/wp/2014/10/15/architects-oma-and-olin-studio-selected-to-
    design-11th-street-bridge-park/.
——. 2016. "Can D.C. Build a $45 Million Park for Anacostia without Pushing People
    Out?" *Washington Post Magazine*, January 21.
Pearsall, H. 2012. "Moving Out or Moving In? Resilience to Environmental Gentrifica-
    tion in New York City." *Local Environment* 17 (9): 1013–26. doi.org/10.1080/135
    49839.2012.714762.
——. 2013. "Superfund Me: A Study of Resistance to Gentrification in New York City."
    Urban Studies 50 (11): 1–18. doi:10.1177/0042098013478236.
Reynolds, K., and N. Cohen. 2016. *Beyond the Kale: Urban Agriculture and Social
    Justice Activism in New York City*. Edited by N. Cohen. Athens: University of
    Georgia Press.
Schmelzkopf, K. 1995. "Urban Community Gardens as Contested Spaces." *Geographi-
    cal Review* 85 (3): 364–81.
Smith, C. M., and H. E. Kurtz. 2003. "Community Gardens and Politics of Scale in
    New York City." *Geographical Review* 93 (2): 193–212.
TPL (Trust for Public Land). 2011. "NYC Community Gardens Turned Over to Local
    Land Trusts." https://www.tpl.org/media-room/nyc-community-gardens-
    turned-over-local-land-trusts.
Wennersten, J. R. 2008. *Anacostia: The Death and Life of an American River*. Baltimore:
    Chesapeake Book Co.

Wheeler, L. 1998. "A Future Dependent on the Past." *Washington Post*, July 2. District
    Ward Profiles, Ward 6. http://www.washingtonpost.com/wp-srv/local/longterm/
    library/dcelections/wards/ward6full.htm.
Williams, B. 2001. "A River Runs through Us." *American Anthropologist* 103 (2):
    409–31.
——. 2002. "Gentrifying Water and Selling Jim Crow." *Urban Anthropology and Studies
    of Cultural Systems and World Economic Development* 31 (1): 93–121.
Wolch, J. R., J. Byrne, and J. P. Newell. 2014. "Urban Green Space, Public Health,
    and Environmental Justice: The Challenge of Making Cities 'Just Green
    Enough.'" *Landscape and Urban Planning* 125:234–44. doi:10.1016/j.
    landurbplan.2014.01.017.

Chapter 11

CIVIC STEWARDSHIP AS A CATALYST FOR SOCIAL-ECOLOGICAL CHANGE IN DETROIT, MICHIGAN

Rebecca Salminen Witt, Erika S. Svendsen, and
Marianne E. Krasny

From thirty thousand feet above the ground, much of Detroit appears to be a sea of green. In places its dense tree canopy makes Detroit appear as both city and forest. Elsewhere, a sprawling, verdant landscape is interspersed with homes, offices, and wide boulevards. Comprising nearly a third of Detroit's land area, vacant grasslands punctuated by stands of trees are noticeable even from the air.

At ground level, it becomes clear that the view from the air belies the hardships and struggles embedded in the sprawling open space. Close up, Detroit's urban grasslands are no idyllic native prairie, and the forests emerging along forgotten fence lines bear little resemblance to the oak-hickory savannah that once characterized the area. In fact, many who remain in sparsely populated neighborhoods consider this type of nature as a further sign of abandonment and neglect. Yet residents and organizations have emerged to convert these neglected open spaces into green spaces that offer amenities to local residents and in doing so demonstrate that urban nature's social-ecological benefits do not accrue on their own. They demonstrate that urban green spaces—whether community gardens or greenways, a wildflower meadow or a grassy field, an alleyway of trees or a tree nursery—must be recognized, valued, experienced, and attended to by the people who live nearby. These environmental stewardship groups are defined by their actions to conserve, manage, monitor, advocate, and educate the public about their local environments (Svendsen and Campbell 2008; Fisher, Campbell, and Svendsen 2012). One role for urban environmental stewardship organizations is helping residents to convert and reappropriate space into places of social-ecological meaning (Tidball 2014; Krasny, Crestol, et al. 2014).

Similar to the impression one might have of Detroit from remote aerial imagery, the stories about restoration and revival heard from afar often offer a single perspective of the opportunities that await. Academic design studios and popular press articles have depicted Detroit as a new frontier populated by savvy entrepreneurs and by artists attracted by low rent in a city where they can hone their craft and where there is space to create, invest, and shape one's future. Many Detroiters are glad to have all this attention and welcome the new ideas, energy, and innovation focused on their city. At the same time, this rosy scene of revival is juxtaposed with the realities of gun violence and racial segregation, coupled with displacement and disenfranchisement as a result of gentrification and political maneuvering, which makes it hard for anyone to understand what is really happening in Detroit or where they themselves might fit into this new urban economy. In the end, while each of these representations contains a truth, none of these sentiments captures the whole of this urban landscape. Detroit is a kaleidoscope of cities, constantly changing with the lens that is applied. It is a city of hope and possibilities for many, and for many more it is the city where they have become trapped and left with few options other than to watch as the world around them changes. As evidenced from the history of social unrest globally, this feeling of hopelessness can produce anxiety, disorder, and suffering that can render moot all talk and aspirations of the resilient city.

In such transitioning urban landscapes, whether it be modern-day Detroit or New York City's Lower East Side in the 1970s and 1980s, the defiant acts of guerrilla gardening and tree planting by individuals, friends, and neighbors have often paralleled the emergence of local organizations seeking to connect, support, and expand these actions. These acts and organizations provide mechanisms not simply for neighborhood revitalization but also to help ensure equitable distribution of the benefits of urban greening throughout the community. They find resonance with the South Asian Indian concept of *jugaad*—when government is unable or unwilling to address public welfare, the people are forced to innovate and find solutions on their own (Doshi et al. 2013). In fact, urban environmental stewardship organizations have assumed some of the roles and responsibility of government through a growing professionalization and contribution to urban governance (Connolly et al. 2013; Fisher, Campbell, and Svendsen 2012). By examining the evolution of one such organization, the Greening of Detroit (the Greening), we hope to learn how these groups evolve over time and how they interact with the beliefs, desires, and rights of others to ensure that the green spaces they steward truly become a public resource. In addition to tracing the Greening's evolution over its thirty-year history, we explore its role in urban green-space governance networks and in national social movements, thereby suggesting mechanisms whereby organizations engaged in civic ecology practices can have broader impacts.

Environmental Organizations, Networked Governance, and Social Movements

Sirianni and Sofer (2012) describe three types of environmental nonprofits, including advocacy organizations that pursue an agenda through legislatures, government agencies, and courts; educational organizations working in school and out-of-school settings to foster environmental knowledge and understanding; and ecosystem organizations that focus on place-based work, from the small stream to larger landscape or watershed scale. Ecosystem organizations use holistic management approaches such as stakeholder engagement and building trust and civic respect as they design and implement green infrastructure projects. Although the Greening is best described as an ecosystem organization focusing on the city of Detroit, it also has engaged in educational initiatives such as green jobs training. Consistent with other ecosystem organizations, the Greening plays a role in producing ecosystem services (Pataki et al. 2011; Reyers et al. 2013; Krasny, Russ, et al. 2013), for example, through tree planting and urban agriculture.

However, the importance of local environmental groups such as the Greening of Detroit extends beyond collaborative urban environmental restoration and stewardship to produce ecosystem services. These groups also often emerge as key players in citywide networks of stewardship organizations, thus playing roles in new forms of hybrid or polycentric governance that are critical to addressing complex problems (Fisher and Svendsen 2014; Ostrom 2010; Connolly et al. 2014, 2013; see chapter 8). Some nonprofit organizations occupy key bridging or boundary-crossing positions in governance networks, connecting and sharing knowledge among nonprofit, government, and private actors operating at different scales (Olsson et al. 2007; Ernstson et al. 2010).

In addition to their role in governance, networks of environmental organizations can catalyze larger social or environmental movements (Avina 2002). Political scientists have described a civic environmental movement that in contrast to the polarized, adversarial group politics that traditionally divide corporations and environmentalists, involves reaching across the boundaries that insulate and separate government agencies and divide civil society and business. Civic environmentalism leverages "nongovernmental public-purpose institutions, cultural norms of cooperation and public-spirited behavior, a web of interpersonal ties, and a history of effective local cooperation" to address local environmental problems (John 2004, 230). The movement's work is accomplished through multistakeholder partnerships, such as the Chicago Wilderness, a regional alliance of over three hundred stewardship organizations that seek to improve nature and quality of life in the Chicago area (Chicago Wilderness 2014). In addition to coalescing around a city or metropolitan region like Chicago, such groups may focus on a watershed, where they both complement and provide redundancy for each other's work. Examples include the Chesapeake Bay Foundation, an advocacy group that also engages citizens in watershed restoration, monitoring, and education; and the Alliance for Chesapeake Bay, which builds capacity of local watershed associations, other citizen groups, local government, and businesses to formulate land-use policy, as well as engages volunteers in watershed monitoring and restoration (Sirianni and Sofer 2012).

McAdam and Scott (2005) claim that similar processes govern the emergence and evolution of organizations and social movements; for example, forming networks and building social capital are critical to both (Hasenfeld and Gidron 2005). Fligstein and McAdam (2011) have gone one step further to suggest a blurring of the lines between organizations and social movements. They present the term "strategic action fields" to describe change processes that occur across different levels of social organization, from community group to nonprofit to social movement. Another approach to understanding the evolving nature of civil society is the notion of multipurpose hybrid organizations, which attempt to balance grassroots engagement and professionalism and use the services they provide as a means toward broader social change (Hasenfeld and Gidron 2005). In short, this literature suggests that the boundaries between an organization and a social movement are fluid, and that similar processes of change may operate across multiple levels of social organization.

Below we trace the history of the nonprofit organization the Greening of Detroit. Like many nonprofits, the Greening was launched by a concerned community leader motivated by witnessing a disturbance (cf. Avina 2002). And as with other nonprofits, the Greening's history is one of navigating the "distinctiveness imperative" (what makes it unique) and the "survival imperative" (what it has to do to survive) (Salamon 2012). In tracing the Greening's history, we also explore its role in governance networks and as part of larger urban agriculture (Reynolds and Cohen 2016), ecological restoration (Tomblin 2009), and civic environmental movements (John 2004; Sirianni and Friedland 2005).

The Greening of Detroit: A History

Scholars have identified stages of the nonprofit life cycle including start-up, expansion, and consolidation. We use these nonprofit life-cycle stages to explore the history of the Greening of Detroit while recognizing that such stages may not be linear and may occur simultaneously (Avina 2002).

Start-Up

Between 1950 and 1980, about five hundred thousand of Detroit's trees were lost to Dutch elm disease and urban expansion. Troubled by the deforestation of a great city and in the face of inaction by city government, community leader Elizabeth Gordon Sachs launched an initiative to restore Detroit to its early twentieth century grandeur as the "City of Trees" and the "Paris of the Midwest." In 1989, Sachs founded the Greening of Detroit with a single focus in mind—to restore the city's once tree-lined boulevards and wooded neighborhoods. For a decade, the Greening maintained this singular focus, planting nearly thirty thousand trees in its first ten years of existence.

Expansion: Forging Networks

In 1999, the Greening of Detroit was still a small and relatively unknown organization operating in a city under financial duress. It moved to new offices in Detroit's Historic Corktown neighborhood on Michigan Avenue, a major thoroughfare that, although once tree-lined, had been devoid of trees for decades. Consistent with its original mission, the organization launched a tree-planting initiative. However, working in a new community brought new challenges. An active community group in Corktown had been trying to plant trees for years without success because of property jurisdiction issues; this group was not convinced that a new initiative was worth the effort. Further, Michigan Avenue was a state trunk line maintained under contract by the city, and the sidewalks were public property. This meant that tree planting would require coordination with multiple agencies, none of which had regular contact or experience working together. To make matters more difficult, municipal agency positions turned over rapidly in those days, meaning that the Greening had to build collaboration from the ground up, with no one inside city administration to provide support and guidance.

Using its newcomer status to its advantage, the Greening of Detroit began to work with whomever was interested in improving conditions along Michigan Avenue. Many individuals attended meetings simply to air grievances and

FIGURE 11.1 Michigan Avenue and downtown Detroit, 1964. Collection of the Detroit Historical Society.

frustrations. Groups were often fragmented and disjointed in their mission. But as time went on, community groups from opposite ends of Michigan Avenue joined in the conversation about the trees that would connect them. Those early discussions created a core group of collaborators who brought a new spirit to the project and a sense of unity that had been missing from the area for years. When a radical change was required in the plan to allow for new road construction, the group was able to pivot and adapt to a new scenario that would still meet the goal of increasing Historic Corktown's tree canopy. In fact, the change led to a planting that was eight times the size of the original plan.

In an example of how grassroots collaborations can lead to more powerful networks (Avina 2002), the Michigan Avenue Reforestation Project created new partnerships that persist to this day. Active neighborhood groups were legitimized and strengthened as they improved relationships with local decision makers. In one example, new connections within city government built support for the neighborhood Community Development Corporation, which then launched a decade-long project to refurbish homes and build new houses on vacant properties. Although the Community Development Corporation dissolved during the subsequent housing crisis, its connections survived, and another version emerged as the Corktown Business Association several years later. As a result of establishing rapport and trust with the community, government agencies started to bring improvements to the area. For example, the Public Lighting Authority installed historically appropriate and pedestrian-scaled streetlights along Michigan Avenue, which like many Detroit neighborhoods had suffered for years from lack of functioning streetlights and associated crime. These collaborations extended to residents, who found a collective voice that continues to inform development decisions. In one instance, home gardeners transitioned into vacant-lot community gardeners and environmental advocates, choosing to remain a part of the community even in the face of rising real estate values that might previously have tempted them to cash out. Historic Corktown has become one of Detroit's hot spots, with new residential lofts selling rapidly and longtime residents renovating historic cottages and forming a welcoming core for newcomers endeavoring to save derelict buildings from demolition. A new restaurant, brew pub, or distillery seemingly opens every weekend, creating employment opportunities for residents and economic opportunities for local farmers. And there are exciting redevelopment plans for almost every vacant space along Michigan Avenue, a street that once again boasts a lovely canopy of trees.

However, similar to the situation in other cities experiencing green and community revitalization, gentrification has led to concern over displacement and disenfranchisement (see chapter 10). In Detroit, gentrification generally takes a form different from that in other cities. In Corktown, as in most neighborhoods in Detroit, property values are not so high that longtime families are being forced out. However, in one notorious instance, new residents circulated a memo, addressed to the "Conquistadors," that described the tactics they were considering to close a neighborhood business and the local soup kitchen and shelter thought to be contributing to "drugs, crime and general malcontent." The tone-deaf memo was particularly offensive, given the many Hispanic families in the area. In short, gentrification took on the form of neighborhood revitalization gone terribly askew, with the collaboration and common voice created by the initial collaboration reemerging as a force of exclusion and displacement.

North Corktown, located adjacent to gentrifying Historic Corktown, faces a different challenge. As a result of being bisected by a freeway, it has not experienced the same reinvestment as its sister neighborhood to the south. North Corktown is still a place where vacant land is abundant and wild; it remains a "gap-toothed" residential area that has come to epitomize much of the city. Occupied homes are interspersed with grassy expanses that can span as little as two or three lots or as much as half a block. This neighborhood has experienced significant change and uncertainty in recent years. Redevelopment plans have come and gone; its community development organization floundered and then failed; schools that were once anchors for the community have closed, reopened, and closed again; and a casino was built on its eastern edge. Residents in the area grew breathless just trying to keep up. They wanted more certainty in their lives and their neighborhood, and it seemed that the land was the only thing remaining unchanged.

The Greening of Detroit had worked with North Corktown for many years, and in 2011 launched a community-led initiative that gave residents the opportunity to engage in land-use planning at a sidewalk scale. North Corktown residents came together around grassroots greening concepts that they could apply to stabilize their neighborhood and improve their quality of life. Community gardens, production farming, pocket parks, and public-art-filled gathering spaces joined street tree planting as the preferred interventions. Neighborhood social networks acted first as a catalyst for planning and then for the collective volunteer effort necessary to implement the greening initiatives. Further, the changes have attracted the attention of the city government, which turned attention and investment plans to the area. Most recently, a Corktown architecture firm announced plans to build market-rate housing in North Corktown, reflecting a rise in appraisal values. The multiple actions of this engaged community have played a significant role in building the fair market value of their neighborhood. At the same time, the neighborhood's networks, ability to adapt, and collective efficacy will be important as it faces this new wave of development.

Expansion: Broadening the Mission

In 2002, a new destructive insect, the emerald ash borer, was identified in Detroit and quickly decimated Detroit's ash trees. The Greening was ready to respond with the tools it had developed in the wake of Dutch elm disease. This time, however, the Greening decided not only to attend to the dying trees, but to use the new disturbance as a rallying call to address problems at a watershed scale. For example, the city's combined sewer system was experiencing unregulated overflows negatively impacting the local watershed and leading to federal oversight. The Greening decided to overhaul its program from neighborhood-scale street tree plantings to massive plantings at the landscape scale, with the objectives of vacant land stabilization, environmental decontamination, storm-water reclamation, and forest restoration (SEMCOG 2013).

The Greening's role in Corktown neighborhood networks had helped it recognize that Detroit had much broader needs than reforestation alone. Teachers had commented on the lack of outdoor and environmental education in Detroit's stressed public schools. The maintenance capacity of the municipality's forestry and parks operations was severely diminished. Food insecurity was on the rise in many parts of the city. As a nonprofit organization, the Greening felt a duty to focus its capacity and expertise in the areas where the need was most intense and modified its programs accordingly. This led the organization to amend its mission, initially by moving to an ecosystem-based planting protocol and, in 2006, by formally eliminating the restriction to tree planting. This opened the door for urban agriculture and gardening programs, which eventually would serve over fifteen thousand urban and community gardeners who produce over two hundred tons of food annually. The Greening also expanded to incorporate environmental education and green workforce development. In 2012, the Greening revised its mission again to specifically acknowledge the role of each program in attaining the organization's broad goal of growing a sustainable urban community in Detroit, and adopted the motto "Planting tomorrow's Detroit, from peas to trees." By remaining fluid, the Greening has been able to embrace emerging opportunities.

By 2016, after twenty-six years of operation, the Greening was actively pursuing the goal of a healthy urban community not only through tree planting but through all manner of green-space stewardship, supported by community engagement activities and youth employment and workforce development. To accomplish its goals, the Greening had responded repeatedly to changing community needs with innovative programs and collaborative partnerships that now stretched far beyond traditional park and open-space relationships. Acting as a bridging organization (Olsson et al. 2007; Bodin and Crona 2009), the Greening had also collaborated with the City of Detroit and hundreds of block clubs, nonprofit organizations, and businesses, relying on broad partnerships, including with the faith-based community, nontraditional political actors, health organizations, and universities. Today the Greening positions itself as an organization that *does things*. It relies on its hard-won reputation as a doer to enable its work as a bridging organization that brings individuals and organizations together to implement projects that would not be completed otherwise.

Crisis and Consolidation

All organizations undergo planned or unintended consolidations at various times in their evolution. During a consolidation, an NGO analyzes its performance to better align its operative capacity to its external reality. . . . [Consolidation may] be the direct outcome of an internally or externally generated crisis, such as a failed expansion.

(Avina 2002, 136)

As the Greening's programs and partners grew, they eventually created a threat to the organization. The threat took the form of internal strife within the Greening itself and of significant competition from its collaborators. Rapid growth had created an organizational silo of the Greening's urban agriculture program, which was passionately embraced by its staff and collaborators but did not feel connected to the Greening's broader mission of environmental sustainability. Race and class also entered into the conflict. African Americans, who have historically played a prominent role in grassroots agriculture in Detroit, felt ownership over the city's urban agriculture movement, and the growth of the Greening's agriculture programs was perceived as infringing on their proprietary rights. Although the Greening itself has a diverse staff through all levels of leadership, its status as a well-established organization contrasted with the more grassroots African American urban agriculture groups. For the urban agriculture program to thrive, it needed to become a separate entity that could reclaim the grassroots mantle in the eyes of Detroit's broader urban agriculture community. Desperate to regain the balance it had lost, the Greening initiated the most difficult maneuver in its history: it spun off its major urban agriculture program, along with the staff and a significant amount of the funding, to become a new organization (Keep Growing Detroit 2017). This move was met with both criticism and praise, which eventually helped the Greening to refocus itself as an organization and to find a way to reshape its remaining urban agriculture programs to better reflect its organizational mission.

Expansion: Broadening Services

Responding to an increasingly competitive environment, many nonprofits have recently begun charging for their services. This can necessitate a more managerial style that emphasizes efficiency and cost containment as well as innovation.

Balancing "commercialism" and "managerialism" with a grassroots tradition poses challenges (Salamon 2012).

The Greening often found itself in the position of having ample program funds for planting, education, and training, but inadequate funds for administration and operations. Inadequate support for core functions threatened its ability to continue to act as a bridging organization; its core staff were critical to building understanding of the places where they worked, to building trust, and to establishing reciprocity between organizations and communities. The Greening turned to its network for ideas and received feedback that the services it offered as a component of its grant-funded activities would be valuable on a contract basis. Thus, the Greening began to engage in fee-for-service work. The new contracts generated a sustainable source of revenue that stabilized operations, allowing the Greening to continue its bridging role. The Greening also expanded its workforce development program in collaboration with two other nonprofits by launching a landscaping services firm with the capacity to complete larger city and state projects. With this shift, the Greening transitioned into a multipurpose hybrid organization (Hasenfeld and Gidron 2005) that fulfills both private and public-sector roles. Such professionalization and hybridity in urban greening organizations is becoming common in a new "ecological restoration economy" (BenDor, Lester, et al. 2015; BenDor, Livengood, et al. 2015).

The Greening: Organizational Change, Networks, and Social Movements

Next we place the history of the Greening of Detroit within the contexts of organizational change, governance networks of environmental stewardship and community development organizations, and larger social movements (see also chapter 12).

Organizational Change

Throughout its history, an organization faces the dual challenge of balancing mission fidelity and securing resources (Mitchell 2015) or of navigating the "distinctiveness imperative" along with the "survival imperative" (Salamon 2012). Further, challenges arise when nonprofits emerge in response to a specific need, yet widespread support for their narrow mission is lacking (McAdam and Scott 2005). This tension between mission and survival over time emerged in a study of leaders of transnational NGOs who were asked to identify attributes that make NGOs effective. Among attributes of effective organizations topping the list were sound vision, principles, and strategy; grassroots approach; collaborative approaches; and singleness of focus. Near the bottom of the list were nimbleness and diversity of strategies. However, when the same researchers compared attributes of specific organizations with reputations for being effective, a contradiction emerged: diversity of strategies, which ranked low in the first, more generic question, was the third-most-important predictor of attributes of specific organizations with a reputation for being effective. Further, sound vision, principles, and strategy, the most highly ranked attribute in the initial analysis, was marginally yet significantly negatively associated with an organization's reputation. Another contradiction emerged in that NGO leaders claimed both a grassroots approach and large size and scale were important in determining organizational effectiveness (Mitchell 2015). These conflicting findings reflect the tensions organizations like the Greening constantly navigate—on the one hand they should instantiate sound vision, principles, and strategies, but on the other hand they should employ a diversity of strategies. Further, the study found that organizations that employ hybrid strategies, like combining service delivery and advocacy, have higher reputational effectiveness relative to those that pursue only advocacy. In light of these results, it is perhaps not surprising that ecosystem organizations like the Greening strategically pursue hybrid strategies (Mitchell 2015), integrating, for example, serving as a bridging organization and green job training.

Over time, the Greening of Detroit has responded to a series of threats and opportunities by adapting its programs, processes, relationships—and mission. These adaptations have changed the very core of the organization's programs such that today the organization is no longer defined by a single tree-planting focus but instead is committed to creating a resilient Detroit through engaging communities and providing environmental and nutrition education, green infrastructure, and workforce development. Regardless of these changes in program focus and strategies, the Greening has consistently served as a bridging organization in governance networks of community development and greening organizations.

To garner support for its changing mission and mobilize collective action, the Greening has drawn on so-called cognitive and relational mechanisms (Campbell 2005). Framing is one cognitive mechanism, which emphasizes the role of the actor in diagnosing and suggesting solutions for problems (Benford and Snow 2000; see also chapter 12). Elizabeth Gordon Sachs originally framed tree planting as a means to restore Detroit's grandeur as a "City of Trees" and the "Paris of the Midwest." Even in this original call to action over an acute disturbance (i.e., the loss of tree canopy), we see reference to a larger, systemic disturbance (i.e., urban decline). The effort around community tree planting was linked not only to the potential environmental benefits but to something more distant—the hopes and dreams of Detroit's residents. In fact, the organization even took to describing its plantings as "tangible expressions of hope for the future" (cf. Tidball 2014). With every tree planted, participants hoped for a better city and that the hardships endured by so many would finally come to an end.

In addition to a strategy for garnering support, the Greening's changing mission can be viewed as a strategic expansion adaptation strategy (Alexander 2000). As nonprofits expand, they need to take into account sustaining trust with established constituencies, which requires a certain consistency. Rapid change might jeopardize such relationships with stakeholders, who also play a role in determining organizational direction (Shea and Hamilton 2015). We have seen how what at one point might have seemed like strategic expansion—the Greening's urban agriculture program—posed new threats over time, including those related to the trust of other actors who were leaders in Detroit's urban agriculture movement. More recently, the Greening has pursued strategic expansion into the ecological restoration economy through its fee-for-services initiatives; while perhaps needed for survival, such expansion into the commercial sector can again pose threats to a nonprofit organization's reputation and established relationships (Salamon 2012).

Networks

Early on, the Greening took on networking and boundary-crossing activities, which can be a relational means of garnering support for an organization's mission and mobilizing collective action (Campbell 2005) and an expansion strategy (Alexander 2000). Boundary-crossing actions also can serve a broader purpose of helping to create governance networks that fill roles beyond those internal to the nonprofit organization (Ernstson et al. 2010; Olsson et al. 2007; Connolly et al. 2014; Fisher, Campbell, and Svendsen 2012; Hasenfeld and Gidron 2005). Such networks can support community-wide greening goals and, through forming polycentric and adaptive governance systems, contribute to the adaptability and social resilience of a block, neighborhood, or larger city (Ostrom and Cox 2010; Dietz, Ostrom, and Stern 2003; see also chapter 8). While social resilience may be difficult to measure, McMillen et al. (2016) suggest using empirically observable stewardship practices as indicators of social resilience, including place attachment, social cohesion, collective identity, social networks, and knowledge exchange.

A governance network is made possible in part by trust and a recognition of complementary roles among participating agencies and organizations. The Greening spent its early years trying out all sorts of urban greening models while growing a constituency of trusted residents, organizational partners, and policy makers. Through the years, the Greening has been asked to leverage its community contacts and relationships to ensure that voices of individuals throughout Detroit are included in planning efforts and to undertake new projects on behalf of neighborhoods around the city (American Forests 2006; SEMCOG 2013). The Greening brings to the table its reputation as a capable representative for greening ideas, its design skills, and its ability to secure funding and permission to implement new projects.

The Greening also has assumed roles of civic environmental, bridging organizations, such as empowering residents to take action (Gooch 2004; Slater 2001) and including more voices and local knowledge in urban planning and community development (Eizenberg 2012). It has used greening programs as a means to engage local people in local action, and to leave residents with lasting connections and resources that enable them to act collectively in the future. This process has spurred government and other actors to overcome the inertia that plagued certain government departments and neighborhoods. Because community members have seen results from past participation in the Greening's efforts, they are more willing to engage in additional civic efforts; such ability to foster civic engagement is further evidence of the Greening's role in facilitating governance networks.

Social Movements

Both urban agriculture (Reynolds and Cohen 2016) and urban ecological restoration (Tomblin 2009) have emerged as twenty-first-century social movements. Thus, while the Greening has played a bridging role in local environmental governance networks, on a broader scale it is an actor in national and transnational social movements. Further, given the Greening's central position in Detroit and Detroit's position as emblematic of the decline of rust belt cities and subsequent greening renewal efforts, the Greening's experience provides important lessons and perhaps even has helped frame these social movements. Conversely, these social movements may have influenced the discourses and frames used by the Greening to mobilize local resources (cf. Zald, Morrill, and Rao 2005).

The Greening also can be considered a local actor in the civic environmental movement, which emphasizes collaborative approaches to addressing local and watershed-scale environmental issues. Whereas earlier environmental movements used confrontational tactics and focused on preservation, civic environmentalism can be considered as part of a broader, participatory civic renewal movement in the United States (Sirianni and Friedland 2005). The Greening's ability to connect its practices to civic renewal in Detroit, from its earliest days of tree planting to more recent job training and fee-for-service programs, is consistent with this recent form of environmentalism.

Emerging from moments (and decades) of crisis is a new social-ecological landscape characterized by the number and type of organizations engaged in urban environmental stewardship and its governance (Svendsen and Campbell 2008; Romolini et al. 2016; Wolf et al. 2011). How can the Greening and other bridging organizations in these governance networks share this space with new organizations, accurately identify opportunities appearing on the horizon, and create new ways to address threats that range wildly from invasive insects to predatory urban land speculators? And how do these organizations help shape and contribute to broader social movements?

What we learn from the legacy of the Greening is that these ecosystem organizations create environmental stewardship hubs in the communities where they work. From these hubs emerge community leaders who help shape stewardship networks and, more recently, the demand for an urban restoration economy. Through processes of social contagion and mimicry, other individuals and groups adapt urban greening strategies on their blocks and in their vacant spaces. Suddenly, we find new organizations similar to the Greening emerging to support initiatives ranging from greenways to urban farms, from gardens to plant nurseries, and from tree planting to green roofs. We find that these organizations have helped to professionalize the civic urban greening sector while retaining a focus on local participation and engagement of diverse stakeholders. They have seized on opportunities not only to restore vacant land but to create jobs, generate revenue, and even provide legal counsel. Starting with mobilizing volunteers to perform roles traditionally considered the responsibility of city agencies, stewardship groups like the Greening of Detroit have expanded to incorporate activities associated with the private sector.

Parallel to these changes in the Greening's stewardship and educational practices has been its bridging role in Detroit's environmental governance network. Further, the Greening of Detroit has expanded to play a role in, as well as help shape, larger urban agriculture, restoration economy, and civic environmental movements. In this way, the story of the Greening of Detroit can be seen as a first attempt to expand work describing the overlap in processes governing the emergence and evolution of environmental organizations and social movements to encompass processes at the level of individual greening practices and citywide environmental governance and community revitalization networks.

REFERENCES

Alexander, J. 2000. "Adaptive Strategies of Nonprofit Human Service Organizations in an Era of Devolution and New Public Management." *Nonprofit Management and Leadership* 10 (3): 287–303. doi:10.1002/nml.10305.

American Forests. 2006. *Urban Ecosystem Analysis SE Michigan and City of Detroit.* Washington, DC: American Forests.

Avina, J. 2002. "The Evolutionary Life-Cycles of Non-governmental Development Organizations." In *The Earthscan Reader on NGO Management*, edited by M. Edwards and A. Fowler, 123–45. New York: Earthscan.

BenDor, T. K., T. W. Lester, A. Livengood, A. Davis, and L. Yonavjak. 2015. "Estimating the Size and Impact of the Ecological Restoration Economy." *PLoS ONE* 10 (6): e0128339. doi:10.1371/journal.pone.0128339.

BenDor, T. K., A. Livengood, T. W. Lester, A. Davis, and L. Yonavjak. 2015. "Defining and Evaluating the Ecological Restoration Economy." *Restoration Ecology* 23 (3): 209–19. doi:10.1111/rec.12206.

Benford, R. D., and D. A. Snow. 2000. "Framing Processes and Social Movements: An Overview and Assessment." *Annual Review of Sociology* 26:611–39.

Bodin, O., and B. Crona. 2009. "The Role of Social Networks in Natural Resource Governance: What Relational Patterns Make a Difference?" *Global Environmental Change* 19:366–74.

Campbell, J. L. 2005. "Where Do We Stand? Common Mechanisms in Organizations and Social Movements Research." In *Social Movements and Organization Theory*, edited by G. F. Davis, D. McAdam, W. R. Scott, and M. N. Zald, 41–68. Cambridge: Cambridge University Press.

Chicago Wilderness. 2014. "Chicago Wilderness." www.chicagowilderness.org/.

Connolly, J. J., E. S. Svendsen, D. R. Fisher, and L. K. Campbell. 2013. "Organizing Urban Ecosystem Services through Environmental Stewardship Governance in New York City." *Landscape and Urban Planning* 109:76–84. doi:10.1016/j.landurbplan.2012.07.001.

——. 2014. "Networked Governance and the Management of Ecosystem Services: The Case of Urban Environmental Stewardship in New York City." *Ecosystem Services* 10:187–94. doi:10.1016/j.ecoser.2014.08.005.

Dietz, T., E. Ostrom, and P. C. Stern. 2003. "The Struggle to Govern the Commons." *Science* 302 (5652): 1907–12. doi:10.1126/science.1091015.

Doshi, A., A. Khanna, V. Mahadevan, N. Rao, and N. Shukla. 2013. "From Jugaad to Justice: Endemic Corruption and the Possibility of an Indian Spring." Knowledge@Wharton.

Eizenberg, E. 2012. "The Changing Meaning of Community Space: Two Models of NGO Management of Community Gardens in New York City." *International Journal of Urban and Regional Research* 36 (1): 106–20. doi:10.1111/j.1468-2427.2011.01065.x.

Ernstson, H., S. Barthel, E. Andersson, and S. T. Borgström. 2010. "Scale-Crossing Brokers and Network Governance of Urban Ecosystem Services: The Case of Stockholm." *Ecology and Society* 15 (4): 28.

Fisher, D. R., L. Campbell, and E. S. Svendsen. 2012. "The Organisational Structure of Urban Environmental Stewardship." *Environmental Politics* 21 (1): 26–48. http://dx.doi.org/10.1080/09644016.2011.643367.

Fisher, D. R., and E. S. Svendsen. 2014. "Hybrid Arrangements within the Environmental State." In *Routledge International Handbook of Social and Environmental Change*, edited by S. Lockie, D. A. Sonnenfeld, and D. R. Fisher, 179–89. London: Routledge.

Fligstein, N., and D. McAdam. 2011. "Toward a General Theory of Strategic Action Fields." *Sociological Theory* 29 (1): 1–26.

Gooch, M. 2004. "Volunteering in Catchment Management Groups: Empowering the Volunteer." *Australian Geographer* 35 (2): 193–208. doi:10.1080/0004918042000 249502.

Hasenfeld, Y., and B. Gidron. 2005. "Understanding Multi-purpose Hybrid Voluntary Organizations: The Contributions of Theories on Civil Society, Social Movements and Nonprofit Organizations." *Journal of Civil Society* 1 (2): 97–112. doi:10.1080/17448680500337350.

John, D. 2004. "Civic Environmentalism." In *Environmental Governance Reconsidered*, edited by R. F. Durant, D. Fiorini, and R. O'Leary, 219–54. Cambridge MA: MIT Press.

Keep Growing Detroit. 2017. "Cultivating a Food Sovereign Detroit." http:// detroitagriculture.net/.

Krasny, M. E., S. R. Crestol, K. G. Tidball, and R. C. Stedman. 2014. "New York City's Oyster Gardeners: Memories, Meanings, and Motivations of Volunteer Environmental Stewards." *Landscape and Urban Planning* 132:16–25. doi:10.1016/j.landurbplan.2014.08.003.

Krasny, M. E., A. Russ, K. G. Tidball, and T. Elmqvist. 2013. "Civic Ecology Practices: Participatory Approaches to Generating and Measuring Ecosystem Services in Cities." *Ecosystem Services* 7:177–86. doi:10.1016/j.ecoser.2013.11.002.

McAdam, D., and W. R. Scott. 2005. "Organizations and Movements." In *Social Movements and Organization Theory*, edited by G. F. Davis, D. McAdam, W. R. Scott, and M. N. Zald, 4–40. Cambridge: Cambridge University Press.

McMillen, H., L. Campbell, E. Svendsen, and R. Reynolds. 2016. "Recognizing Stewardship Practices as Indicators of Social Resilience: In Living Memorials and in a Community Garden." *Sustainability* 8 (8): 775.

Mitchell, G. E. 2015. "The Attributes of Effective NGOs and the Leadership Values Associated with a Reputation for Organizational Effectiveness." *Nonprofit Management and Leadership* 26 (1): 39–57. doi:10.1002/nml.21143.

Olsson, P., C. Folke, V. Galaz, T. Hahn, and L. Schultz. 2007. "Enhancing the Fit through Adaptive Comanagement: Creating and Maintaining Bridging Functions for Matching Scales in the Kristianstads Vattenrike Biosphere Reserve Sweden." *Ecology and Society* 12 (1): 28.

Ostrom, E. 2010. "Polycentric Systems for Coping with Collective Action and Global Environmental Change." *Global Environmental Change* 20:550–57.

Ostrom, E., and M. Cox. 2010. "Moving beyond Panaceas: A Multi-tiered Diagnostic Approach for Social-Ecological Analysis." *Environmental Conservation* 37 (04): 451–63. doi:10.1017/S0376892910000834.

Pataki, D. E., M. M. Carreiro, J. Cherrier, N. E. Grulke, E. Jennings, S. Pincetl, R. V. Pouyat, T. H. Whitlow, and W. C. Zipperer. 2011. "Coupling Biogeochemical Cycles in Urban Environments: Ecosystem Services, Green Solutions, and Misconceptions." *Frontiers in Ecology and Environment* 9 (1): 27–36. doi:0.1890/090220.

Reyers, B., R. Biggs, G. S. Cumming, T. Elmqvist, A. P. Hejnowicz, and S. Polasky. 2013. "Getting the Measure of Ecosystem Services: A Social-Ecological Approach." *Frontiers in Ecology and Environment* 11 (5): 268–73. http://dx.doi.org/10.1890/120144.

Reynolds, K., and N. Cohen. 2016. *Beyond the Kale: Urban Agriculture and Social Justice Activism in New York City*. Edited by N. Cohen. Athens: University of Georgia Press.

Romolini, M., J. M. Grove, C. L. Ventriss, C. J. Koliba, and D. H. Krymkowski. 2016. "Toward an Understanding of Citywide Urban Environmental Governance: An Examination of Stewardship Networks in Baltimore and Seattle." *Environmental Management* 58 (2): 254–67. doi:10.1007/s00267-016-0704-4.

Salamon, L. M. 2012. "The Resilient Sector: The Future of Nonprofit America." In *The State of Nonprofit America*, 2nd ed., edited by L. M. Salamon, 3–87. Washington, DC: Brookings Institution Press.

SEMCOG (Southeast Michigan Council of Governments). 2013. *Green Infrastructure Progress Report*. Detroit: Michigan Department of Environmental Quality.

Shea, M., and R. D. Hamilton. 2015. "Who Determines How Nonprofits Confront Uncertainty?" *Nonprofit Management and Leadership* 25 (4): 383–401. doi:10.1002/nml.21136.

Sirianni, C., and L. A. Friedland. 2005. *The Civic Renewal Movement: Community Building and Democracy in the United States*. Dayton, OH: Charles F. Kettering Foundation.

Sirianni, C., and S. Sofer. 2012. "Environmental Organizations." In *The State of Nonprofit America*, 2nd ed., edited by L. M. Salamon, 294–328. Washington, DC: Brookings Institution Press.

Slater, R. J. 2001. "Urban Agriculture, Gender and Empowerment: An Alternative View." *Development Southern Africa* 18 (5): 635–50. doi:10.1080/0376835012009747 8.

Svendsen, E. S., and L. K. Campbell. 2008. "Urban Ecological Stewardship: Understanding the Structure, Function and Network of Community-Based Land Management." *Cities and the Environment* 1 (1): 1–32.

Tidball, K. G. 2014. "Trees and Rebirth: Social-Ecological Symbols and Rituals in the Resilience of Post-Katrina New Orleans." In *Greening in the Red Zone: Disaster, Resilience and Community Greening*, edited by K. G. Tidball and M. E. Krasny, 257–96. New York: Springer.

Tomblin, D. C. 2009. "The Ecological Restoration Movement." *Organization & Environment* 22 (2): 185–207. doi:10.1177/1086026609338165.

Wolf, K. L., D. J. Blahna, W. Brinkley, and M. Romolini. 2011. "Environmental Stewardship Footprint Research: Linking Human Agency and Ecosystem Health in the Puget Sound Region." *Urban Ecosystems* 16:13–32. doi:10.1007/s11252-011-0175-6.

Zald, M. N., C. Morrill, and H. Rao. 2005. "The Impact of Social Movements on Organizations: Environment and Response." In *Social Movements and Organization Theory*, edited by G. F. Davis, D. McAdam, W. R. Scott, and M. N. Zald, 253–79. Cambridge: Cambridge University Press.

Chapter 12

FROM PRACTICE TO FLEDGLING SOCIAL MOVEMENT IN INDIA

Lessons from "The Ugly Indian"

Aniruddha Abhyankar and Marianne E. Krasny

In cities across India, encountering incredible filth in public spaces—piles of garbage accompanied by the stench of urine and stains of tobacco and *paan* spit—is a daily occurrence. Everyone dislikes it, yet many Indians contribute to the filth. Politicians and social organizations have tried clean-up drives and campaigns, but in a matter of days garbage and filth return. As India transforms into a modern society, many wonder how to start cleaning up and eradicating ugly public spaces.

Eight years ago, an anonymous group of tech-savvy professionals in Bangalore began experimenting with ways to "nudge" citizens away from their littering, urination, and spitting behaviors. They realized that modern-day Indian attitudes and behaviors are at the root of the problem—"We Are All Ugly Indians"—and that until Indians accept that "we tolerate this filth and hence it prevails," the problem will not be solved. Calling themselves "The Ugly Indian" (TUI), since 2010 this group has doggedly pursued the question: "What does it take to keep one city street clean?"

This is the story of how TUI purposefully focuses on one small practice—cleaning up public spaces through short-term, volunteer "spot fixes." But it is also the story of how TUI has forged an organizational and collective identity that reflects Indian cultural traditions of *jugaad* or self-help, as well as the competencies and values of a new Indian middle class. And because TUI spot fixes have spread so rapidly across India and more recently Pakistan, this is also a story that illustrates how one can move from a civic ecology practice to collective—and Internet-mediated *connective*—action. Integral to the growth of TUI has been how it has skillfully framed its organizational and collective identity, while adopting features of inclusive, Internet-mediated forms of organization. Below we tell the story of TUI and then examine its work through the lenses of identity, framing, and attitudes and social norms. Finally, we use practice, organizational, and social movement theories and recent writing about connective action to answer the question, What are the larger impacts of new forms of hybrid organizations like TUI?

The Ugly Indian Spot Fix

A typical TUI spot fix lasts three hours. Volunteers ranging from slum dwellers to IT and corporate professionals congregate at a filthy space along a street or sidewalk and haul away trash. They then paint adjacent walls a terracotta color to hide spitting stains and add small pathways and planters. Upon completing a spot fix, volunteers publish visually dramatic before-and-after photos on social networking platforms. Any expenses are generally covered by the volunteers themselves. Throughout the process, volunteers remain anonymous; talking is not permitted during a spot fix.

TUI has developed multiple strategies for stakeholder engagement and maintaining cleaned-up spaces. Spot fixes generally entail minimal government involvement, as local officials tend to ignore or even passively support commercial uses and homeless persons encroaching on public spaces and the resulting degradation. However, gaining acceptance and involvement from local stakeholders and community members is critical, because antagonism toward a spot fix from a single squatter, policeman, or local business can pose a threat to sustaining the cleanup beyond the immediate spot fix. In planning a spot fix, TUI asks those contributing to filth on the targeted public space for advice on how to transform it. For example, engaging people who left food for stray animals led TUI and the animal lovers to find alternative sites to feed cows, crows, and other creatures. TUI also asks local stakeholders to contribute simple things such as a broom, a bucket, or a place to store materials. And TUI has taken advantage of an Indian tradition whereby housemaids draw beautiful patterns with rice flour, which are respected across Indian society as auspicious designs (locally called *kolam* or *rangoli*). These same maids take out the garbage, often dumping it in public spaces. TUI invites the maids to draw the *rangoli* on a cleaned-up public space for several days after a spot fix, thus helping reinforce the perception of the space as beautiful rather than a dumping ground. Through such engagement, the maids and others feel part of a group working together, and the space remains clean long enough to change local habits. TUI also encourages use of cleaned-up public spaces by installing plants and benches, which creates feelings of ownership and discourages littering and other negative behaviors, thus helping ensure that the cleanups are sustained.

Although government is generally only minimally engaged before and during the spot fix (e.g., officials may be asked for a verbal "go-ahead"), TUI ensures that volunteers thank government staff and authorities afterward and recognize any low-level staff who have contributed. This helps form ties with government employees, who may be unable to participate in spot fixes as part of their official duties but may be willing to take part anonymously.

What started as one spot fix on one street in Bangalore in 2010 had grown to five hundred spot fixes by 2015 in Bangalore alone. As citizens across India have started to take charge of their "ugly, filthy" surroundings and to transform them into beautiful spaces, TUI's social media presence has also grown. In 2015, TUI had a fan-follower base of 320,000 on Facebook, equal to that of some Indian film stars.

How, within five years, did a loosely organized, Internet-based, anonymous group focused on cleaning up small public spaces expand to a fan base of several hundred thousand? How did the idea of spot fixes resonate with so many and yet not become diluted by other social agendas? And might TUI have triggered a change in social norms, even a social movement? To address these "broader impacts" questions, we first examine TUI's actions through the lenses of identity, framing, and changing Indian attitudes toward waste, and then through the perspectives of practice, organizational, and social movement theory (see also chapter 11).

Identity, Framing, Attitudes, and Social Norms

When asked to reflect on factors critical to the transition of spot fixes from short-term practice to what may be emerging as a social movement, TUI volunteers immediately responded "identity." For social-movement activists, the movement itself becomes an important part of one's identity, and identity in turn can lead to action (Stern et al. 1999). While it is not clear what type of identity TUI volunteers are referring to, social-movement theorists emphasize *collective identity*, which is defined as "an individual's cognitive, moral, and emotional connection with a broader community, category, practice, or institution" (Polletta and Jasper 2001, 285). Relevant to understanding TUI as an organization, *organizational identity* is defined as "the central and enduring attributes of an organization that distinguish it from other organizations" (Whetten 2006, 220). In today's world, identity and the related concept of framing (Campbell 2005; Benford 1993) are increasingly constructed through the Internet (Loader 2008).

Organizational Identity

As implied in its definition, organizational identity consists of three components: *central*, or claims about what is core to an organization; *enduring*, organizational elements that have withstood the test of time and are often embedded in the telling of an organization's history; and *distinctiveness*, which identifies how the organization differs from others and is esteemed as a social actor (Whetten 2006). Organizational identity is critical because it enables an organization to define its unique "social space" in a competitive field of other organizations and provides guidance about fork-in-the-road decisions. Because a major threat to organizations is "acting out of character," this distinctiveness feature of identity is often communicated as a moral or categorical imperative. Further emphasizing the importance of organizational identity, Whetten (223) stated that "although chronic mistaken identity is troublesome for individuals, it is a fatal flaw for organizations."

The central, distinctive, and enduring elements of organizational identity are evident in how TUI maintains its purposeful focus on cleaning up public spaces and distinguishes itself from other players in the waste management field. As cities across India struggle to handle garbage, solid waste management (SWM) has become a hot issue. In this context, any initiative to clean up public spaces may get labeled as SWM, which implies a government-directed, large-scale, institutional approach not amenable to citizen initiative and grassroots innovation. Similar to how citizen-driven grassroots recycling initiatives in the United States developed an identity that distinguished them from industrial SWM (Lounsbury, Ventresca, and Hirsch 2003), and reflected in TUI's goal "to present stories of hope and optimism and thereby inspire citizen-action in public spaces," TUI has homed in on how citizens can address the issue of visible filth in public spaces to distinguish itself from SWM.

TUI's organizational identity has helped guide its decisions about how to work with mainstream media and other groups (cf. Whetten 2006). When invited by film star Amir Khan to present on a popular TV show an episode about SWM, TUI turned down the offer. But when another network ran a show dedicated to the Clean-India Campaign, TUI agreed to represent Bangalore and organized a major spot fix in subway stations in the heart of the city. TUI has avoided getting involved in issues such as the health and welfare of workers maintaining urban spaces, stray dogs and animal care, and reduce-reuse-recycle, regardless of their importance and potential to attract funding. Rather, TUI supports other groups focused on issues related but not central to its mission. In 2011, when TUI installed its first male non-smell urinal at a cleaned-up site, complaints arose about discrimination against women. But for TUI, the focus was rescuing the wall and footpath from urination—and males, not females, commonly urinated on the site. TUI did, however, offer to support others in setting up female urinals on cleaned-up sites.

TUI has learned from the India Against Corruption movement about being vigilant in protecting its core identity. When this movement encouraged people to take to the streets to protest and form groups under the name "India Against Corruption," several groups deviated from its original agenda, resulting in the movement's image being tarnished. TUI decided not to allow volunteers to open TUI chapters in their respective cities. Rather it helps them set up Facebook pages with different names (e.g., Gurgaon Rising, Mumbai Rising) and that include text about being "inspired by The Ugly Indian."

Similarly, TUI is wary of collaborations with social, academic, political, and media organizations labeled as activist, to avoid being seen as a troublemaker and losing government cooperation. TUI also refuses to talk to traditional media, except to request that they conduct their own investigations of spot fixes and that they not associate TUI with antigovernment forces. As a *Forbes India Magazine* journalist reported: "I had reached out twice earlier to [TUI] to get no response only to read on their Facebook page the following: 'There is enough material on this FB page for any journalist to talk about.' . . . Indeed, there is" (D'Souza 2013). In short, with the exception of offering spot fixes as activities in corporate employee social responsibility programs and working strategically with municipal governments, TUI declines collaboration opportunities, in order to safeguard its organizational identity.

Collective-Action Framing

TUI has drawn on Indian traditional and more recent social norms to strategically frame its identity as a group engaged in collective action around spot fixes. Collective-action frames are "action-oriented sets of beliefs and meanings intended to inspire and legitimate the activities and campaigns of a social movement organization" (Benford and Snow 2000, 614). Successful collective-action frames make a compelling case for what is unjust or wrong, and how collective action can address the problem while distinguishing agents of change from those maintaining the status quo (Polletta and Jasper 2001). They are constructed collaboratively as social movement actors perform three framing tasks: diagnostic, or defining the problem and where the blame lies; prognostic, identifying solutions and strategies for attaining them; and motivational, intended to mobilize people to action (Benford and Snow 2000).

TUI's diagnostic frame claims that litter, urination, spitting, and defacing public property with bills and posters constitute the visible filth in public spaces, and that the perpetrator, rather than being a government decision maker, business, or other antagonist, is "all" Indians, along with their attitudes and behaviors toward public space. This differs from most social movements, where frames focusing on injustice clearly distinguish the perpetrators from the problem solvers (Benford and Snow 2000). By framing the issue of filthy public space in terms of "We Are All Ugly Indians," TUI avoids us-versus-them terminology used in more adversarial social movements.

FIGURE 12.1   Gopi garage corner before the spot fix. Photo by Aniruddha Abhyankar.

FIGURE 12.2 Gopi garage corner after the spot fix. Photo by Aniruddha Abhyankar.

The second task in TUI's framing—prognosis—claims that citizen volunteers can solve the problem of visible filth in local public spaces through low-cost and self-funded volunteer activities—namely, spot fixes. In addressing the problem of visible filth, volunteers discover their capacities, bury assumptions about "ugly Indians," come to understand the complexities in a seemingly simple problem, and come to own the problem in order to solve it. Because spot fixes do not depend on outside funders, volunteers also develop feelings of ownership of public space and satisfaction related to their role as stewards, as well as a sense of self-determination and freedom. As a result, volunteers often maintain cleaned-up public spaces until the root cause—or the original diagnosis that we are all responsible for filthy public spaces—is addressed. This entails changing attitudes and behaviors toward public spaces beyond the participants involved in the spot fix, providing alternatives to defacing public spaces such as no-smell urinals and dustbins (trash cans), and provoking action on the part of the municipality. In that 80 percent of the spot fixes TUI conducted in Bangalore remain clean public spaces, it appears the prognosis for the problem has been effective.

The third framing task—motivating action—attempts to convey the severity and urgency of the problem alongside the efficacy of and ownership for taking action (Benford 1993). TUI uses visual images—before-and-after photos of spot fixes—that, perhaps by shock value, viscerally communicate the severity and urgency of the problem and the efficacy of citizen action. The notion of ownership—that we have a moral duty to take action—is conveyed through the meme "We Are All Ugly Indians."

Attitudes and Social Norms

Framing a collective or organizational identity to resonate with the values or "cultural narratives" of participants, the public, and politicians (Benford and Snow 2000; Campbell 2005) helps recruit and mobilize group members (Polletta and Jasper 2001). Cultural beliefs, attitudes, values, and norms also influence environmental behaviors (Schultz and Kaiser 2012). TUI takes into account the cultural narratives of Indian citizens from different walks of life in "nudging" citizens to take action.

Given that TUI has its roots in Bangalore, it is not surprising that it frames its identity to reflect the values, attitudes, and competencies of India's twenty-five-to-forty-year-old, tech-savvy, urban middle class. Not only are those in this demographic well educated and relatively well paid; they are accustomed to clean modern office buildings, have an interest in Western ways of life, and often have traveled or worked abroad. In addition, as a result of seeing ongoing government corruption and the government's seeming abandonment of the middle class in favor of the poor, the new middle class has a disdain for government employment and sees the future in the private sector (Fuller and Narasimhan 2007). TUI's focus on action outside formal government is consistent with these middle-class attitudes. Further, spot fixes do not require organizational affiliation, and participation is facilitated by online registration, Google Maps, and the ability to see what others are doing on Facebook—elements that fit well with the lifestyle of India's middle-class "wired" demographic. Other ways in which TUI leverages contemporary Indian social norms include strategically conducting spot fixes near the homes of film stars or near fields where famous cricket stars play, and on Women's Day to enable women to express their power and equality in India's male-dominated society. By using these and similar strategies, TUI tries to "nudge" and "provoke" people from all walks of life to participate in spot fixes.

TUI's strategy also reflects an Indian tradition of self-help or *jugaad*. *Jugaad* arises when government is unable or unwilling to address public welfare and people are forced to innovate and find solutions on their own (Doshi et al. 2013). A traditional expression of *jugaad* would be "sweepers make their own brooms." TUI expresses *jugaad* when volunteers clean up public spaces and install pictures of deities on walls to deter urination; design no-smell urinals, trash cans (Tere-Bins), and spitting-deterrent pillar wraps; or cover walls with boulders and sharp glass fragments to prevent people from defacing them. This spirit of self-help is consistent with TUI's beliefs that the solution to negative attitudes toward public spaces lies within ordinary citizens (Radjou 2014).

TUI's leadership is anonymous, and the rule prohibiting talking at clean-up events reflects a guiding principle of *kaam chalu mooh bandh* (only work, no talk). Ideas about anonymity may stem from ancient traditions of Indian artists, craftsmen, and designers (e.g., temple architects) who rarely left their names on their works. Even the popular TUI TED talk (TUI 2014; Parekar 2015), which has over one million views, was presented by an individual wearing a face mask to hide his identity and who was given the name Anamik Nagrik—"anonymous citizen."

TUI also has had to confront aspects of spot fixes that are not congruent with Indian attitudes and social norms. For example, certain spaces are unofficially designated by local communities as preferred spots for spitting, urination, and litter, and norms dictate against doing "someone else's job" (including cleaning, a task reserved for the lowest castes). In addition, Indians have a history of drawing lines between their home and spaces outside the home. Once rubbish is out of sight on the street, it is no longer of concern; rather, lower castes ritually absorb the waste "pollution" produced by upper castes (Mawdsley 2004).

TUI's approach to "nudging" people away from these social norms reflects its "wired generation" and more traditional demographic. It uses its website and Facebook to reinforce notions of *jugaad*, egalitarianism, and other aspects of Indian society. To "enter" TUI's website, the viewer answers a question about who is responsible for India's "filth"—with the correct answer being "We Are All Ugly Indians" (TUI 2010). Further, the website uses a clever inversion of a famous saying attributed to Mahatma Gandhi ("Be the change you want to see"), asking its followers to "SEE the change YOU want to BE." Simple, memorable language and images reinforce TUI's message about degraded public space, such as "Filth on footpath," "Stains on wall," "Posters on public property," "Trash on trees," and "Death trap." TUI also uses short, visually dramatic stories and photos to bring attention to the cascading effects of trashed spaces, such as deterioration of public infrastructure and damage to the neighborhood's and city's image. By asking volunteers to publish before-and-after photos of spot fixes and share how they have come up with locally appropriate solutions on Facebook, TUI applauds all efforts equally and incites participants to come up with their own approaches. Volunteers are asked to post between 9 a.m. and 4 p.m. to maximize views, and to personalize their posts, for example by posing and answering questions like "What did you do Sunday morning?" "We fixed the ugly corner in the neighborhood." Using visual images also helps address barriers to action related to India's high illiteracy rate, linguistic diversity, and the fact that ethnic minority city dwellers who are treated as outsiders fear going against social norms, including those related to trash.

Further, TUI considers how it might have a larger influence on changing Indian social norms (see also the notion of "culture building," chapter 3). As city dwellers start to notice cleaned-up public spaces, TUI instructs them to observe the space twice daily and befriend the government staff who are maintaining it, and offers guidelines for conducting new spot fixes. Although only 10 percent of people who send TUI a picture of an ugly spot they want to fix actually end up conducting a spot fix, TUI hopes its strategy will provoke the public to reconsider their assumptions about who is responsible for, and can address the problem of, filthy public spaces.

TUI summarizes barriers related to social norms and its response as follows:

> We walk where more people are walking.
> We jump the signal if others do.
> We remove footwear where others do.
> Similarly we spit and litter where others have left the cues, and
> We respect all the spaces that others have left untouched or clean.

Practice, Organizational, and Social Movement Theory

On the one hand, TUI is a simple spot fix practice. Yet TUI's use of identity framing and attempts to influence social norms reflect aspects of changing organizations and social movements, including those resulting from the Internet. Here we draw on practice, organizational, and social movement theory, as well as recent writing on the role of the Internet in social movements, to answer the question, What is TUI? By exploring TUI as a hybrid incorporating elements of practice, organization, and social movement, we can better understand its potential broader impacts (table 12.1).

Practice Theory

In one sense, TUI is defined by its hands-on collective practice—spot fixes. Practice theory views practices as the unit of analysis, and thus offers a middle ground between individual agency or behavior on the one hand, and social or institutional structures on the other (Hargreaves 2011; Reckwitz 2002). Although scholars agree that practices are composed of the interactions of multiple elements, they differ in what elements are deemed important (Kemmis and Mutton 2012; Pantzar and Shove 2010; Gram-Hanssen 2011). In a study of civic ecology practices, Krasny et al. (2015) identified four practice elements: competencies (technical know-how, relationship building, and volunteer management); physical or biological resources (e.g., a plot of land); meanings (including those attributed to the resource and to the practice per se); and technology (e.g., the Internet and DIY). These elements can be used to understand spot fix practice. The volunteers who constitute TUI's anonymous backbone have multiple competencies: how to engage local government and stakeholders, use of the Internet, technological design (e.g., designing low-technology solutions to alleviate littering and impacts of public urination and spitting), and the creation and framing of an organizational identity. Other elements of TUI's spot fix practice include the resource (small public spaces); the technologies (e.g., the Internet, no-smell public urinals, steal-proof dustbins); and the meanings attributed to the resource (filthy, beautiful) and to the practice per se (e.g., We Are All Ugly Indians, cleaning up India). As these elements vary somewhat from one spot fix to another, the practice assumes slightly different forms; thus, sharing local spot fixes over the Internet enables volunteers from different cities to learn from each other. Scholars writing about social practices have focused on how by combining existing elements in new configurations—such as technologies and the competencies of ordinary citizens—practices evolve and become grassroots social innovations (Seyfang and Haxeltine 2012; Shove and Pantzar 2005).

Whereas practice theory is useful for understanding spot fixes per se, other theoretical perspectives are needed to understand how TUI has grown beyond a collection of spot fixes in cities across the Indian subcontinent. Here organizational and social movement theories are helpful.

Organizational and Social Movement Theory

Whereas early social movement theorists viewed labor and other 1900s protests as spontaneous and unruly and protesters as irrational and reactive, scholars studying the civil rights and peace movements of the 1960s incorporated ideas about organizational capacity, resources, and rational actors (Weber and King 2014). For example, resource mobilization theory emphasizing the role of incentives, cost-reducing mechanisms, and benefits in collective action (McCarthy and Zald 1977) and work on strategic framing of collective identities (Weber and King 2014) assumed importance in the mid-1900s. At about this time, organizational studies also emerged to understand hierarchical organizations such as businesses and industries. As organizational theorists came to realize that contemporary organizations, rather than being stable bureaucracies, shared characteristics associated with social movements including "fluid boundaries, transient existence, and network forms of governance" (Weber and King 2014, 10), they began to incorporate notions of identity and social action (Whetten 2006). Today, both social movement and organizational theorists employ parallel concepts, including identity, framing, and networks, in understanding mechanisms for collective action (Campbell 2005; Whetten 2006; Benford and Snow 2000; Polletta and Jasper 2001).

TUI, as a network of volunteers who conduct specific actions while changing the way local governments and Indian society address waste, integrates characteristics of both organizations and social movements. Organizations are characterized by their membership, hierarchy, rules, and right to monitor compliance and decide about sanctions (Ahrne and Brunsson 2010). TUI is largely nonhierarchical, sets rules, and monitors compliance through volunteer-generated reports about spot fixes, but it does not offer certifiable membership and has limited ability to impose sanctions; for these reasons, it might be considered a "partial organization" (Ahrne and Brunsson 2010). Although it may not yet be recognized as a social movement—such movements traditionally have multiple organizational players (Zald and McCarthy 2009)—TUI has grown from a single practice to influencing social norms related to public space and civic responsibility. TUI in fact calls itself a movement, but one that avoids social activism by focusing on noncontroversial practices. In this way, it reflects aspects of the civic environmental movement, which emphasizes cooperative rather than contentious politics (Sirianni and Friedland 2005).

Hasenfeld and Gidron's (2005) outline of the steps involved in the transformation of volunteer-run associations to social movements is useful in understanding TUI. Organizations begin by stating a mission to promote alternative cultural values—in TUI's case, cleaning up filthy public spaces. Next, they "offer services to members and the public that express their distinct values, using the services as a model and catalyst for social change" (Hasenfeld and Gidron 2005, 98). TUI offers the know-how to clean up public spaces, including how to engage government and other local stakeholders. Finally, transitioning or so-called "multipurpose hybrid voluntary" organizations promote a collective identity, in TUI's case one of responsible citizens who address the issue of visible filth in public spaces.

Whereas the literature linking organizations and social movements is helpful in understanding TUI, it focuses largely on protest actions such as petition drives or demonstrations, rather than on hands-on practices. (An exception is the work of Lounsbury, Ventresca, and Hirsch [2003], who describe how through the hands-on practice of recycling, countercultural environmental groups positioned their identity in opposition to that of the hegemonic solid waste management industry.) Further complicating our understanding of TUI is how the rise of the Internet has enabled new forms of organization and social movements.

The Internet and Connective Action

As people have abandoned traditional formal organizations and identities associated with labor, religious, social justice, and other issues, they have joined looser, Internet-enabled networks (Bennett and Segerberg 2013). In addition to facilitating mass mobilization (Earl et al. 2016; Earl and Kimport 2011), the Internet has enabled *connective* action, a new form of protest that responds to people's interests in flexible associations embracing a cause (Bennett and Segerberg 2013). Rather than starting with a formal organization that extends its ability to mobilize people using the Internet ("one to many"), connective action begins with individual actions that are then aggregated through sharing and shaping narratives via the Internet in a process called "peer-production" ("many to many"). An example of connective action comes from the 2011 Occupy protests, where no one cause was identified as central, but a movement identity emerged from thousands of people being asked: "What is our one demand?" Eventually an individual posted "I have type 1 diabetes. How can I afford COLLEGE when I may not be able to afford my INSULIN? I *am* the 99%." This led to the overarching protest frame: the 1 percent versus the 99 percent (Bennett and Segerberg 2013, 7). As opposed to more polarizing frames that demand major identity shifts, like "Eat the bankers," connective action frames such as "We are the 99 percent" accommodate diverse individual identities and require minimal persuasion to bridge attitudinal differences. In short, in connective action, action frames develop organizational structure through social media (Bennett and Segerberg 2013).

TUI incorporates features of connective action networks, including inclusive framing ("We Are All Ugly Indians"), user-generated content aggregated via Facebook (e.g., before-and-after photos of spot fixes), and a spirit of DIY or *jugaad* as embodied in volunteer-generated solutions to problems. Further, like

TABLE 12.1 The Ugly Indian as a practice, organization, and movement

PRACTICE	**Spot fixes**
	Practice elements (Krasny et al. 2015):
	Competencies: technologically savvy, networking, working collaboratively rather than in opposition, low-cost design
	Meanings: traditional and new Indian values (self-help, anticorruption, Western standards of cleanliness)
	Resource: public spaces
	Technology: Internet (web, Facebook), DIY innovations like no-smell public urinals
ORGANIZATION	**Anonymous network of volunteers with small group of core organizers**
	Partial organization: nonhierarchical, sets rules, and monitors compliance through volunteer-generated reports about spot fixes, but does not offer certifiable membership and has limited ability to impose sanctions (Ahrne and Brunsson 2010)
	Multipurpose hybrid organization: organization transitioning from offering services to social movement (Hasenfeld and Gidron 2005)
SOCIAL MOVEMENT	**Spread across India and to some extent in Pakistan**
	Linking strategically with government, media, and entertainment sector to expand while focused on core message
	Collective action: "organizationally brokered collective action" where core leadership uses the Internet to help frame cause and to cultivate loose network of volunteer "followers"
	Connective action: inclusive framing ("We Are All Ugly Indians"), aggregated user-generated content, DIY spirit (Bennett and Segerberg 2013)

other connective-action networks that assume features of organizations, TUI allocates resources (e.g., small amounts of money to fund spot fixes), responds to short-term external events (e.g., capitalizes on media personalities), and has developed long-term adaptive responses (e.g., working with municipal governments that neglect public-space upkeep but appreciate credit when such spaces are cleaned up). Other features of TUI more closely resemble "organizationally brokered collective action" in that the leadership, although anonymous, consists of a core group of professionals who have defined a cause and who depend on the Internet to help them frame that cause and to cultivate a loose network of volunteer "followers" (cf. Bennett and Segerberg 2013).

By engaging ever greater numbers of citizens in spot fixes and by using framing and other strategies to challenge existing social norms, the TUI case provides insights into how civic ecology practices can have impacts beyond thousands of individual cleaned-up public spaces. TUI creatively deploys online and on-the-ground tactics to make visible not only the cleaned-up spaces, but also the role citizens from multiple walks of life play in "fixing" those spaces, thus attempting to change social norms related to public space and citizen engagement. By quietly working around government neglect and collusion, and then giving government credit for what was accomplished by volunteers, TUI also has started to turn around government attitudes toward public space. In some instances, local government has enlisted TUI's help to beautify public spaces, such as engaging volunteers to paint and install plants around freeway pillars. Further, TUI has started to influence policy, as for example by inventing the expression nGOG (no garbage on ground) to emphasize that citizens are concerned not just about waste collection but also about the cleanliness of public spaces, which led to TUI recommendations being incorporated into an expert committee report about handling Bangalore's garbage crisis (*Bangalore Mirror* 2014).

Despite or perhaps because of its significant impacts, attaching a label to TUI is difficult. Central to its work are volunteer spot fixes that replace signs of neglect with symbols of respect and care. From this perspective, TUI is a collection of practices and can be understood through the lens of practice theory. But TUI also sees spot fixes as a means to reframe social norms about the importance of public spaces and citizen responsibility for stewardship of these spaces, and thus aspires to become a social movement. Social movements, however, are generally broader than one issue and involve multiple organizations. In between practice and social movements are organizations; but even here TUI may be less of an organization than a loose network of volunteers and practices. In fact, TUI incorporates features of organizationally brokered networks, which use the Internet as a means to connect formal organizations and foster traditional forms of mobilization, and of connective-action networks, in which the very structure of the movement is generated by possibilities opened up by the Internet—such as peer production and sharing of content and ideas (Bennett and Segerberg 2013).

Perhaps its hybrid positioning at the intersection of multiple levels of activity and action is integral to what the TUI case can teach us. Understanding how practices, organizations, movements, identities, and framing are changing in the age of the Internet may be useful in teasing out how civic ecology practices more broadly can scale up in numbers and scale out to influence social norms and even government policies.

Acknowledgments

The authors thank Danny Daneri Rosenberg for reviewing an earlier version of this chapter.

REFERENCES

Ahrne, G., and N. Brunsson. 2010. "Organization outside Organizations: The Significance of Partial Organization." *Organization* 18 (1): 1–22. doi:10.1177/1350508410376256.

Bangalore Mirror. 2014. "From Trash to Tidy." January 24. http://www.bangaloremirror.com/bangalore/civic/From-trash-to-tidy/articleshow/29262622.cms.

Benford, R. D. 1993. "'You Could Be the Hundredth Monkey': Collective Action Frames and Vocabularies of Motive within the Nuclear Disarmament Movement." *Sociological Quarterly* 34 (2): 195–216.

Benford, R. D., and D. A. Snow. 2000. "Framing Processes and Social Movements: An Overview and Assessment." *Annual Review of Sociology* 26:611–39.

Bennett, W. L., and A. Segerberg. 2013. *The Logic of Connective Action: Digital Media and the Personalization of Contentious Politics.* New York: Cambridge University Press.

Campbell, J. L. 2005. "Where Do We Stand? Common Mechanisms in Organizations and Social Movements Research." In *Social Movements and Organization Theory,* edited by G. F. Davis, D. McAdam, W. R. Scott, and M. N. Zald, 41–68. Cambridge: Cambridge University Press.

Doshi, A., A. Khanna, V. Mahadevan, N. Rao, and N. Shukla. 2013. "From *Jugaad* to Justice: Endemic Corruption and the Possibility of an Indian Spring." Knowledge@Wharton.

D'Souza, N. 2013. "Spot Fixing You Can Bet On." *Forbes India,* May 30. http://forbesindia.com/blog/economy-policy/spot-fixing-you-can-bet-on/.

Earl, J., J. Hunt, R. K. Garrett, and A. Dal. 2016. "New Technologies and Social Movements." In *The Oxford Handbook of Social Movements,* edited by D. Della Porta and M. Diani, 355–66. Oxford: Oxford University Press.

Earl, J., and K. Kimport. 2011. *Digitally Enabled Social Change: Activism in the Internet Age.* Cambridge, MA: MIT Press.

Fuller, C. J., and H. Narasimhan. 2007. "Information Technology Professionals and the New-Rich Middle Class in Chennai (Madras)." *Modern Asian Studies* 41 (1): 121–50. doi:10.1017/S0026749X05002325.

Gram-Hanssen, K. 2011. "Understanding Change and Continuity in Residential Energy Consumption." *Journal of Consumer Culture* 11 (1): 61–78. doi:10.1177/1469540510391725.

Hargreaves, T. 2011. "Practice-ing Behaviour Change: Applying Social Practice Theory to Pro-environmental Behaviour Change." *Journal of Consumer Culture* 11:79–99. doi:10.1177/1469540510390500.

Hasenfeld, Y., and B. Gidron. 2005. "Understanding Multi-purpose Hybrid Voluntary Organizations: The Contributions of Theories on Civil Society, Social Movements and Nonprofit Organizations." *Journal of Civil Society* 1 (2): 97–112. doi:10.1080/17448680500337350.

Kemmis, S., and R. Mutton. 2012. "Education for Sustainability (EfS): Practice and Practice Architectures." *Environmental Education Research* 18 (2): 187–207. doi: 10.1080/13504622.2011.596929.

Krasny, M. E., P. Silva, C. W. Barr, Z. Golshani, E. Lee, R. Ligas, E. Mosher, and A. Reynosa. 2015. "Civic Ecology Practices: Insights from Practice Theory." *Ecology and Society* 20 (2): 12.

Loader, B. D. 2008. "Social Movements and New Media." *Sociology Compass* 2 (6): 1920–33. doi:10.1111/j.1751-9020.2008.00145.x.

Lounsbury, M., M. Ventresca, and P. M. Hirsch. 2003. "Social Movements, Field Frames and Industry Emergence: A Cultural-Political Perspective on US Recycling." *Socio-Economic Review* 1:71–104.

Mawdsley, E. 2004. "India's Middle Classes and the Environment." *Development and Change* 35 (1): 79–103.

McCarthy, J. D., and M. N. Zald. 1977. "Resource Mobilization and Social Movements: A Partial Theory." *American Journal of Sociology* 82 (6): 1212–41. doi:10.2307/2777934.

Pantzar, M., and E. Shove. 2010. "Understanding Innovation in Practice: A Discussion of the Production and Reproduction of Nordic Walking." *Technology Analysis & Strategic Management* 22 (4): 447–61. doi:10.1080/09537321003714402.

Parekar, S. 2015. "Why Is a Video That Talks about India's 'Filth' the Most Popular TED Talk Video from Our Country?" http://www.folomojo.com/why-is-a-video-that-talks-about-indias-filth-the-most-popular-ted-talk-video-from-our-country/.

Polletta, F., and J. M. Jasper. 2001. "Collective Identity and Social Movements." *Annual Review of Sociology* 27:283–305.

Radjou, N. 2014. "Jugaad: The Art of Converting Adversity into Opportunity." *Forbes* (blog). http://www.forbes.com/sites/ashoka/2014/03/23/jugaad-the-art-of-converting-adversity-into-opportunity/.

Reckwitz, A. 2002. "Toward a Theory of Social Practices: A Development in Culturalist Theorizing." *European Journal of Social Theory* 5 (2): 243–63.

Schultz, P. W., and F. G. Kaiser. 2012. "Promoting Pro-environmental Behavior." In *The Oxford Handbook of Environmental and Conservation Psychology*, edited by S. Clayton, 556–80. Oxford: Oxford University Press.

Seyfang, G., and A. Haxeltine. 2012. "Growing Grassroots Innovations: Exploring the Role of Community-Based Initiatives in Governing Sustainable Energy Transitions." *Environment and Planning C: Government and Policy* 30:381–400. doi:10.1068/c10222.

Shove, E., and M. Pantzar. 2005. "Consumers, Producers and Practices: Understanding the Invention and Reinvention of Nordic Walking." *Journal of Consumer Culture* 5 (1): 43–64. doi:10.1177/1469540505049846.

Sirianni, C., and L. A. Friedland. 2005. *The Civic Renewal Movement: Community Building and Democracy in the United States*. Dayton, OH: Charles F. Kettering Foundation.

Stern, P. C., T. Dietz, T. Abel, G. A. Guagnano, and L. Kalof. 1999. "A Value-Belief-Norm Theory of Support for Social Movements: The Case of Environmentalism." *Research in Human Ecology* 6 (2): 81–97.

TUI (The Ugly Indian). 2010. "The Ugly Indian." http://www.theuglyindian.com/.
——. 2014. "Why Is India So Filthy?" TEDxBangalore. https://www.youtube.com/
    watch?v=tf1VA5jqmRo.
Weber, K., and B. King. 2014. "Social Movement Theory and Organization Studies."
    In *The Oxford Handbook of Sociology, Social Theory, and Organization Studies:
    Contemporary Currents*, edited by P. Adler, P. du Gay, G. Morgan, and M. Reed,
    487–509. Oxford: Oxford University Press.
Whetten, D. A. 2006. "Albert and Whetten Revisited: Strengthening the Concept
    of Organizational Identity." *Journal of Management Inquiry* 15 (3): 219–34.
    doi:10.1177/1056492606291200.
Zald, M. N., and J. D. McCarthy, eds. 2009. *Social Movements in an Organizational
    Society: Collected Essays*. New Brunswick, NJ: Transaction.

AFTERWORD
Toward a Collaborative Engagement

David Maddox

From where does innovation emerge and thrive? From which sources flow novel ideas that can make a difference? In my own experience (in science, theater, and civil society), real innovation most often flourishes when novel collections of different types of people gather to collaborate on problems that demand solutions. Together they create something that they never would have produced working by themselves. They innovate in unexpected ways.

Cities are full of people with wide-ranging points of view. Indeed, extensive engagement and collaboration among individuals with different points of view is a reasonable description of any city, town, or human settlement. Every city is a gathering of people trying to negotiate their vision for the future, and who, despite disagreements, want to make their communities better. Novel collaborations for the public good is also a good description of the fundamental idea of this book, which gathers together representatives from various civil society organizations—civic ecology groups focused on a broad vision of environmental stewardship—and academics interested in scientific studies of change, ecosystems, and society.

The process that led to *Grassroots to Global: Broader Impacts of Civic Ecology* starts with people—people from civil society and people from academia paired to explore a fundamental and potentially transformative question: *Do small-scale civic ecology practices make a difference beyond the small spaces that they immediately transform?* At its most basic, this is a straightforward (if generally underexplored) question of impact assessment and monitoring. However, a more vivid answer involves an interrogation of scale: Can such practices make a difference *over time*, and can they influence actions in *other places*? Can they persist? Can they spread? The short answer is "yes they can," but don't always. One avenue for success is sharing and innovation. Such practices can make a difference by discovering through collaborative and collective action and by sharing ways to act on and improve places for both people and nature.

The chapters in this book are an important exploration of these ideas about innovation and collective action. Their power lies in their collaborative invention, produced by interrogating different points of view to find what works and why it works, and communicating their findings and insights to others. As the facilitator for the workshop that brought the chapter authors of this book together for the first time, I was able to witness this innovation take root. We made a film of each participant sharing his or her definition of civic ecology (Maddox 2015). In experiencing the compilation of ideas, one can appreciate how the richness of this collaborative concept emerges from diverse approaches and points of view but related values.

In recent years, research on the connection between people and nature in human communities—urban spaces, variously defined—has flourished. Many examples from around the world can be found at *The Nature of Cities* blog (*TNOC* 2017), which I founded and edit. In 1990 fewer than five thousand papers were published with a keyword of "urban"; in 2016 there were nearly seventy thousand (Wolfram, Frantzeskaki, and Maschmeyer 2016). But it is not only urban research that is flourishing. Cities and communities around the world increasingly benefit from participation and activism by civil society, practitioners in various arenas of environmental stewardship and community building, and regular citizens. Examples of such work are illustrated in this book.

The civic ecology activism richly exemplified here, especially when wedded to scientific ways of knowing, has three broad benefits for societies. First, it facilitates the grounded practice of making better cities through not just knowledge, but knowledge-based action and lived experience. This is reflected in the actual design of neighborhoods, infrastructure, and open spaces—that is, *places*—that are better for both people and nature, and reflect the desires and work of members of the community. The knowledge of civil society can inform the work of scientists by grounding it and connecting it to outcomes. In turn, for civil society, the methods of science can help evaluate the methods of practice and potentially make then generalizable.

Second, the civic ecology practices in this book lay a foundation for a knowledge based on lived experience that can drive the policy realm of city building. Understanding such lived experience and practitioner knowledge can be a basis from which to connect academic research and civil society, and make research legible to policy makers. Sometimes policy-relevant knowledge is academically generated; sometimes it is gathered from lived experience; and sometimes, hopefully, these two ways of knowing can be connected. But rarely do academic ideas and civil society find a connection as they do in this book. Indeed, what are the communities that people want for themselves? How can they support nature, and in turn be supported by nature in ways that make cities more resilient and sustainable, but also more livable and just? What knowledge do civil society organizations themselves feel they need to be successful? How can this knowledge be generalized and shared more broadly for a greater good and to wider effect?

Third, collaborative engagement among ways of knowing—as here, for example, with science and civil society—can explore the role for imagination in the creation of cities, in the form of not only art, but innovation. Imagination is not a word typically associated with science, nor even with civil society. But imagination is a key ingredient for collaboration—for reaching across ways of knowing to unveil something new to all partners. It is a core foundation to the inspiration of this book—that is, scientists and practitioners from civil society meeting in pairs to discover something new through an act of imagination, of reaching across difference. Imagination is the essence of sharing, of discovery. It unveils the values that support our lives, and matures the generative methods that we use to create our communities.

So, what comes after this book? Where do we go from here? Some key observations and provocations emerge in the chapters of this collection. One overarching message is the growing vibrancy of civil society and communities of practice around the world, which put people at the center of movements to make cities better. The book also points to new ways forward to make civil society movements more effective. Three such ways are reflected in the structure of the collaborations included here.

First, we could use greater understanding of what makes civil society effective and lasting in solving problems. Are there patterns across organizations that suggest effectiveness and lasting impact? Far too often, but for understandable reasons, civil society organizations operate in isolation, away from wider dialogues in city building. Their ideas and experience need to be disseminated. Second, in the realm of policy, science can seem very abstract, often existing far from the concerns of regular people. A forthcoming publication, of which I am an editor, puts academic and practitioner essays together in a book about the future sustainability of cities (Elmqvist et al., forthcoming). The two ways of knowing seemed to exist in entirely different universes. Engagement between scientists and civil society practitioners has the potential to enrich both ways of knowing, but it happens too infrequently. The conversations in *Grassroots to Global: Broader*

Impacts of Civic Ecology are the start of an improved model for collaboration between academics and practitioners. Third, we need more engagement among civic ecology organizations, more sharing platforms by which we can learn from, and innovate with, each other. This is especially important in the Global South, where the ecological and social needs are great, and a rapidly developing civil society faces numerous existential threats (Civicus 2016).

There is much work to be done in communities near and far. It is work that makes communities better for both nature and people. It is fundamentally embedded in issues of livability, justice, sustainability, and resilience. Let's get to work. Let's keep it going. Let's push farther. Let's do it together.

REFERENCES

Civicus. 2016. Civicus: World Alliance for Citizen Participation. http://civicus.org/.
Elmqvist, T. X. B., N. Frantzeskaki, C. Griffith, D. Maddox, T. McPhearson, S. Parnell, P. Romero-Lankao, D. Simon, and M. Watkins, eds. Forthcoming. *The Urban Planet: Knowledge towards Livable Cities.* Cambridge: Cambridge University Press.
Maddox, D. 2015. "What Is Civic Ecology? 25 Definitions." *The Nature of Cities* (blog). https://www.thenatureofcities.com/2015/04/15/what-is-civic-ecology-25-definitions-tnoc-podcast-episode-004/.
TNOC (The Nature of Cities). 2017. Blog. https://www.thenatureofcities.com/.
Wolfram, M., N. Frantzeskaki, and S. Maschmeyer. 2016. "Cities, Systems and Sustainability: Status and Perspective of Research on Urban Transformations." *Current Opinion in Environmental Sustainability* 22:18–25.

Notes on Contributors

Aniruddha Abhyankar
The Ugly Indian
Bangalore, India

Martha Chaves
MINGAS Research Group
Filandia, Quindío, Colombia

Louise Chawla
Program in Environmental Design
University of Colorado Boulder
Boulder, Colorado, USA

Dennis Chestnut
Washington, District of Columbia, USA

Nancy Chikaraishi
Hammons School of Architecture
Drury University
Springfield, Missouri, USA

Zahra Golshani
Institute for Health and the Environment
University at Albany
Albany, New York, USA

Lance Gunderson
Department of Environmental Sciences
Emory University
Atlanta, Georgia, USA

Keith E. Hedges
Hammons School of Architecture
Drury University
Springfield, Missouri, USA

Robert E. Hughes
Eastern Pennsylvania Coalition for
    Abandoned Mine Reclamation
    (EPCAMR)
Ashley, Pennsylvania, USA

Rebecca C. Jordan
School of Environmental and Biological
    Science
Rutgers University
New Brunswick, New Jersey, USA

Karim-Aly Kassam
Department of Natural Resources
Cornell University
Ithaca, New York, USA

Laurel Kearns
Drew Theological School
Drew University
Madison, New Jersey, USA

Marianne E. Krasny
Department of Natural Resources
Cornell University
Ithaca, New York, USA

Veronica Kyle
Faith in Place
Chicago, Illinois, USA

David Maddox
The Nature of Cities
New York, New York, USA

Mila Kellen Marshall
Department of Biological Sciences
University of Illinois at Chicago
Chicago, Illinois, USA

Elizabeth Whiting Pierce
Center for Ethics
Emory University
Atlanta, Georgia, USA

Rosalba Lopez Ramirez
Brooklyn, New York, USA

Michael Sarbanes
Collins Avenue Streamside
   Community
Baltimore, Maryland, USA

Philip Silva
The Nature Conservancy
New York, New York, USA

Traci Sooter
Hammons School of Architecture
Drury University
Springfield, Missouri, USA

Erika S. Svendsen
United States Forest Service
Newton Square, Pennsylvania,
   USA

Keith G. Tidball
Department of Natural Resources
Cornell University
Ithaca, New York, USA

Arjen E. J. Wals
Education and Competence Studies
   Group
Wageningen University
Wageningen, the Netherlands

Rebecca Salminen Witt
Detroit Historical Society
Detroit, Michigan, USA

Jill Wrigley
Collins Avenue Streamside Community
Baltimore, Maryland, USA

Index

Page numbers followed by letters *f* and *t* refer to figures and tables, respectively.

Tocqueville, Alexis de, vii
transformative learning, 105–6; Aula Viva
network (Colombia) and, 115; boundary
crossing and, 106; outscaling of, 117–20,
121; principles of, 107–12, 108f, 114, 120;
ultimate goal of, 107
trash: in Anacostia, Washington, DC, 197; in
Baltimore, Maryland, 142, 148; behavioral
norms regarding, efforts to change, 6–7;
in India, 231, 235–36, 236f; in Iran, 66, 67;
neighborhood efforts to manage, 149. *See
also* cleanups
tree planting: in Detroit, Michigan, 217–19,
220–21, 224–25; after Hurricane Katrina,
186; in New York City, 35–36, 187, 214
Trinity United Church of Christ, Chicago,
Illinois, 60
Trust for Public Land (NGO), 169, 203
Turner, Nap, 194
Twelver Shi'ism, in Iran, 66; and personalism, 67

Ugly Indian. *See* The Ugly Indian (TUI)
United Church of Christ, toxic waste report
of, 47
United States: civic activism and race in,
23–24; grassroots recycling initiatives
in, 234; revitalization of cities in, civic
ecology practices and, 195–96; rural
mining communities in, and civic ecology
practices, 7. *See also specific cities and
states*
universities, and civic ecology practices, 178,
187–88
urban agriculture movement, 11; in Detroit,
221, 222, 225; minority representation in,
36; as social movement, 226
urban areas: changes in, 159; community
gardens in, 130; green spaces in, 196,
197, 198, 213; revitalization of, civic
ecology practices and, 195–96; stressed
communities in, 21, 22–23, 25, 127–31.
See also abandoned buildings/spaces;
specific cities
urban ecological restoration, as social
movement, 226
urban environmental stewardship
organizations: local, importance of, 215;
professionalization and hybridity of, 216,
223; roles of, 213–14

urgent biophilia, 178
USDA Forest Service, 183

vacant lots. *See* abandoned buildings/spaces
Vadala, C., 91, 92, 99
Van Jones, Anthony Kapel, 60
Van Wieren, Gretel, 51, 54, 61–62
Vella, Jane, 136
Ventresca, M., 243
Victory Gardens, 169
volunteers: African American, 24, 25, 36;
data collectors, 9, 10; diversity of, 188;
motivations of, 72–73; Nature Cleaners
(Iran) and, 70–73; novice vs. committed,
187; short-term, importance of, 178, 183,
185, 187; social media and, 12; The Ugly
Indian (TUI) and, 232, 237–38, 237f, 239,
241
Volunteer Women's Community Health
Workers Organization, Iran, 69

Wals, Arjen, 4, 9, 112
Walters, C. J., 125
Warburton, J., 73
Washington, DC: Anacostia neighborhoods
in, 11, 194–96; 11th Street Bridge Park in,
200, 204–9, 209f; history of segregation in,
196–97; Navy Yard in, 194, 200; Potomac
neighborhoods in, 194. *See also under*
Anacostia
Washington Parks and People (NGO), 198
water quality, concerns about, in New Jersey,
141–42, 147–48, 149
watershed restoration, EPCAMR and, 85, 98
Wenger, É., 145
Western Pennsylvania Coalition for
Abandoned Mine Reclamation, 93
Whetten, D. A., 234
Williams, Anthony A., 199
Williams, Debbie, 51
Witt, Rebecca Salminen, 5, 10, 14
Worden, J. W., 185
Workforce Housing Group, New York City, 131
Wrigley, Jill, 3–4, 7, 15, 21–22, 23, 26–28, 29f,
31–34, 35, 36–38

Zamora, Stephenie, 43
Zawacki, Gabby, 99
Zoroastrianism, ritual cleanliness in, 73